How to Do *Everything* with

Paint Shop Pro® 8 ™

Dave Huss

McGraw-Hill/Osborne

New York   Chicago   San Francisco   Lisbon
London   Madrid   Mexico City   Milan   New Delhi
San Juan   Seoul   Singapore   Sydney   Toronto

The McGraw·Hill Companies

McGraw-Hill/Osborne
2100 Powell Street, 10th Floor
Emeryville, California 94608
U.S.A.

To arrange bulk purchase discounts for sales promotions, premiums, or fund-raisers, please contact **McGraw-Hill**/Osborne at the above address. For information on translations or book distributors outside the U.S.A., please see the International Contact Information page immediately following the index of this book.

How to Do Everything with Paint Shop™ Pro® 8

34567890 FGR FGR 019876543

ISBN 0-07-219107-4

Publisher	Brandon A. Nordin
Vice President &	
Associate Publisher	Scott Rogers
Acquisitions Editor	Megg Morin
Project Editor	Patty Mon
Acquisitions Coordinator	Tana Allen
Technical Editor	Steve Bain
Copy Editor	Sally Engelfried
Proofreader	Emily Hsuan
Indexer	Valerie Robbins
Computer Designers	Carie Abrew, Tara A. Davis, Elizabeth Jang
Illustrators	Kathleen Fay Edwards, Melinda Moore Lytle, Lyssa Wald
Series Design	Mickey Galicia
Cover Series Design	Dodie Shoemaker
Cover Illustration	Tom Willis

This book was composed with Corel VENTURA™ Publisher.

Dedication

This book is dedicated to Mary Snow
A marvelous, caring woman whose love of children is beyond measure
and who is both my sister-in-law and dear friend

About the Author

Dave Huss is the author of more than a dozen best-selling books on digital photo editing that have been translated into eight languages. He's an avid digital photographer and photo editor whose photo compositions have won several prestigious international art competitions, and he's a popular conference speaker who has taught workshops in both the U.S. and Europe and has been interviewed on CNN and Tech TV.

Contents at a Glance

Contents

Foreword

There's never been a better time to enjoy the world of digital imaging. Digital cameras have changed the way we take pictures, giving us the freedom to capture life anywhere, anytime. For most of you, taking the picture is only the beginning. You want to do more, to go beyond what the camera produces without breaking the bank or struggling with a steep learning curve. Paint Shop Pro is the software that will help you get started on the right foot. Whether you're new to digital photography or a seasoned professional, Paint Shop Pro has what you need. With its unique combination of automatic and precision tools, Paint Shop Pro will grow with you as your needs and abilities change. No matter where you are in your digital imaging journey, there will always be something new to inspire you in Paint Shop Pro.

How to Do Everything with Paint Shop Pro 8 by Dave Huss is packed with inspirational examples and straight-shooting information. Dave takes you on a digital imaging journey, imparting tricks and tips along the way, getting you started on the road to better photos and creative graphics. A seasoned digital photographer and graphics guru, Huss captures the essence of Paint Shop Pro 8 and shows that unlike the expensive, high-end graphics programs that take a lifetime to master, Paint Shop Pro is the photo and graphics editor for all users at every level.

Throughout this book, Dave teaches you how to use Paint Shop Pro 8 to transform ordinary snapshots into beautiful photographs using automatic enhancement tools, professional correction filters, and powerful retouching brushes. Dave shows off the power of new tools, including the precision selection tools, warping brushes, and lens correction filters, plus old favorites: Picture Tubes,™ picture frames, text on a path, and much more. Paint Shop Pro 8 produces many special effects to rival the results that previously only a graphics professional could generate. With a robust feature set in one easy-to-use program, Paint Shop Pro gives you the ability to enhance, edit, create, paint, draw, animate, and organize your images for home and business.

How to Do Everything with Paint Shop Pro 8 will teach you everything you need to know about the most popular image editor on the market, and then some. Now it's up to you to start doing more with your photos and graphics—the creative possibilities are endless with Paint Shop Pro.

—Bonnie Hollenhorst
Paint Shop Pro Senior Product Manager

Acknowledgments

All books are a team effort, and this book is no exception. First of all, there are several people at Jasc who were of immeasurable assistance as I worked with Paint Shop Pro 8. Bonnie Hollenhorst and her crew worked so hard to ensure that Paint Shop Pro 8 was the world class product that they had envisioned. Nancy Peterson was amazing in somehow finding the time to provide me with answers to some of my seemingly endless questions about the product, all while heading up both the private and public beta testing. I especially appreciated all of the gracious hospitality afforded this author when visiting the Jasc facility in Minnesota. I still use my Minnesota coffee cup!

From the Osborne team, there are many people to thank. Many of these people I have worked with on other books. At the top of my list is Megg Morin, my acquisitions editor, for the critical part of the book. She would have worked with me through the entire book, but she took some time off to have her first son— Cooper the cute little kid in the Easter basket in Chapter 11. Next on the list is Lyssa Wald, who did a fantastic job laying out the color insert for this book as well as the other graphics—thank you, thank you, thank you. As usual, I am deeply indebted to my friend and technical editor, Steve Bain, who is himself a best-selling author. I appreciate all of his efforts in not only making sure the materials and techniques described in the book are accurate but also lending his considerable wealth of graphics knowledge in the form of suggestions and recommendations about topics. My thanks to Tana Allen for her contributions, which are always appreciated. Patty Mon deserves a medal for dealing with all of the logistic nightmares we had reviewing chapters multiple times to ensure they were not only accurate but contained useful information. Thanks go also to Sally Engelfried for making it appear that this third-generation Texan actually has a firm grasp of the English language. I also want to mention the five chapters (1, 2, 4, 12, and 13) written by Rowena Portch.

Several other companies graciously lent equipment for use in this book. I appreciate all of the help I received from Amy K. Podurgiel of the MWW Group in all of my dealings with the digital camera side of Nikon. I also want to acknowledge Jane Bolhorst of Walt & Company for her tireless efforts in obtaining the Epson Stylus Photo 960 that was used for testing in this book.

I would be remiss if I didn't thank all of the people in my church who let me take photos of them and use them in the book. Special thanks to Cindy Ryan, the lovely lady with the flower in her hair in the color insert, and Kelly Pound, the precocious youngster who poses at the drop of a hat. (She is the one in Chapter 10 who is sticking her (snow-cone blue) tongue out at the camera.) Last on this list, but first in my life, is my lovely wife of almost 30 years* Elizabeth, who must put up with continued and repeated absences of her hubby as he buries himself in his laptop or runs off to some remote location to get some photos for the book.

*I am often asked what it takes to stay married for nearly three decades—it is just two little words—Yes, dear. Everything else is details.

Introduction

How to Do Everything with Paint Shop Pro 8

By the mere fact that you are reading this introduction, you are in a minority. Most computer book readers immediately jump into the middle of the book, after which the reader gets lost and sheepishly returns to Chapter 1. Because you are reading the introduction, I congratulate you and, because it is just the few of us here, let's get informal and talk about what is and what is not between the covers of this book.

Who Should Read This Book?

The purpose of this book is to show you how to do things with Paint Shop Pro 8. While writing this book I used several major assumptions:

- You, the reader, may not have ever worked with photo editing software before but you want to use it to make your photos look better.

- You haven't won a Nobel Prize but you also are not a dummy or an idiot[1].

- You are more interested in discovering what you can do with a tool or feature than reading a detailed explanation of how it works.

> **TIP** *If you are interested in a book that offers detailed explanations of every tool, always go for the heaviest one.*

[1] "Suppose you were an idiot. And suppose you were a member of Congress. But I repeat myself."
—Mark Twain, a Biography

Being that I am (among my many other transgressions) a photographer, you will discover that my approach to Paint Shop Pro 8 is more focused (pun intended) on using it for working with photographs rather than drawing heart-shaped vector shapes or as a paint tool to create semi-realistic flowers. Most of the pages are dedicated to improving, preserving, and printing photos and having some fun in the process. There are also tips scattered throughout on how to prevent some of the more common problems that photographers face. Did you know people who have had too much to drink are much more susceptible to red-eye? One of the many reasons flash photography and bars rarely mix.

As a digital photographer, I am impressed with the vast array of digital image correction tools that up until now have only been available as expensive Photoshop plug-ins. For example, one of the inherent problems with digital cameras is the distortion created by the wide-angle lenses used by the cameras. In this book, you will discover that Paint Shop Pro 8 includes a set of tools to correct perspective distortion (the distortion that makes the top of a building appear smaller than the bottom), as well as the rounded corner distortion produced by wide-angle lenses.

Paint Shop Pro is also about having fun with your photos and while Jasc improved the performance, they didn't forget about important features such as thinfy (in Paint Shop Photo Album, which ships with the product), which could make Harry Potter's cousin Dudley look 30 pounds thinner. You discover how to use the wide assortment of really cool picture-edge effects so that your next Christmas newsletter might end up as a Pulitzer candidate.

If you just want to make photos look better, you will learn how to use the powerful set of image enhancement tools to give both beginners and power users the ability to make even poor quality photos look great with only a few keystrokes.

One of the benefits of digital cameras—that you can take as many pictures as you want—can really become a nuisance when you return from your family vacation with 600 images instead of the usual 60. This is probably why the folks at Jasc have added a lot of new scripting features for commonly repeated tasks in addition to some great new, easy-to-use batch processing features.

How to Do Everything with Paint Shop Pro 8 is written in nontechnical, everyday language for the beginner-to-intermediate user. A special effort was made to focus on the realistic use of program features on real-world projects and problems. I take issue with authors and others who demonstrate how a feature works with an example that leaves the reader wondering why in the world they would ever want to do that. I also do not believe in wasting precious pages providing detailed information about how every tool works. If you want to learn how a tool or feature works, Jasc has included an excellent 448-page printed user manual which can also be accessed by clicking the Help button in Paint Shop Pro 8. If you are not a beginner, I have included a wealth of techniques, ideas, and suggestions for the advanced user, digital photographer, or photo editor.

Conventions Used in This Book

As you follow the procedures contained in this book, you're bound to encounter terms specific to manipulating tools, using shortcuts, or applying or accessing commands. The following brief list may help define some of these terms:

- **Click-drag**   This action involves clicking the left mouse button and subsequently dragging the tool or cursor while holding down the button. You often find this action described as simply a "drag." Click-dragging is often used for moving objects, manipulating control or object handles, or drawing with tools.

- **CTRL-click**   This term describes the action of holding the CTRL (Control) key in combination with a mouse click.

- **CTRL-SHIFT-drag**   This action describes holding the CTRL (Control) and SHIFT keys together, while dragging an object or Tool cursor.

- **CTRL-drag**   This term describes holding the CTRL (Control) key while dragging, which can have different effects depending on which tool you are using and the action you are performing.

- **Marquee-select**   This term describes the action of click-dragging using the Object Selection Tool and is often used as a technique for selecting objects within a defined area. As you drag, a dotted marquee-style line appears to indicate the defined area.

- **Menu | Submenu | Submenu**   This commonly found annotation is used to describe the action of accessing application menus and further selecting submenus. The first entry describes the main application menu, while subsequent entries describe further menu access with each menu/submenu name separated by a vertical bar.

- **Right-click**   This term is used to describe the action of clicking your *right* mouse button as opposed to the typical left mouse button; this action is most often used for accessing context-sensitive commands contained in the pop-up menu. The pop-up menu offers shortcuts to commands or dialogs.

How This Book Is Organized

How to Do Everything with Paint Shop Pro 8 includes 14 chapters organized into 5 parts. Each chapter is designed to guide you through how to use Paint Shop Pro's tools, features, and/or resources. The parts are structured in a sequence for reference and in logical progression, much like a typical learning sequence.

Part I: Get Acquainted with Paint Shop Pro 8

Whether you're just getting acquainted with Paint Shop Pro 8 as a first-time user or you're revisiting this latest version, Part I is designed to cover the basics. If you're new to Paint Shop Pro, Chapter 1, "Meet Paint Shop Pro for the First Time," provides brief summaries of the new tools and features available in version 8 and familiarizes you with how to use various application and document window components including palettes, toolbars, the status bar, and Workspace features. Chapter 2, "Set Up Shop," teaches you how to set up, configure, and customize the program to fit you and your working environment. To round off the quick-start reference, Chapter 3, "Capture and Manage Your Photos," covers essential skills and techniques necessary to manage the vast number of images that either do or will soon exist in your computer. Chapter 4, "See Things Your Way," explores navigating documents and pages, setting page magnification, and creating custom page views, as well as using the Zoom and Pan tools and toolbars that are critical to making your work accurate.

Part II: Basic Image Editing

For users somewhat more familiar with Paint Shop Pro, Part II covers basic skills for working with digital photos, how to fix minor photo problems, and how to add text to photos. Chapter 5, "Simple Image Editing and Printing," offers basic instruction as well as tips and tricks to get photos from the digital camera or scanner into the computer as well as how to set up your photo printer to get the best possible results. Chapter 6 is "Correcting Photographic Problems." All photographs have problems— too much light, too much darkness, color casts caused by cloudy days. This chapter shows you how to correct most of these common photographic problems. Chapter 7, "Add Text to Your Images," details many of the different ways you can add text to add more impact to your photos. You will learn how to add different types of text effects; from adding cartoon-like caption balloons to inserting cool text flowing around or along a curve.

Part III: Advanced Image Editing

Part III is a must-read for users who want to get the most benefit from using Paint Shop Pro's photographic tools to repair, restore, or preserve important family heirlooms or automate repetitive tasks. Chapter 8, "Repairing and Restoring Photographs," offers techniques on how to scan, repair, and preserve damaged photos and other important documents. Chapter 9, "Automating Paint Shop Pro 8," tells you how to take advantage of the built-in automation features to increase your productivity when working on a large number of images.

Part IV: Create Original Images Using Paint Shop Pro 8

Part IV features two chapters specifically dealing with using Paint Shop Pro 8's powerful selection tools to create exciting photo compositions from images drawn from many sources and teaches you how to add dazzling effects to your photos using the fantastic effects filters and other features built into Paint Shop Pro. Chapter 10, "Creating a Photo Montage" covers a lot of ground by explaining in detail how to select, add, remove, and manipulate people and objects from photos. Learn to add special, cool effects to your photos in Chapter 11, "Add Dazzling Effects to Your Photos." You will learn how to add photo edges and photo frames to your photos, how to create stunning effects with the Picture Tube brush, and much more.

Part V: Create Web Graphics

In Part V, you'll discover how to unlock Paint Shop Pro 8's web graphics tools. Chapter 12, "Create Images for the Web" describes the various ways you can create objects to use on your web page. Chapter 13, "Create Animations with Animation Shop" explains how to use Paint Shop Pro resource tools to make web animations add zest to your web page.

Appendix: Everything You Need to Know About Digital Images

Some readers know a lot about digital images, others know next to nothing, and a majority are right in the middle. To accommodate Paint Shop Pro 8 users who want to learn more about the how and why of digital images, I included this appendix, a complete course in digital images basics, from soup to nuts. If you think a pixel is a character in the *Lord of the Rings* or resolution is something passed by Congress, this appendix is for you.

Part I

Get Acquainted with Paint Shop Pro 8

Chapter 1

Meet Paint Shop Pro 8 for the First Time

How to…

- Become familiar with Paint Shop Pro 8's new features
- Understand the conventions used in this book
- Get around in the Paint Shop Pro 8 workspace

Paint Shop Pro 8 offers powerful digital-imaging tools that enable you to create eye-catching images, dazzling effects, and exciting photo enhancements in a short amount of time. Because this program is very easy to learn and use, it is perfect for the scrap-booking hobbyist as well as for the digital-imaging entrepreneur. In this chapter, you'll get acquainted with the Paint Shop Pro 8 workspace and gain an overview of how to create some digital magic.

New Features of Paint Shop Pro 8

If you're familiar with Paint Shop Pro 7, you're going to be pleasantly surprised with what Paint Shop Pro 8 has to offer. A team of almost 50 people at Jasc spent over two years enhancing Paint Shop Pro based on customer feedback. So let's take a peek at what's in store for your digital-imaging potential.

Play it Again, Sam

Have you ever done something really cool but couldn't remember how you did it? Now you don't have to worry about that. Paint Shop Pro 8 records those steps at your command. How does it do this? Paint Shop Pro 8 offers a full-blown scripting engine, based on the Python programming language. Okay, in English what this means is that you can record your steps while creating a particular effect you may want to use again. Each recording is called a script. When you want to apply the same set of effects to another object or image, all you need to do is run the script you recorded. It's that simple.

Printing Like a Pro

The printing functionality has been enhanced to give you greater flexibility regarding print size, layout, and scalability. There are a variety of built-in templates to choose from, or you have the resources to create your own. For proofing purposes, you can use the Paint Shop Pro browser to print thumbnails of images stored in a given folder.

Selecting the Right File Format

Paint Shop Pro 8 supports a variety of new formats to broaden your possibilities. Selecting the right format for the job is like selecting the right wine for a meal. Any wine would do, but the right wine enhances the flavor and overall eating experience. Likewise, the appearance of your image can change depending on the format you choose. The following new formats are bound to do your digital images justice:

AutoFX (AFX)	Brooktrout Fax (BRK)
CALS Raster (CAL)	Microstation Drawing (DGN)
AutoCAD Drawing (DWG)	JPEG 2000 (JP2)
Kofax (KFX)	Lazer View (LV)
NC G4 (NCR)	Portable Document File (PDF)
Scalable Vector Graphics (SVG)	Wireless Bitmap (WBMP)
X Windows Bitmap (XBM)	X Windows Pixmap (XPM)
X Windows Dump (XWD)	

Paint Shop Pro 8 also supports Exchangeable Image Format (EXIF) data. This ensures that information such as shutter speed, exposure compensation, F number, metering system and flash settings, ISO number, date and time the image was taken, white balance, and resolution is not lost when the original JPEG file is saved as a native Paint Shop Pro (PSP) file.

You can even edit and save JPEG images without losing quality because Paint Shop Pro 8 now supports reading and writing of lossless JPEG files.

Converting and Renaming Multiple Files

Remember having to change those convoluted filenames your camera selected for you? With Paint Shop Pro 8, you can convert and rename all of the files in a given directory with one simple batch command. The Batch Convert feature has even been enhanced to include the option of running a script during conversion.

Exporting Custom Picture Frames

If you have an image that meets specific requirements, now you can export that image as a custom picture frame, and then use it to frame something extra special.

Automating Your Preferences

Paint Shop Pro 8 enables you to specify which actions to perform automatically, prompt you about, or disable all together. Simply open the programming Preferences under the File menu and click the Auto Actions tab.

Learning as You Go

The Learning Center cleverly displays short tutorials directly in the application. These quick guides use scripts to automate some or all of the steps in the tutorial, so you can watch and observe how a technique is done.

Conventions Used in This Book

Look for the following styles to quickly identify specific types of information:

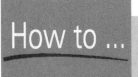 Procedures in these boxes step you through a project so you can practice some of the techniques explained in the chapter.

 *Read this content for additional information you may find helpful or noteworthy.*

 *Use this content to wow and impress your friends. It often reveals alternate methods for achieving a specific effect or task.*

 *This information could save you from unforeseen headaches.*

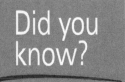 *These little tidbits offer quicker ways for getting a job done.*

Did you know? This content provides useful, fun-to-know information about a given subject.

Windows and Dialog Boxes

Throughout this book, you'll encounter terms such as windows and dialog boxes. So, what's the difference? A window enables you to change a file directory and select a file or similar functions, but it does not offer command buttons, such as OK or Cancel.

Dialog boxes enable you to set options or specify text. To apply the choices you make, you are usually given the chance to save the changes by clicking the OK command button, or clicking Cancel to ignore and discard your changes.

Touring the Paint Shop Pro 8 Workspace

Getting to know the Paint Shop Pro 8 workspace will save you time when it comes to getting a project done. Think of it as a kitchen. If you know where to find the pots, pans, and required utensils, you can concentrate more on creating a meal fit for a king. You may even want to bookmark this area of the book for quick reference.

When you start Paint Shop Pro 8 and open an image, your workspace will resemble Figure 1-1.

Toolbars

The toolbars offer buttons that perform common functions. Of course, unless you use these buttons frequently, it is easy to forget what each one does. To spark your memory, you can position your cursor over the button and a tool tip will display the name of the tool. If that's not enough information, look at the left portion of the status bar to read a description of what the tool does. Some tools offer additional options. To access these options, click the down arrow to the right of the button.

To add a button to a toolbar, complete the following steps:

1. Right-click the toolbar and select Customize.

2. In the Commands tab, select the button you want to add and click and drag the button to the appropriate toolbar.

3. When the cursor changes to an I-beam, release your mouse button.

To remove a button from a toolbar, complete the following steps:

1. Right-click the toolbar and select Customize.

2. On the toolbar, click the button you want to remove and drag it to the Commands pane.

The toolbars can be either docked in the toolbar area or made to float over the workspace. To move the toolbar, click and drag the toolbar handle to the desired location. The toolbar handle is depicted by a series of gray dotted lines.

Photo toolbar   Menu bar   Tool Options palette   Effects toolbar

Standard toolbar   Title bar   Script toolbar

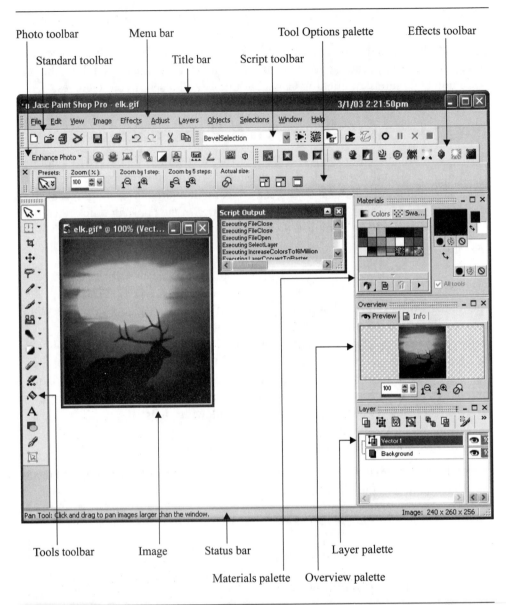

Tools toolbar   Image   Status bar   Layer palette

Materials palette   Overview palette

FIGURE 1-1   The Paint Shop Pro 8 workspace

Standard Toolbar

The Standard toolbar enables you to perform a set of common file functions.

The functions are

- Create a new image
- Open an existing image
- Browse all files on your computer
- Acquire an image from a scanner or other TWAIN device
- Save your image

- Print your image
- Undo the last action
- Redo the last action
- Move the selected object to the clipboard
- Copy the selected object to the clipboard

Web Toolbar

The Web toolbar enables you to perform common functions for web objects.

The functions are

- Optimize the image as JPEG
- Optimize the image as GIF
- Optimize the image as PNG
- Preview the image in a web browser
- Slice the image

- Map the image
- Offset the image
- Create a seamless tile with the image
- Convert the image to a button

Photo Toolbar

The Photo toolbar enables you to perform common photo enhancements.

These enhancements include

- Enhance the photo
- Distort the image
- Adjust brightness
- Adjust contrast
- Apply a fade correction
- Adjust black and white points
- Adjust the colors
- Remove JPG artifacts
- Blur the image

Effects Toolbar

The Effects toolbar enables you to apply common effects.

These common effects include

- View a library of preset effects
- Apply button effects
- Add a drop shadow
- Create an inner bevel
- Apply a Gaussian blur
- Create a hot wax effect
- Create brush strokes
- Apply a colored foil effect
- Emboss the image
- Create a fur effect
- Define a light source
- Create a polished stone effect
- Create a sunburst effect
- Create a topographic effect

Browser Toolbar

The buttons in this toolbar are only active when the file browser window is open.

These buttons enable you to

- Copy the selected image file into the Clipboard
- Delete the selected image file

- Move the selected image file to another location
- Rename the selected image file
- Open the selected image file
- Find an image file based on the filename
- Refresh the folder tree

- Shrink the browser window to one thumbnail height
- Change the default browser folder
- Select a thumbnail based on specific criteria
- Sort thumbnails based on specific criteria
- Update the thumbnail display

Palettes

Palettes may appear to take up a lot of your workspace, but they are fantastic tools to have readily available. Palettes can be docked on the right, left, or top portions of the workspace, or they can float over the workspace area.

To view a palette that is hidden, open the View menu and select Palettes, or press the associated function key. By default, the palettes are docked on the right side of the workspace, with the exception of the Tools toolbar (see Figure 1-2).

Tools Toolbar

The Tools toolbar contains the basic tools required for most digital imaging. The down arrow at the right of a button indicates the tool button is part of a group of similar tools. When you click the down arrow, the group opens and you are able to select another tool from that group. You will also notice that when you select a tool, the options in the Tool Options palette change to reflect the options available for the selected tool.

These tools enable you to:

- **Control your viewing area**   Click the arrow to the right of this button to access the following tools:

    - **Pan**   Enables you to move the canvas around so you can see various areas at a time. This is especially useful when you are working with large images.

    - **Zoom**   Enables you to enlarge or shrink the image you are viewing so that you can see either greater detail or more of the whole image. This tool does not affect the actual size of the image, only the way you view it.

Floating palette   Docked palettes

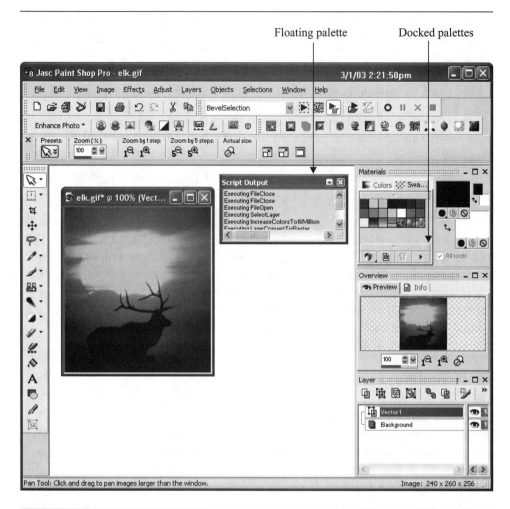

FIGURE 1-2   Floating and docked palettes

■ **Reshape or reorient the image**
Click the arrow to the right of this
button to access the following tools:

■ **Deform**   Enables you to deform,
rotate, resize, or skew the image.

■ **Straighten**   Rotates a crooked image so that it appears straight.

■ **Perspective Correction**   Enables you to add perspective to your image.

■ **Mesh Warp**   Warps the image to a mesh frame, thus giving the image dimension and depth.

■ **Crop**   Enables you to define the areas of an image you want  to crop.

■ **Move**   Moves the selected object or image.

■ **Select an area in the image**   This button displays the last tool you selected from the following list. These tools enable you to select various areas of an image so they can be moved or manipulated without affecting the areas that are not selected.

> ■ **Selection**   Draws lines from one anchor point to another, enabling you to select areas of an image with greater precision than the Freehand tool. Each time you click your mouse button, another anchor point is placed.
>
> ■ **Freehand Selection**   If you have a steady hand, this tool enables you to draw an area around the object you want to select.
>
> ■ **Magic Wand**   Selects areas of an image based on color shades.

■ **Select color**   This button displays the last tool you selected from the following list. These tools enable you to select colors based on a color in the image or a color on the color swatch.

> ■ **Dropper**   Enables you to change the foreground color swatch based on a color in the image.
>
> ■ **Color Replacer**   Replaces a color in the image with the one selected as the foreground color.

■ **Paint**   Displays the last tool you selected from the following list. These tools enable you to select various types of artistic brushes.

> ■ **Paint Brush**   Offers a wide, smooth stroke, very much like a normal paint brush.

- **Airbrush** Offers a soft blending stroke like an ordinary airbrush or paint can.

- **Warp Brush** Paints areas of distortion to create an underwater effect.

- **Repair** Displays the last tool you selected from the following list. These tools enable you to select areas of an image to repeat or to blend away cracks and creases from an old photo.

  - **Clone** Repeats an area of your image to create a symmetrical look. This tool is often used for photo retouching.

  - **Scratch Remover** Blends away cracks and creases from old photos.

- **Add an artistic touch** Displays the last tool you selected from the following list. These tools create artistic effects.

  - **Dodge** Lightens shadowed areas to reveal more detail.

  - **Burn** Darkens areas that are too light.

  - **Smudge** Smudges the colors as if you were running your finger through wet paint.

  - **Push** Blends a color over the canvas to spread it around.

  - **Soften** Softens the edges so they blend into the background.

  - **Sharpen** Creates greater contrast to bring an area of an image into greater focus.

  - **Emboss** Creates an embossed effect.

- **Play with light and color** Displays the last tool you selected from the following list. These tools enable you control the light source in your image.

  - **Lighten/Darken** Adds more light or darkness to a selected area.

  - **Saturation** Gives the colors in a selected area a richer look.

- ■ **Hue** Adjusts the color shades of an image.

- ■ **Change to Target** Makes an image look as if it were painted on a canvas or some other selected material.

- ■ **Erase** Displays the last tool you selected from the following list. These tools enable you to remove areas of an image.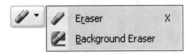

  - ■ **Eraser** Erases an image area.

  - ■ **Background Eraser** Removes areas of a layer to reveal the background.

- ■ **Paint with 3D Object** Enables you to paint with picture tube images.

- ■ **Flood** Fills the selected area with the foreground color.

- ■ **Add text** Opens the text box where you can type your text. **A**

- ■ **Preset Shape** Offers a library of preset shapes in the Tool Options palette.

- ■ **Pen tool** Enables you to draw straight lines.

- ■ **Select** Enables you to select vector objects to move or resize them.

Brush Variance Palette

The Brush Variance palette controls how a brush behaves. For example, if you have the Airbrush tool selected, you can adjust how much paint is applied each time you click the mouse button.

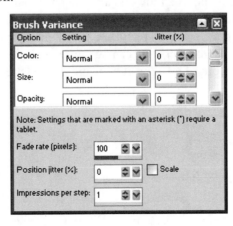

 *To show and hide the Brush Variance palette, press* F11.

Histogram Palette

The Histogram palette represents the color and brightness values of the active image. By analyzing the detail distribution of shadows, midtones, and highlights, you will know where to make corrections.

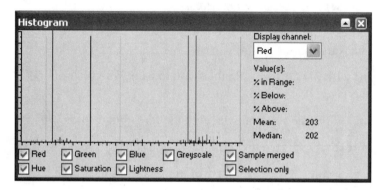

 *To show and hide the Histogram palette, press* F7.

Layers Palette

The Layers palette displays the individual layers that make up an image. Layers are like clear sheets of paper, each with a picture on it. When you lay the pieces of paper on top of one another, it forms a complete image. The fun thing about layers is that you can treat each one as its own individual entity. For example, let's say you have this majestic photo of a redwood and the only thing that would make it better is adding that bear from the picture Uncle Al took on his trip to Yosemite. Copy the bear image from Uncle Al's photo and paste it into your image of a redwood, and voila, you now have two layers that can be moved and blended with one another to form one awesome work of art. You'll be using this palette quite a bit.

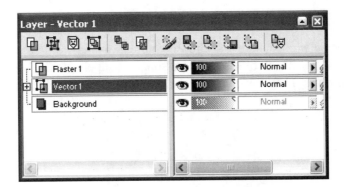

 *To show and hide the Layers palette, press* F8.

Learning Center Palette

The Learning Center palette provides a quick guide of simple tutorials designed to quickly get you started with common tasks. If you need to jump start your creative juices, this may be a good place to start.

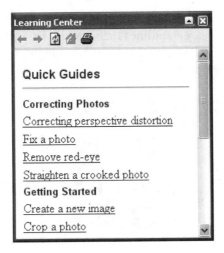

 *To show and hide the Learning Center palette, press* F10.

Materials Palette

The Materials palette is where you choose your canvas material, paint swatches, patterns, and styles. Think of it as your personal art supply store. This is definitely a palette you want to have available all the time.

 *To show and hide the Materials palette, press* F6.

Overview Palette

The Overview palette offers a thumbnail view of your image. If you are zoomed into a specific area, a rectangle outlines the area you are currently working on. Click on the Info tab to see information regarding height, width, color depth, memory used, and cursor position.

 *To show and hide the Overview palette, press* F9.

Script Output Palette

The Script Output palette shows the result of a script as it runs. This ensures you that all steps in a given script were executed completely, or warns you of which steps could not complete due to a given condition. If this window starts to look as cluttered as a child's playroom, you can clean it up with a simple command: open the File menu, select Script, and click Clear Output Window. Don't you wish cleaning the playroom was this easy?

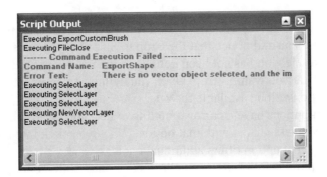

 *To show and hide the Script Output palette, press* F3.

Tool Options Palette

The Tool Options palette is like a chameleon; it changes contents to reflect the selected tool. The options it presents enable you to fine-tune the tool to create the look you envision.

 *To show and hide the Tool Options palette, press* F4.

Menus

Menus offer the same options provided by the toolbar icons plus additional commands that are not as commonly used. To open a menu, click the menu title. For clues on what a menu option does, position your cursor over the menu item and read the description on the left side of the status bar.

Standard Conventions Are a Beautiful Thing

Most applications follow a standard for shortcut keys. So, if CTRL-S works in one application for Save, it is likely to work the same way in other applications.

If a menu item is grayed out, that option is not available. For example, if you open the Image menu and notice that the Crop to Selection option is grayed out, that's because a selection has not been defined in the image, and the program doesn't know what you want to crop. Once you define a selection area, the Crop to Selection option will be available to you.

Some menu options have an arrow pointing to the right (▶). This means that there is a submenu associated with that option. When you click that menu option, the submenu for that option offers additional choices.

If a menu option is followed by an ellipsis (...), that option opens a dialog box. The dialog box enables you to specify parameters for a given action. For example, if you open the File menu and select Print, the Print dialog box appears. From here you can define specific output options for the image you want to print.

Shortcut Keys

Some menu options that are used frequently offer shortcut keys. Some shortcut keys are executed with the CTRL key, while others are executed with the ALT key. Menus or options that are executed with the ALT key have a line under the activation key. For example, the File menu has a line under the letter F, so if you press ALT-F, the File menu will open. Likewise, the Save option under the File menu offers two shortcut keys: ALT-S or CTRL-S. To use ALT-S, you must first open the File menu. So if you are working on an image and want to save it by using the shortcut keys, you could press ALT-F and then ALT-S, or just press CTRL-S.

File Menu

Items in the File menu offer options for controlling file functions. Click File or press ALT-F to open this menu.

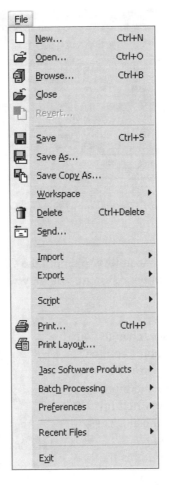

Edit Menu

Items in the Edit menu enable you to perform common editing functions such as Cut, Copy, and Paste. The Edit menu also offers a very useful tool: Command History. This little gem enables you to experiment without being afraid you can't undo what you have done. Of course, Undo and Redo enable you to go back one step at a time, but the ability to undo a series of actions is invaluable.

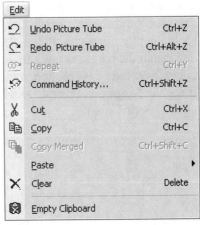

 *To open the Command History window, press* CTRL-SHIFT-Z.

Another useful feature is the ability to empty the Clipboard. If you have a limited amount of memory in your system, you may want to use this feature often.

View Menu

If you don't like what you see, change your point of view. This menu enables you to control how an image displays in your workspace. As you get more and more into detail, this menu becomes very helpful. The View menu is also where you can access various toolbars and palettes.

Another feature worth noting is the Magnifier. If your eyesight isn't what it used to be, or if you are working on ultra-detail that must be absolutely perfect, this is the tool to get familiar with. Press CTRL-ALT-M and watch the magic as you move your cursor over the image. When you are done using the Magnifier, press CTRL-ALT-M again. It's that simple.

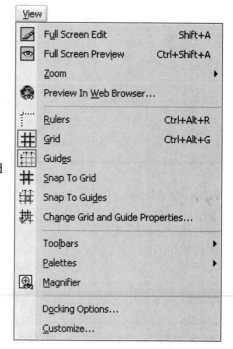

Image Menu

The Image menu gives you the ability to control the image as a whole, including individual layers. Using the options in this menu, you can rotate the canvas, add borders, and add a watermark to the background, among other things.

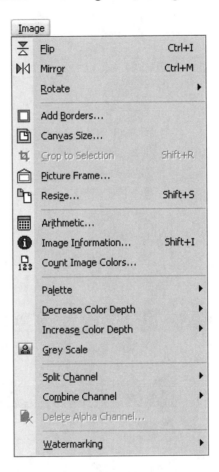

Effects Menu

This fun little menu offers several special effects that make your image leap from the page, or at least appear to. Click the Effect Browser option to view an impressive collection of effect presets that you can apply or modify at will. This browser takes a few moments to load, but it's worth the wait.

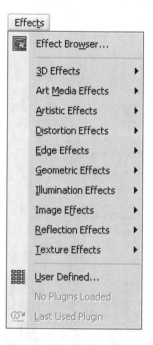

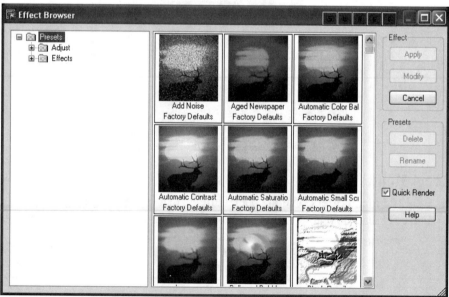

Adjust Menu

As the name implies, this menu enables you to adjust various aspects of your image regarding color, sharpness, brightness, and contrast. Use the options in this menu to fine-tune your work.

Layers Menu

Once you start using layers, you'll wonder how you ever managed without them. Almost every aspect of your layers are managed through the options in this menu. Use it in conjunction with the Layers palette to gain the full effect of this powerful little feature.

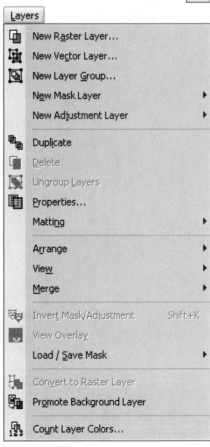

Objects Menu

When you have one or more objects in your image selected, you can use the items in this menu to perform some time-saving tasks. Use it to space the selected objects uniformly, or make them the same size, among other things.

Selections Menu

Use this menu to control selections. You can either select all objects in the active layer, or deselect an object. With selections, you can apply certain effects to only a portion of a layer.

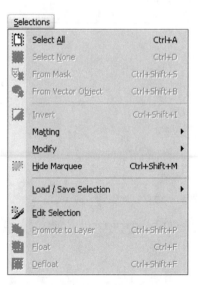

Window Menu

Use this menu to control the open windows in your workspace. One terrific feature in this menu is the ability to create a duplicate of the active image in your workspace.

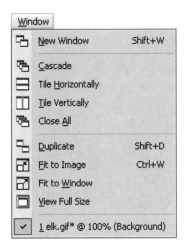

Help Menu

For guidance on how to use a particular feature, click this menu and select the Help Topics option. If you are in a particular dialog box and have no idea what to do, you can press SHIFT-F1 to get help on that specific feature.

Chapter 2

Set Up Shop

How to...

- Install Paint Shop Pro 8
- Customize Your Paint Shop Pro Workspace

In this chapter, you'll learn how to install Paint Shop Pro 8 and set up the workspace. With so many customization options, you are bound to set up a workspace that promotes creativity to the highest degree—or at least, make your working experience a bit more relaxing. So grab a cup of your favorite beverage and let's get started.

Installing Paint Shop Pro 8

Depending on how you purchased Paint Shop Pro 8, there are a couple of different ways to install the program: using a CD or downloading and installing an electronic software distribution (ESD) file. No worries, both techniques are fairly simple.

Installing Paint Shop Pro 8 from a CD

In most instances, your system is set up for Autorun, which causes the installation program to start automatically when the CD is loaded into the drive. If you have this feature disabled for some reason, follow the manual installation instructions.

Use Autorun

To install Paint Shop Pro 8 from the CD, complete the following steps:

1. Insert the Paint Shop Pro 8 Installation CD into your computer's CD drive.

2. If the installation welcome screen appears, that's a good thing. Simply follow the directions until the installation wizard completes. If nothing appears on your screen, you may have Autorun disabled. No worries: just follow the instructions for manual installation.

2

NOTE   *Unless you have specific reasons for doing a custom install, I recommend that you accept all of the defaults presented to you.*

Manual Installation

To manually install Paint Shop Pro 8 from the CD, complete the following steps:

1. Insert the Paint Shop Pro 8 Installation CD into your computer's CD drive.

2. Right-click the Start button, and then click Explore.

3. Click the CD drive containing the installation CD.

4. Double-click Autorun.exe.

5. Follow the directions until the setup wizard completes.

NOTE   *Unless you have specific reasons for doing a custom install, I recommend that you accept all of the defaults presented to you.*

Installing Paint Shop Pro 8 from an ESD File

If you want to save some money or are in a hurry to try the program out, downloading the program from the Internet is the way to go. If you have already downloaded the Electronic Software Distribution (ESD) file, simply double-click the downloaded file to begin the installation process.

To download and install the ESD file from the Internet, complete the following steps:

1. Start Internet Explorer, or your preferred browser, and then go to www.jasc.com.

2. Follow the links to the Paint Shop Pro 8 download page, and then click the Download link.

3. When prompted, save the file to your hard drive. Select a location for the downloaded file that is easy to remember. I suggest creating a folder under your C: drive called JASC and saving the downloaded file there.

NOTE *If you want to close the downloader and install Paint Shop Pro 8 at a later time, click Close. When you are ready to install the program, open the folder where you saved the ESD file and double-click the ESD filename.*

4. When the download completes, click Open. This should start the installation wizard.

5. Follow the directions until the installation wizard completes.

NOTE *Unless you have specific reasons for doing a custom install, I recommend that you accept all of the defaults presented to you.*

6. When the installation completes, you can delete the ESD file you downloaded.

Customizing Paint Shop Pro

Now that you have Paint Shop Pro 8 installed, you are ready to optimize your workspace. Think of it as rearranging the equipment in your virtual digital-imaging lab to make it more efficient for your specific needs. Let the fun begin.

Customizing the Toolbars

As you become more proficient at using the toolbars and buttons, you'll find that you use certain buttons more than others. For this reason, Paint Shop Pro 8 enables you to customize the buttons on each toolbar. You can even move them from one place to another to make them more convenient. The following illustration shows a docked toolbar and the handle used to move it to another location.

Handle ⟶

Move a Toolbar

You can move your toolbars to any side of the workspace, within the workspace, or to the top of the workspace window. When you move a toolbar to the middle of the workspace, the title bar turns into a small window without a handle. To change the window back into a toolbar, click and drag the window's title bar to an edge of the workspace or to the top of the workspace window.

To move a toolbar, click its handle and drag it to the desired location. When you release your mouse button, the toolbar snaps into place.

Hide a Toolbar

If you don't like a lot of clutter in your workspace, you may choose to do a little house cleaning. To hide a toolbar, open the View menu and click Toolbars. The icons that have a frame around them are currently visible. The display state of any toolbar may be toggled on or off by choosing it from the View | Toolbars submenu.

Show a Toolbar

When you are doing something specific, like touching up a photo or creating web elements, you may find it necessary to access those toolbars. To make a toolbar visible, open the View menu and click Toolbars. The icons that do not have a frame around them are currently hidden. To show a toolbar, click its icon in the Toolbar menu.

 *You can also open the Toolbars menu by right-clicking any toolbar and clicking Toolbars.*

Remove Command Buttons from a Toolbar

To save space, you may find it necessary to remove buttons that you don't use very often. Don't worry, you can always add them at a later time.

To remove a button from a toolbar, complete the following steps:

1. Open the View menu, and then click Customize.

2. Click the Commands tab. You do not have to select a category.

3. On the toolbar, click and drag the button you want to remove to the Commands list.

4. To close the Customize dialog box, click Close.

Add Command Buttons to a Toolbar

To add a button to a toolbar, complete the following steps:

1. Open the View menu, and then click Customize.

2. Click the Commands tab.

3. In the Categories list, select the category of the command you want to add. For example, if the command controls a file-related function like Save, that command is under the File category.

4. In the Commands list, select the button you want to add, and then click and drag the button to the appropriate toolbar.

5. When the cursor changes to an I-beam, release your mouse button.

6. To close the Customize dialog box, click Close.

Create Your Own Toolbar

Like having things your way? No worries, simply create your own toolbar. This is extremely helpful when you work on specific tasks and only want to deal with one toolbar instead of several.

To create your own toolbar, complete the following steps:

1. Open the View menu, and then click Customize.

2

2. Click the Toolbars tab, and then click New.

3. In the Toolbar Name text box, type a name for your toolbar, and then click OK.

4. Your new toolbar is added.

5. Click the title bar of your new toolbar and drag it to a more convenient location so you can easily add your command buttons to it.

6. In the Customize dialog box, click the Commands tab.

7. In the Commands list, select the button you want to add, and then click and drag the button to the new toolbar.

8. When the cursor changes to an I-beam, release your mouse button.

9. To close the Customize dialog box, click Close.

10. To move your new toolbar to the toolbar area, click and drag its title bar to the desired location.

Delete a Custom Toolbar

You cannot remove any default toolbar, only custom ones that you created.
To remove a custom toolbar, complete the following steps:

1. Open the View menu, and then click Customize.

2. Click the Toolbars tab.

3. From the Toolbars list, select the toolbar you want to remove, and then click Delete.

4. To close the Customize dialog box, click Close.

Customizing the Menus

The command menus can be as personalized as your filing system at home: you can arrange things so you can find them when you need them without having to remember another person's logic. So customize away, and make those menus your own.

Hide a Menu

You can control which menus display during certain conditions. For example, if you start Paint Shop Pro 8 but have not yet opened an image, you can choose to hide the menus that require an image to be open.

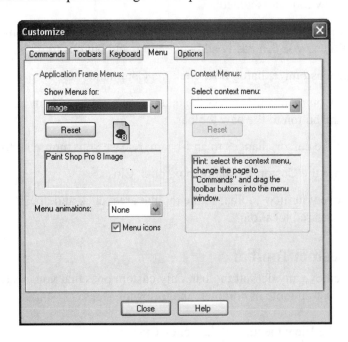

To hide images, complete the following steps:

1. Open the View menu, and then click Customize.

2. Click the Menu tab.

3. Click the arrow to the right of the Show Menus For drop-down box.

4. Click the menu you want displayed, regardless of the situation:

   ■ If you want to view image-related menus whether an image file is open or not, click Image.

   ■ If you want to view browser-related menus whether the browser window is open or not, click Browser.

- The default menu is displayed at all times. It cannot be disabled.

5. To close the Customize dialog box, click Close.

Remove Options from a Menu

There is no real reason for removing items from a menu; however, if you ever feel the need to do so, the option is available.

To remove items from a menu, complete the following steps:

1. Open the View menu, and then click Customize.

2. Click the Menu tab.

3. Open the menu you want to customize. There are a couple of different ways to do this:

- Click the menu title in the menu bar.

- Select a context menu from the Select Context Menu pull-down list.

4. With the menu open, click the Commands tab in the Customize dialog box.

5. In the open menu, click and drag the item you want to remove to the Commands list.

6. To close the Customize dialog box, click Close.

Add Options to a Menu

If you find yourself always looking for a command in a menu but can never seem to find it, you may want to add that command to that menu to save yourself time and possible headaches.

To add items to a menu, complete the following steps:

1. Open the View menu, and then click Customize.

2. Click the Menu tab.

3. Open the menu you want to customize. There are a couple of different ways to do this:

- Click the menu title in the menu bar.

- Select a context menu from the Select Context Menu pull-down list.

4. In the Categories list, select the category of the command you want to add. For example, if the command controls a file-related function like Save, that command is likely to be in the File category.

5. In the Commands list, select the icon you want to add, and then click and drag the icon to the open menu.

6. When the cursor changes to an I-beam, release your mouse button.

7. To close the Customize dialog box, click Close.

Additional Options

To set additional menu options, complete the following steps:

1. Open the View menu, and then click Customize.

2. Click the Menu tab.

3. Menu animations control the way the menus open. If you want to play with the different settings, click the arrow to the right of the Menu Animations drop-down box, and then choose a style.

- **None**   Applies no animations.

- **Unfold**   Displays the menu in chunks.

- **Slide**   Slides the menu down from the top.

- **Fade**   Causes the menu to fade in.

4. Select the Menu icons check box if you want to see the associated command icon next to the menu command. This can help you learn what the command icons do.

Additional Toolbar and Menu Options

You can control how your command icons and menus appear and disable the tool tips from popping up each time you move your cursor over an item.

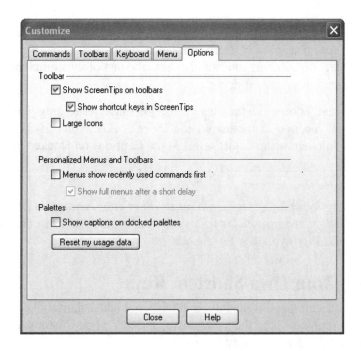

To set additional toolbar and menu options, complete the following steps:

1. Open the View menu and click Customize.

2. Click the Options tab.

3. Under the Toolbar section, you can select one or more of the following options:

   ■ **Show Screen Tips on Toolbars**   Displays a pop-up tip about the tool your cursor is currently suspended over.

   ■ **Show Shortcut Keys in Screen Tips**   Adds the shortcut key to the above tool tip.

   ■ **Large Icons**   Makes the icons in each toolbar larger and easier to see.

4. Under the Personalized Menus and Toolbars section, you can choose to have your most recently used commands appear first on a given menu. If you select this option, you can also hide the rest of the commands on a menu until after a short delay.

5. If you really don't like the idea of using the handles to drag your palettes from one location to another when they're docked, you can choose to show a mini title bar, instead: just select Show Captions on Docked Palettes.

6. To close the Customize dialog box, click Close.

 *Clicking Reset My Usage Data resets all of your customization options to their defaults. It also clears your command history and any other workspace customizations you may have made.*

Assigning Your Own Shortcut Keys

Have you used a command frequently and wished it had a shortcut key? Your wish has been granted. Open the View menu, and then click Customize. Click the Keyboard tab and assign away.

To assign a shortcut key, complete the following steps:

1. From the Category pull-down list, select the category for the command you want to assign a shortcut key for.

2. From the Commands list, select the command you want to assign a shortcut key for.

3. If the command already has a shortcut key assigned, it will display in the Current Keys text box. To assign a new shortcut key, click inside the Press New Shortcut Key text box, and then press your new shortcut key combination.

4. If your shortcut key combination is already assigned, a message appears below the Press New Shortcut Key text box. Unless you want to overwrite the old shortcut key assignment, you need to try another combination.

5. When you are finished, click Assign, and then click Close.

Creating Your Own Workspace

Now that you have made some customizations, you may want to save them as a Workspace preference. For example, if you are working on a project for a client and have set your workspace to bring up their images in the browser and have set the preferences used for their specific images, you can save that workspace and recall it at will. This not only saves you precious time, it keeps your projects organized and promotes professionalism in the eyes of your client.

Saving Your Workspace

To save a workspace, complete the following steps:

1. Open the File menu, click Workspace, and then click Save.

 *To open the Save Workspace dialog box, you can also press* SHIFT-ALT-S.

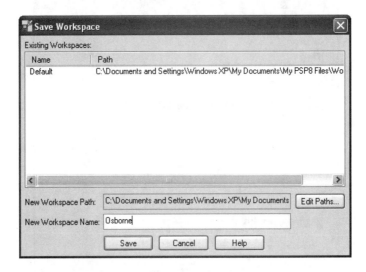

2. Keep the default path, or click Edit Paths to select a new path where you want your workspace settings saved.

3. In the New Workspace Name text box, type the name you want to give to your workspace, and then click Save.

Loading a Custom Workspace

Switching between projects can be a time-consuming task. If you can quickly load specific preferences used for a given project, it will save you time. It's like having one of those luxury cars that remembers driver seat settings, mirror positions, and environment preferences for each driver. Just push a button and voila, you're on your way.

You may not have a luxury car, but you do have a luxury image-editing application that remembers your preferences.

To load a custom workspace, complete the following steps:

1. Open the File menu, click Workspace, and then click Load.

 *To open the Load Workspace dialog box, you can also press* SHIFT-ALT-L.

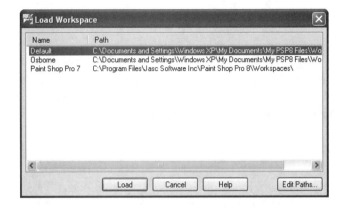

2. From the list, select the name of the workspace you want to load, and then click Load.

Preferences

When you set preferences, you instruct Paint Shop Pro 8 how to handle various aspects of your image-editing needs. Specify default file locations, color settings, format preferences, and much, much more. These preferences become part of the workspace environment and can be set for each workspace you have saved.

 *If you want your preferences saved, make certain you save the workspace when you are done making changes.*

General Program Preferences

When you open the File menu, click Preferences, and then click General Program Preferences. The following dialog appears:

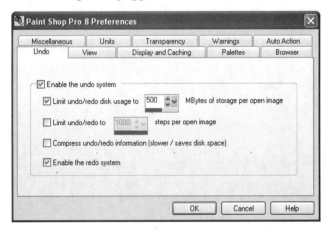

Undo

Click this tab to specify undo limits and how much command history memory you want to reserve for each open image. The higher the limit, the more commands can be stored. You can also compress the undo information to save memory. Depending on the speed of your system, this may or may not be a convenient choice. Unless you have extremely limited memory, I strongly suggest you do not disable the Undo feature.

View

Click this tab to specify zoom and image display preferences. For example, you may want the image to fill the screen rather than fit into a predefined window size. These are just the default settings; you can always change these settings in the program when you need to.

Display and Caching

Click this tab to specify presentation preferences, image, and group layer options. For example, if you prefer using precise cursors as opposed to a traditional pointer, you can choose this preference. If you use a specific font face in your text, you may want to have Paint Shop Pro 8 remember your last font choice for future text objects. In the layers sections, you can define how you want the images in your layers managed.

Palettes

Click this tab to specify how your color palette displays colors and which palettes can and cannot be docked. These options are helpful if you are dealing with a client that uses very specific colors in their design. You can specify how you want the color palette to present the colors. It's a matter of personal preference, so experiment and find one that works well for your particular application.

Browser

Click this tab to specify how your file browser displays image thumbnails and which colors to use. You can change the size of the thumbnail and the style of how it displays.

Miscellaneous

Click this tab to specify the number of recently used files you want to list, and how to handle images stored on the Clipboard. If your system is short on memory, you may want to reduce these values.

Units

Click this tab to specify how to show units of measure. There may be times when inches work better than pixels. You can also specify the default resolution, which is very useful when designing web elements versus printable images.

Transparency

Click this tab to specify how to handle transparent backgrounds.

Warnings

Click this tab to specify the types of warnings you want displayed in given circumstances.

Auto Action

Click this tab to specify which actions you want performed automatically and when they should occur.

CMYK Conversion Preferences

This handy little tool enables you to specify CMYK color conversions for a given project. When you open the File menu, click Preferences, and then click CMYK Conversion Preferences. The following dialog appears:

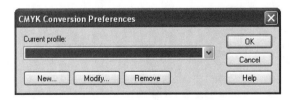

To specify your preferences for the first time, you must first click New. In the Enter Profile Name text box, type a name for your profile, and then click OK.

Once the name of your profile appears as the current profile, click Modify to set your preferences for that profile.

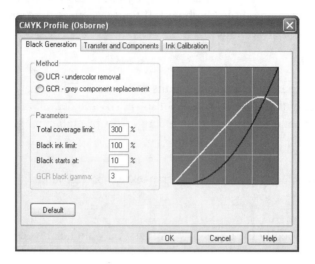

File Format Preferences

To specify how to handle or display specific types of files, open the File menu, click Preferences, and then click File Format Preferences. The following dialog appears:

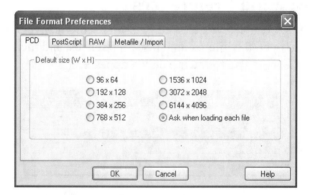

File Format Associations

To select the types of files you want to associate with Paint Shop Pro 8, open the File menu, click Preferences, and then click File Format Associations. The following dialog appears:

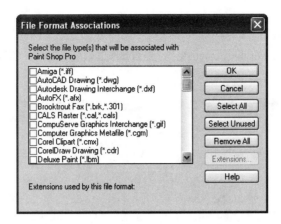

After you make your selections, whenever you double-click files with any of the selected file extensions, they will automatically open in Paint Shop Pro 8.

File Locations

To specify the preferred locations for specific types of files, open the File menu, click Preferences, and then click File Locations. The following dialog appears:

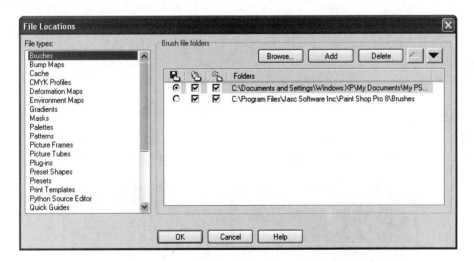

If you are working on a particular project, it is helpful to create a directory for that project and store all associated files under that directory.

Color Management

When you open the File menu, click Preferences, and then click Color Management. The following dialog appears:

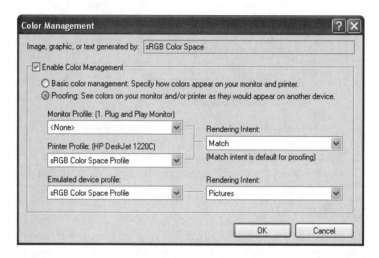

If you have a plug-and-play monitor that can be calibrated, this is where you can adjust the color on your monitor to match your desired output. This enables you to see the colors as they will appear in their final format. This is a great tool for photo enhancements and images that will appear in magazines or other printed documents.

Monitor Gamma

To fine-tune the gamma settings for your monitor, open the File menu, click Preferences, and then click Monitor Gamma. The following dialog appears:

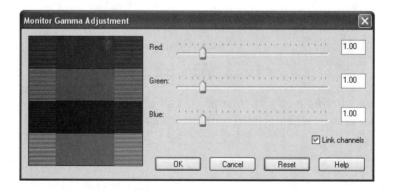

Adjust the color settings until they closely match your desired output.

Autosave Settings

To specify how often you want Paint Shop Pro to save your work, open the File menu, click Preferences, and then click Autosave Settings. The following dialog appears:

If you are not disciplined at remembering to save your work periodically, this feature is a real treasure.

Resetting Application Preferences

To reset various preferences to their original factory settings, open the File menu, click Preferences, and then click Reset Preferences. The following dialog appears:

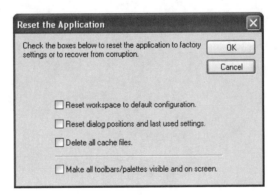

This is a good way to start from scratch if you make many changes that you are not thrilled about.

Chapter 3

Capture and Manage Your Photos

How to...

- Discover all the ways to bring photos into Paint Shop Pro
- Connect and move pictures from digital cameras
- Scan images
- Choose the best graphics format to save your images
- Visually search for photos with the Browser
- Organize your photos with Paint Shop Photo Album

Before you can use Paint Shop Pro to work on photos or any other image, you must first get the images into the computer. With the advent of inexpensive scanners, (relatively) inexpensive digital cameras, and the Internet, you now have the capability to digitize your existing treasured photographs and you also have access to hundreds, if not thousands, of digital pictures. In this chapter, you will learn how to get pictures into the computer from a variety of sources (scanners, digital cameras, and so on) so they can be opened in Paint Shop Pro. We will also look at ways to capture better images with your scanner to obtain improved output and ultimately better pictures.

Putting Photos into Your Computer

Regardless of what you plan to do with or to an image, the first step requires getting the picture into the computer. While it would be nice to just stick your favorite photograph into a slot on your computer and have it appear on the computer screen, it isn't that simple. A photograph must first be converted to a digital file before it can be opened in Paint Shop Pro—and not just any digital file, it must be in a graphic file format. Some images, like photographs taken using digital cameras, are already in a file format that can be opened by Paint Shop Pro, but photographs taken with traditional film cameras must be converted into graphic files using a scanner. In this section, you will learn about available sources of digital images and what equipment is necessary to convert nondigital images (like photographs) into graphic files.

Where Digital Pictures Come From

Digital pictures that can be used in Paint Shop Pro are available from a variety of sources. It would be impossible to list them all, so what follows is a brief summary of some of the more popular sources for digital images.

Digital Cameras

In the span of a few short years digital cameras (also called digicams) have and will continue to change the way we approach photography. Early digital cameras were expensive and produced poor quality photographs. By contrast, today's entry-level digital cameras produce excellent results, cost much less, and give you the ability (after you have paid for the camera) to take thousands of photos at little to no cost. Digital cameras like the ones shown next, come in all sizes and prices but they all produce pictures that can be read by Paint Shop Pro.

Scanners

A scanner can turn almost any photograph, printed image, or even a 3D object (like a coin collection or flowers) into a graphic file that can be brought into Paint Shop Pro for enhancement, correction, or restoration. Even if you own a digital camera, you may still want a scanner. If you have old photo albums with photographs or negatives tucked away, you can scan and convert them into digital images, if only to preserve them.

It may surprise you to know that there are five different types of scanners used in the graphics industry, but only two types of these scanners (Figure 3-1) are of interest to Paint Shop Pro users:

- Flatbed scanners
- Color slide and negative scanners

FIGURE 3-1   A flatbed scanner (left) and a film scanner (right) are used to convert photographs, slides, and negatives into digital images.

Did you know?

Which Scanner Connection Is Best?

Older scanners used a parallel (printer port) or SCSI connection to connect the scanner to the computer. Their connection speed was slow and they were difficult to install. Almost every personal flatbed scanner sold today connects to the computer using a Universal Serial Bus (USB) interface, which offers easy connection hookup and fast data speeds to the computer. Some expensive scanners offer an IEEE-1394 (also called FireWire and iLink) interface, which is much faster than the original USB (also called USB 1.0 or 1.1). Newer scanners use the faster USB 2.0 specification (your computer must support USB 2.0 to get the maximum benefit of the improved scanning speed). Because the connectors are identical, the only way to tell if it is a USB 2.0 port is to check the documentation. If your computer supports only the original USB, your scanner can still scan using it, but the connection speed will only be as fast as USB 1.1.

Flatbed Scanners   Scanners can convert just about anything into a digital image. Many people are unaware that scanning is not limited to flat things like photographs. Scanners capture an image of whatever is placed on the scanner glass, and the captured image is sent to the computer in the form of a digital graphics file.

Film Scanners   Film negatives and slides require a film scanner that is specifically designed to scan very small 35mm originals. Some of the more expensive flatbed scanners offer transparency adapters for scanning color slides and negatives. Dedicated film scanners have traditionally provided noticeably superior results compared to flatbed scanners but that's now beginning to change. Today's combination flatbed scanner with transparency adapter is producing adequate-to-good results. Like scanners in general, the price of film scanners has dropped over the past few years, but they still cost more than the equivalent-quality flatbed scanner. The Pacific Image Electronics PrimeFilm 1800 film scanner shown in Figure 3-2 was the first film scanner to sell for under $200.

FIGURE 3-2   The availability of low-cost film scanners allows consumers to scan their existing film and slide collections. Photograph courtesy of Pacific Image Electronics.

Importing Digital Photos into Your Computer

Whichever type of camera you use, you need a way to get the pictures from the camera into the computer. To do this you need a physical connection between the camera and the computer using one of the following:

- Serial connection (very old and very slow)
- Dedicated card reader
- USB connection to the camera
- 1394/FireWire/iLink connection to the camera

The type of connection determines how long it will take to move pictures from your camera to the computer. Outside of buying a different camera, you cannot control the type of connection your camera has.

How your digital camera is hooked up to the computer and which operating system is used determines what methods can be used to copy pictures from the camera into the computer. When your camera is attached to the computer, it appears in Windows as a hard disk drive. For example, in the Paint Shop Pro Browser window shown below, my Nikon D-100 appears as Drive H.

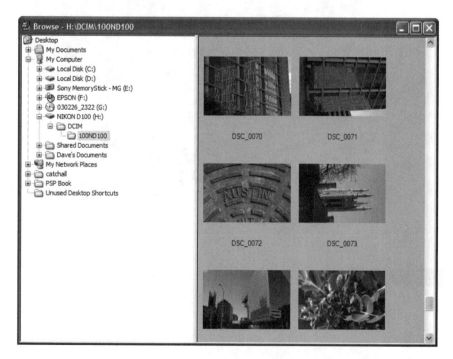

Generally, to copy pictures directly from the camera into your computer you can use any of the following methods:

- Read directly from the camera using File | Open (CTRL-O), and then open the File Browser. The camera then reads its memory device (flash card, MemoryStick, and so on) holding the pictures. This method is very slow, even if you're using a fast connection like USB or 1394.

- Use File | Import, choose Twain, and from the Select Source dialog box, select the camera from a list, where the camera will appear as a WIA (Windows Imaging Acquisition) device. From the same Twain menu, select Acquire. A message box briefly opens, telling you it is communicating with the camera (or scanner), and then thumbnails of the pictures in the camera appear in the Get Pictures dialog box (shown next). This feature works pretty fast. Double-clicking an image copies it from the camera into Paint Shop Pro.

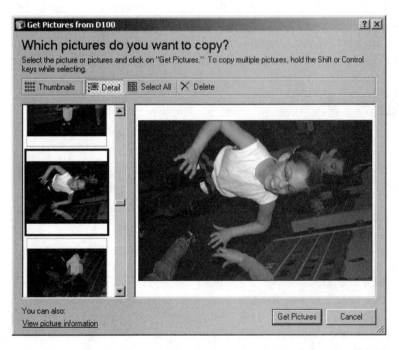

- Read directly from the digital camera media by plugging the camera's memory card into a card reader attached to your computer. This method is much faster than reading through the camera.

- Transfer the pictures to your computer's hard drive using Windows Explorer or the software that came with your camera. This is faster than trying to view the images through the camera but slower than using a card reader.

All of the methods for getting images we have looked at up until now involved navigating through menus, here is a faster way to do the same thing. Click the Twain Acquire button (shown left) in the standard toolbar. This opens the Get Pictures dialog box without the need to open the File and Import menus.

 *If you have used earlier versions of Paint Shop Pro, you may notice that there is no longer a dedicated digital camera interface. This is no longer necessary now that digital cameras are recognized by the operating systems.*

Using Digital Camera Software

Most software that comes bundled with digital cameras provides a range of features such as image management, camera control, and the ability to rotate, flip, and name pictures and to move them to and from the camera. Nikon View 5 (shown in Figure 3-3) is a good example of full-featured camera software that makes getting pictures into the computer a breeze.

The camera's software is often launched automatically when a digital camera (with a USB interface) is plugged into the computer.

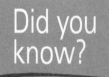

The Disadvantages of WIA

If your digital camera or scanner is attached to a computer that uses Windows XP or Me, each time you attach your camera to the computer you will be asked what application the operating system should use to talk with your camera. One of those choices will be the Windows Imaging Acquisition (WIA) interface. While this provides a simple way to move pictures directly from your digital camera or scanner to the computer, WIA is a generic, no frills control interface and is therefore not as full-featured as the software controls that come with your camera. This is especially true of the WIA scanner interface. Many of the features in your scanner that allow you to get the best possible scan are not usually available in the WIA interface.

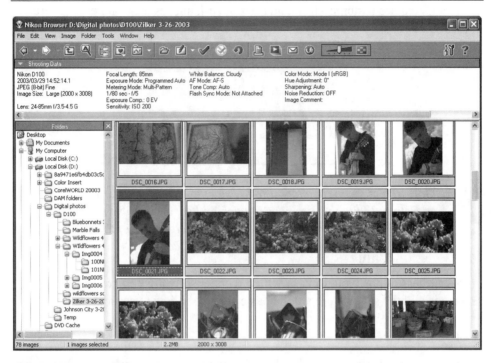

FIGURE 3-3   Some digital cameras offer special software to import and sort camera images.

    Your digital camera software may not automatically launch when you connect a camera—you see this most often in older computers that have early versions of USB hardware. However, the software still works, it just doesn't start automatically.

Scanning Photos with Your Scanner

Even with a digital camera, you still can use a scanner to capture existing photographs, memorabilia, and important documents like diplomas. Scanning can be accomplished in one of two ways. You can press a button on the front of the scanner that launches the scanning software that was put into your computer when you installed the scanner, or you can start the scanner directly from Paint Shop Pro by choosing File | Import | Twain | Select Source. This opens a list (shown next) of installed imaging devices (cameras and scanners). Note that two of the scanners use WIA, as indicated by the letters preceding their name. Selecting a scanner from the list and then clicking the Twain Acquire button in the standard toolbar launches the scanner software in Paint Shop Pro.

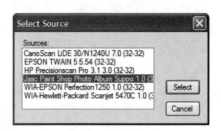

 *Many scanners on the market today start in a fully automatic mode of operation. While this provides a quick and easy way to scan an image, it does not always produce the best quality scans. For optimum scans, I recommend that you not use the automatic feature.*

Regardless of how you do it, or which scanner software you are using, the process is still the same. Here are the basic steps to follow to scan an image.

1. Preview and Select the image.

2. Select the Correct Input Mode and scan the image.

3. Review the scanned image and Rescan the image if necessary.

The following sections discuss each of these steps.

Previewing the Image

Most scanning software produces a preview image as soon as the scanner is started. In some cases, the preview scan will not occur immediately because the software is waiting for the lamp in the scanner, which assures the color accuracy of the scan, to warm up. In some cases the scanner may be waiting for you to initiate the preview scan.

All preview scans, like the one shown in Figure 3-4, are low resolution representations of the scanned image. Even though the preview is a low-quality image, you use it to select the area to be scanned and to verify the color mode setting of the scanner.

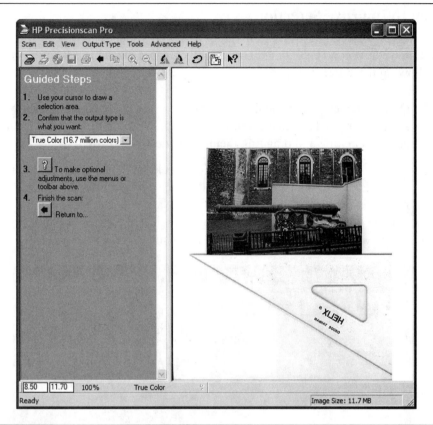

FIGURE 3-4   Preview scans are low-resolution images.

Select the Area to Be Scanned (Crop)

From the preview, you select the area that you want to scan. Your scanner may attempt to automatically select the image area for you, and most of the time it will do a good job. The two situations where this doesn't work are when the border color of the image being scanned is similar to the color of the color of the inside of the scanner lid and when you are scanning only a part of the image placed on the scanner.

Zoom to Improve Selection

When you are selecting a single item out of many on a sheet of paper, or when the selection of the area to be scanned is critical, you can make an accurate selection by following these steps:

1. On the preview, click and drag a rectangle of the area that you want to scan. After you have made a rough selection, you can move the selection bars by clicking and dragging them to the desired position.

2. After you have made the first selection, click the button or command that zooms in the selected area. (On the HP PrecisionScan Pro dialog box, shown next, it is the button with the magnifying glass with the plus sign in it.) The scanner will scan the image again, and the selected area will fill the preview window and you can make any final adjustment to the selection bars.

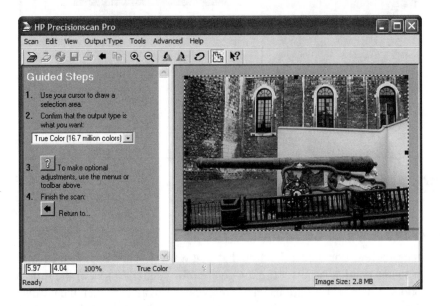

3. If the photo isn't oriented correctly, you can rotate it using the scanning software, or you can scan it into the computer and rotate it using Paint Shop Pro. Rotations in multiples of 90 degrees do not degrade image quality.

Once the image looks the way you want it to, there are only a few more selections to make.

Selecting the Correct Input Mode

Not so long ago, the dialog box that controlled the scanner asked the user to select the color input mode with choices like line art, halftone, grayscale, 256-color, or RGB color, plus all of the possible naming variations of these modes used by different scanner manufacturers. Current scanner software tries to determine what kind of image it is you are scanning and then describes the scanner color mode in terms of what the image is, as shown here:

However, even the more full-featured scanners that cost a little more tend to describe the mode rather than the type of image being scanned.

The following table illustrates some of the more popular terms for various color input modes:

Technical Term	Commonly Described as
Line art	Black-and-white document, OCR, bitmap (1-bit)
Grayscale	Black-and-white photo, 256-gray shades
Grayscale with d-screening	Black-and-white document
256-color	Web graphics, web palette
RGB color	Color photo, millions of colors
RGB color with descreening	Color document
48-bit color	Billions of colors

Scanning printed material can create moiré patterns, so most scanners offer a feature that eliminates, or at least greatly reduces, these patterns. The process is called descreening, *and it is usually selected automatically by the scanner depending on your input mode selection.*

As a general rule, the scanning software is pretty accurate in guessing the correct color mode. Here are a couple guidelines:

- **Web color graphics** Even though the images you are bringing into Paint Shop Pro might eventually be converted to 256-color, you should still scan these as RGB color images because many of the filters and features in your Paint Shop Pro require RGB color images to work.

- **Line art** These are black-and-white images that you usually find on business cards. Line art should not be confused with grayscale.

Change the Size of Your Photo with the Scanner

A great scanner feature is its ability to change an image's size. Although the physical size of an image can also be changed in Paint Shop Pro through a process called resampling, this method visibly degrades the image so that it loses sharpness and detail. This is as true for Adobe Photoshop as it is for Paint Shop Pro. However, if the original photo is scaled by the scanner, it can be made several times larger without the accompanying loss of detail. Scaling is accomplished by having the scanner scan at a higher resolution, which produces more pixels and creates a larger picture. If the original photo is of poor quality, the resulting larger image will also be poor quality and the defects will be more apparent because it's larger. The best use for scaling is when you are scanning a photo for a particular publication like a newsletter and need a photo that is a specific size for placement. After you crop the photo with the selection, you can tell the scanner software what size the output needs to be, and it will do all of the math and produce a scanned image at the desired size. You can usually specify either the percentage or what the finished size is supposed to be. In the Resize dialog box shown next, the size of the original is being doubled (200 percent).

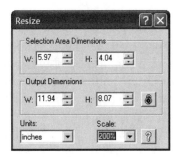

If you're going to be doing a lot of retouching or restoration work on a photo, it is recommended you scale it to twice the original size to make it easier to work on detail areas. When the image is finished, you can still print it at the original size by doubling the resolution before sending it to the printer.

Scanning the Image

The next step is to scan the image. If the scanning software was launched from within Paint Shop Pro, the scanned image appears in an image window within the program. If the scanner was started using a button on the scanner or by launching the scanning software from the computer, most scanning software will offer you the choice of sending the image to Paint Shop Pro, printing it, or saving it as a file. Later in this chapter, you will learn about the different formats available to save scanned images and the advantages and disadvantages of each type.

Reviewing the Scanned Image

Before you remove the photo from the scanner, you should look at the finished scan in Paint Shop Pro. This step is important because you have been looking at the low resolution preview image. You need to look at a high-quality image to evaluate the scan. Here are a couple of things to look for when evaluating the scan.

Does the Image Have Fingerprints, Dust, or Debris on It?

These may appear as tiny blotches of white or black. If there are more than a few, remove the photo and clean it. Verify that the scanner glass is clean, position it back on the scanner glass and scan it again. If there are only one or two small dirty defects and the scan appears to be otherwise in good shape, it may take less time to use Paint Shop Pro to remove them.

Does the Scan Appear to Be Crooked?

Even though you aligned the photo on the scanner, sometimes replacing the lid has a whoosh effect, and the air being displaced by the lid moves the image ever so slightly. Even though your image editing program can correct a crooked scan, it does so at the price of slight image degradation. In addition to this, with most photo editors, getting the correct rotation angle can take as long as or longer than realigning and rescanning the image. Your best action is to remove the photo, realign it, and scan it again.

Saving Your Digital Images

After going to all this work to get a digital image into Paint Shop Pro, you need to save the image, and there are many different image types to choose from. In this section, you will learn about several options for saving your photos and the tradeoffs involved in making large image files as small as possible. The procedure for saving Paint Shop Pro files isn't complicated:

1. Select the format for saving the scanned image.

2. Choose the settings for the selected graphic format.

3. Save the image file.

Types of Graphic Files

The first decision you must make before saving any scanned image is what graphics format to use. Images are saved in Paint Shop Pro just as a letter is saved in your word processor or any other Windows program. What makes it seem complicated is that you can save the files in many different formats. If you are new to computer graphics, the list of graphic formats that Paint Shop Pro supports (Figure 3-5) can almost take your breath away. However, despite all of these choices, there are only a few formats that you will actually ever need to use.

Don't let all of the names of these formats confuse you. Essentially, all of the formats can be categorized into one of the following groups:

■ **Internet formats**   These formats are used to send with e-mails and post on web pages. Most Internet browsers recognize and display them.

■ **Graphic standard formats**   When you need to save the file in a format that someone else can open, you use of one the formats that are considered industry standards for graphic exchange.

3

■ **Native formats**   Any file format that is unique to the program that saved it is called its native format. Saving an image in a native file format maintains all of the information that is unique to that particular application, such as layers, selections, and so on.

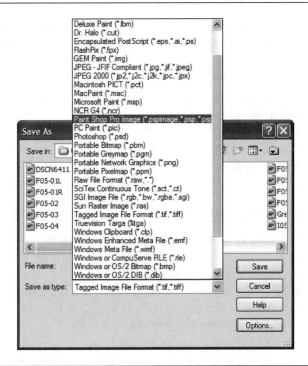

There are many different file formats that can be used to save images.

Internet Formats

The size of graphic files sent over the Internet should be as small as possible so they can be downloaded quickly. To make the images smaller, some form of compression is applied to the files. The two most popular formats that have built-in file compression are GIF and JPEG (including JPEG 2000). There are two types of compression used in file formats: *lossless*, which reduces file size by roughly 50 percent and preserves the image, and *lossy*, which achieves a great amount of compression (up to 90 percent) with some image degradation (called lossy).

When to Use JPEG or GIF   While JPEG is great, it isn't going to replace GIF anytime soon; for some types of images, GIF is the best choice for image quality, file size, or both. To understand when to use JPEG requires that you know which kinds of images work best with it. Overall, JPEG is superior to GIF for storing full-color or grayscale images like scanned photographs, continuous-tone artwork, and similar material. Any scanned image containing smooth variation in color, such as occurs in highlighted or shaded areas, will be represented more accurately and in less space with JPEG than with GIF.

What GIF works best is when saving scanned images containing only a few distinct colors, such as simple logos, line drawings, and cartoons. For these types of images the compression in GIF is not only lossless, but in most cases it actually compresses them more than JPEG can. This is because large areas of pixels of identical colors are compressed more efficiently by GIF, while JPEG can't compress this type of data as much as GIF does without introducing artifacts.

Graphic Standard Formats

When you need to send a scanned image to a printer or a service bureau, they will most likely ask for it in the graphics format that has become the de facto standard for publishing. Its official name is Tagged Image Format File but everyone refers to it by its initials TIFF or TIF (they're both pronounced the same). TIFF files also offer several lossless compression options but, as with GIF files, you can only expect a 40 percent to 50 percent reduction in file size.

Another format that is used a lot in the Windows environment is BMP. When you want to save a scanned image for use as wallpaper on your Windows platform, you should save it as a BMP file.

To preserve the quality of scanned images that are important or require photo editing, you should always save a copy using Paint Shop Pro's native format (*.PSP) or a nonlossy format like TIF.

Paint Shop Pro's Native Formats

Saving a file in Paint Shop Pro's native format allows it to be opened later without losing any special features or information that can only be interpreted and used by Paint Shop Pro. This is the format of choice for important images that you may want to revisit at a later date. Why not save all of the images in native format? Well, first of all, the files can get quite large, especially if the image contains lots of layers. Secondly, not everyone has a copy of Paint Shop Pro, which is necessary to open the file.

Saving your scanned images in any format other than those already mentioned should only be done if you have a specific request for them; otherwise, don't use them.

Paint Shop Pro now offers the option to save the image as a JPEG 2000 (JP2) which offers greater compression than JPEG with less image degradation. Before you get all excited and begin to save images in this format, I recommend that you wait until most of the major Internet browsers support this new JPEG standard or others will not be able to open or view the file.

Now that the images are captured and stored, let's consider image management.

Using the File Browser

Paint Shop Pro's File Browser is a great visual picture manager that provides an easy way to move, view, and manage images on your computer. Using the Browser couldn't be simpler:

1. With Paint Shop Pro open, launch the Browser by either selecting File | Browse, clicking the Browse button in the standard toolbar (looks like a little file cabinet), or typing the keyboard shortcut (CTRL-B). The Browser

window (shown next) opens and displays the currently selected folder on the left and thumbnails of its contents on the right.

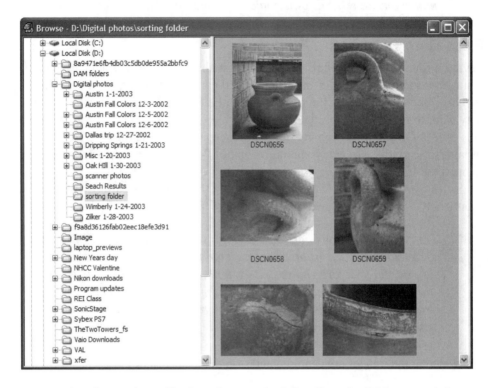

2. Using the Explorer-like interface on the left, select the folder containing the pictures you want to work with. The first time you open a folder you will see blank icons in the right pane, and Paint Shop Pro will take a few moments to generate the preview thumbnails in the area on the right side of the window. Once Browser has created the thumbnails, it saves them in a special file in the same folder so that the next time you open it, the thumbnails appear instantly.

3. Select individual pictures by clicking them one time. Select multiple individual pictures by holding down CTRL while clicking the thumbnails, or select all of the pictures in the folder by pressing CTRL-A.

4. Once selected, drag the pictures into Paint Shop Pro either by clicking one of the selected thumbnails and dragging it into the Paint Shop Pro Image window, or double-clicking the thumbnail.

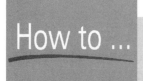 **Set Browser Preferences**

3

You can customize several features in the Browser by right-clicking anywhere in the thumbnail side of the Browser and choosing Preferences. The Paint Shop Pro Preferences dialog box opens on the Browser page with several customizable features. You can change the size of the thumbnails so that they are large enough to recognize the image but small enough to fit the maximum number of thumbnails per screen. I recommend using 100 pixels, but if you have photos on which you need to see greater detail, use the maximum setting of 150 pixels. The other choices are mainly concerned with the overall appearance of the Browser.

TIP   *Place the cursor over a thumbnail in the Browser and, after a moment, a pop-up window will appear and display a lot of information about the picture, as shown here:*

DSCN0656.JPG
1920 x 2560 x 16 Million, 1.56 MB
Kodak Photo-CD Image Pac
12/25/2002 8:02:27 PM

Picture Management Solutions

One of the big advantages of digital cameras is their capability to take an almost unlimited number of pictures at little to no additional cost. As a result, most of us end up with many photos on our computers; I have over 25,000 photos on mine. Keeping track of all of those pictures can be a real challenge, so here are some ideas to help you with that.

Using Paint Shop Photo Album

With the release of Paint Shop Pro 8, Jasc included a 30-day evaluation copy of a full-featured image management program called Paint Shop Photo Album. For a 30-day preview period, you have access to all of the Paint Shop Photo Album Premium features. After the 30-day preview period, many of the features no longer function unless you purchase the upgrade, but even after the preview period is over you will still be able to do the following:

- Transfer photos from your digital camera into Album

- Organize and find your photos using the search options

- Print using standard (not custom) photo sizes

- E-mail photos to friends and family

- Create slide shows

Paint Shop Photo Album is a powerful visual image management tool that helps you catalog and later locate your photos. It also has a wealth of other goodies like a program that lets you make panoramas, slide shows, or video CDs. This program is launched by choosing File | Jasc Software Products and selecting Launch Paint Shop Photo Album (Figure 3-6).

Understanding Albums and Images

Paint Shop Photo Album keeps information about all of the images in collections called albums, as shown in Figure 3-7.

The first time you open the Album program, it collects information about the photos in your computer and stores information (for example, filename, type of image, and file size) in a special database file. This process of collecting information is called cataloging, and it happens automatically. Any media connected to your system can be cataloged, including removable media (such as Zip disks, CD-ROMs, and DVDs, to name a few).

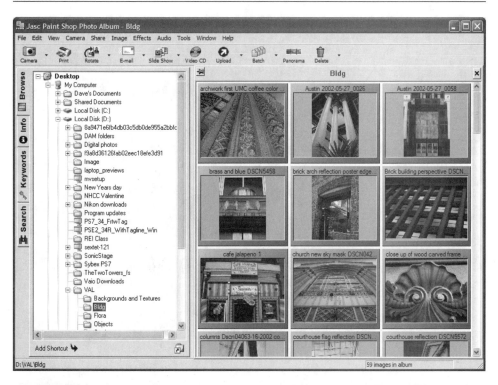

FIGURE 3-6   Paint Shop Photo Album provides powerful visual image
management tools.

You must allow the program to catalog your drives before you are able to use
the Album Search tools. Once your drives are cataloged, you can quickly find images
based on such criteria as file type, size, date created, and so on. You can also assign
keywords (like Betty's Birthday, Christmas, cow tipping), so you can search for
photos in the album based on the content of the image.

Even though an album appears to physically contain the images because you
can see the thumbnails, it is really only a visual representation of images located
elsewhere on your computer.

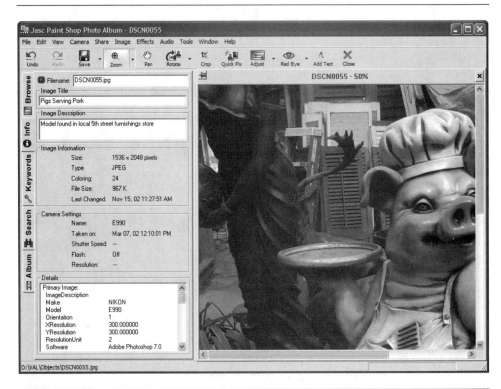

FIGURE 3-7   Paint Shop Photo Album displays EXIF camera data for each photo.

Getting the Pictures Out of the Album

Once you find an image or images that you want to use, you can do one of several things with them. Double-clicking a thumbnail opens the image window, as shown in Figure 3-8.

The following is a list of some of the things you can do to the photo:

■ Crop it

■ Rotate it

- Apply Quick Fix to it

- Launch the Adjust Wizard, which performs image tonal and color correction using a wizard-style approach

- Remove red eye from it

- Add text to it

- Send it into Paint Shop Pro (CTRL-])

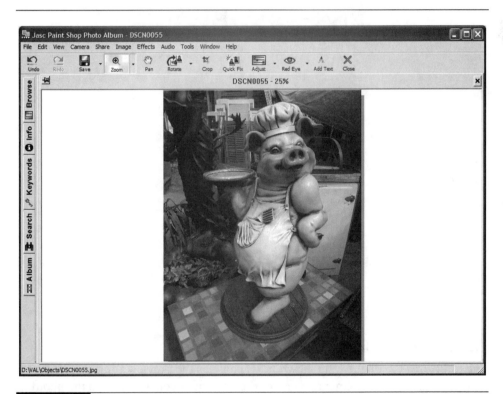

FIGURE 3-8   From this window you can do lots of cool stuff.

Selecting the Info Tab

Clicking the Info tab on the left (see below) displays all of the information about the file, including its title, description, and all of the technical information from the digital camera (if it is available).

Tracking and Assigning Keywords

The Keywords tab on the left (shown next) changes the preview for the selected photo and displays checkmarks by all of the keywords you assigned to the photo. If I forgot where this photo was, for example, I'd just open the Search tab and look for all photos with the keyword Pig (under pets), and the album will display them. Fortunately, I have only one.

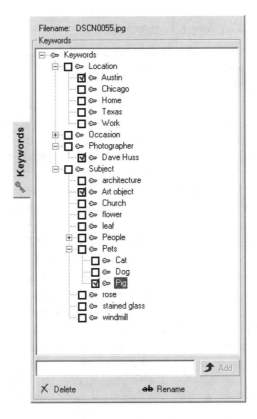

The Album program has so many features that it is beyond the scope of this book to do anything but whet your appetite. There are several excellent tutorials in the online Help files for the Album program. For those of you who don't want to use Album to organize your photos, here are some general organizational tips I have learned over the years.

Other Ways to Categorize Photos

Keep photos organized in folders named for the event, for example, Amanda's Wedding, Baby's First Birthday. If they are not photos of events, then use subject matter with dates, for example Bluebonnets 03-04-2001, or Clouds 12-15-2001. The best time to do this is when transferring the photos from the camera to the computer. I recommend maintaining a master folder on a hard drive in which you keep all of the digital photo folders.

Naming Pictures—A Real Timesaver

I have a few suggestions for naming pictures as well. All digital cameras automatically assign numbers to photos when the pictures are taken. Some cameras reset the numbers each time the media is removed from the camera. This can be a problem because you'll end up with many photo files with a label like AGF0001.JPG. If your camera works this way, having photos categorized in individual folders keeps the duplicate names from being a problem.

Other cameras make life a little easier by not resetting the picture number counter each time so each photo has a unique number. Regardless of how your camera works, you will want to give your pictures unique names that identify the picture. This brings up another potential headache. Let's say you have six pictures of Uncle Bob sitting in front of a fireplace. There are two possible solutions that prevent duplicate file names. You can use sequential numbers following the description, for example, Uncle Bob fireplace 01, Uncle Bob fireplace 02, and so on. But I like to keep the original photo files under the original number assigned by the camera, so I give the picture file a name by adding a descriptive name in front of the number. For example, Uncle Bob's photos would be Uncle Bob fireplace DCN0001, Uncle Bob fireplace DCN0002, and so on. I do this because I apply all changes, enhancements, or corrections to the named copy of the picture. Having the original photo number as part of the name allows us to locate the original picture file when necessary—and believe us, it is often necessary. Without the number, I would have to wade through dozens of images trying to see which original image is Uncle Bob fireplace 01.

A Lot of Information

I have covered a lot of material in this chapter. You have learned how to import pictures into Paint Shop Pro from many different imaging devices, whether it's a digital camera or a scanner. You also discovered how to save those images and how to organize them so you can locate them later. Phew. The next chapter is very brief, but it shows you how to control the important task of viewing and navigating around images in Paint Shop Pro.

Chapter 4

See Things Your Way

How to...

- Zoom in and out of an image
- Use the visual alignment tools
- Control your actions

Images and computer monitors come in various sizes. For this reason, Paint Shop Pro 8 provides many tools to enhance your ability to see great detail and preview an image before you commit it to print. In this chapter, you will learn how to use different zoom features and other tools that make getting around the image a breeze. You will also learn how to use the visual alignment tools, ruler guides, and grids and discover how easy it is to undo and redo your actions.

Resizing the Image Window to Fit Your Workspace

Depending on the size of your monitor or how your palettes are docked, your workspace size may vary. To get the most out of your workspace, there are several options to consider. Changing the zoom level changes your current view magnification. To get a true feel for how the image will look in its final format, view the image at 100 percent. While you're working on the image, however, it is very helpful to view the details of the area you're enhancing.

Fitting Your Image to the Window

If you want to work with a specific window size, you can resize the window and then instruct Paint Shop Pro 8 to fit the image inside the window, as shown in the following illustrations.

Click Fit to Window button

Resize Window

Image resized to fit the window

To resize an image to a specific window size, complete the following steps:

1. Position your cursor on the corner of the image window. When the cursor changes to a double-headed arrow, click and drag the window to the desired size and then release your mouse button.

2. On the Tools toolbar, make certain you have the Pan tool selected.

3. In the Tool Options palette, click the Fit to Window button.

> **TIP**   *If the Fit to Window button is unavailable, you can also open the Window menu and click Fit to Window.*

Fitting Your Window to the Image

Sometimes, when you resize the image window and then fit the image to that window, you are left with gaps in the window frame. This happens when you make the window an odd size for the actual image. These gaps are easily remedied with the Fit to Window command.

Click Fit to Window button

Gap between the image and the window

Window resized to fit the image

To resize the window to fit the new image size, complete the following steps:

1. On the Tools toolbar, make certain you have the Pan tool selected.

2. In the Tool Options palette, click the Fit to Window button.

Fitting the Image to Your Workspace

If you want to make the most of your workspace, click the View Full Size button (shown left) in the Tool Options palette. This action resizes the window and image to fill the entire workspace area minus the space reserved for your palettes (see Figure 4-1).

Changing Your Point of View

There may be times when you need to zero in on a specific area in an image. For example, you may want to change the color of a person's eyes, or remove a blemish. To do the best possible job, you need to zoom in on the image, but still have the ability to see the big picture. Paint Shop Pro 8 offers many tools to ensure you get the best possible view for the effect you desire.

Image resized to fit the workspace area

FIGURE 4-1   Image resized to fit the workspace

Zooming with the Scroll Wheel

If your mouse has a scroll wheel, you can use it to quickly zoom in and out of an image. To zoom in, position your cursor over the image and roll the scroll wheel up. To zoom out, position your cursor over the image and roll your scroll wheel down.

Zoom In Steps

4

If your mouse does not have a scroll wheel, or you find it cumbersome to use, there are other options for increasing the size of your image. You can open the View menu, click Zoom, and then click any one of the zoom levels from the submenu. An easier way, however, is to simply press the + or − key on your numeric keypad. These keys zoom you in or out one step at a time.

If you have your Pan tool selected, you can also click the Zoom buttons in the Tool Options palette, or specify a zoom level in the Zoom (%) text box as shown in the following illustration.

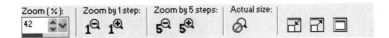

Moving Around in the Image

Once you zoom in on an area, you may need to move around the image to apply various levels of detail. There are a couple of different ways to move the image canvas. If your Pan tool is selected, you can hold your right mouse button and then drag the hand cursor over the image to move it, as shown in Figure 4-2.

If you have another tool selected, switching between the Pan tool and the tool you are using is not always convenient or practical. In that case, it is best to use the Overview palette. Position your cursor over the zoom area in your Overview palette and click and drag that area to the next location you want to detail, as shown in Figure 4-3.

If your Overview palette is not visible, press F9.

Previewing Your Work

As you apply detail to the image, that detail is reflected in the Overview palette. Depending on the size of your monitor, however, this overview may be too small to see much of anything. For this reason, Paint Shop Pro 8 offers other ways to view your work before committing it to print or screen.

FIGURE 4-2 Panning the image with the Pan tool

Increase the Size of Your Digital Darkroom

In the View menu, there is a Full Screen Edit option that increases your window size to fill your entire screen area and hides your application window and status bars. It may not sound like much, but it does increase your workspace real estate. Give it a try. Open the View menu and click Full Screen Edit (SHIFT-A). Repeat these steps to return to normal edit.

 *To toggle between full screen and normal screen edit, press* SHIFT-A.

Seeing the Big Picture

Any time you change the zoom level of an image, you are going to get a certain amount of distortion. A detail change you made may look great when zoomed in at 1000 percent, but it may not look so great when the image is viewed at 100 percent.

FIGURE 4-3   Panning the image in the Overview palette

Although you can see the effects of your work in the Overview palette, you are still not viewing that image at 100 percent.

 If you have the Pan tool selected, you can click on the Normal View button in the Tool Options palette to change the view to 100 percent. If you have another tool selected, open the View menu, click Zoom, and then click Zoom to 100%.

 *To view the image at 100 percent, you can also press* CTRL-ALT-N.

Image Display Basics

To understand why an image is distorted when the size is changed, you must first understand how an image is displayed by your monitor. Images are made up of small square elements called pixels. The number of pixels in an image defines the level of detail that makes up the image. This level of detail is referred to as pixels per inch (ppi), which is also known as dots per inch (dpi). The level of detail also defines the size of the image.

Most computer monitors offer a resolution of 72dpi, defined by the physical size of the phosphor dots on the screen. Printed images vary in their level of detail, depending on how they are printed. Just like the phosphors on your computer monitor limit the amount of detail they can display, the printer that produces your image will also have a limiting factor. For example, if your printer only prints at 150dpi, an image set to 300dpi will not print any clearer than 150dpi. To produce true photographic quality, your image must be set to at least 300dpi, but displaying this image at 100 percent would be much larger than your screen could handle. Although the image would be very clear, you would only be able to see a portion of it at a time.

Your digital camera also plays a roll in how your image displays. For example, if your camera takes 4 × 6 pictures at only 72dpi, your pictures will look great on your monitor but horrible when printed. You can change the resolution of those photos to 300dpi; however, what you make up in detail, you lose in physical size, and your 4 × 6 photo will be more like 2 × 3.

Some monitors offer very high resolution. The higher the resolution, however, the smaller the image size on the screen. If you set the resolution too high, you may not be able to read the text on most screens without increasing the font size. To see what resolution your monitor offers, right-click a blank area on your desktop and click Properties. On the Display Properties dialog box, click the Settings tab.

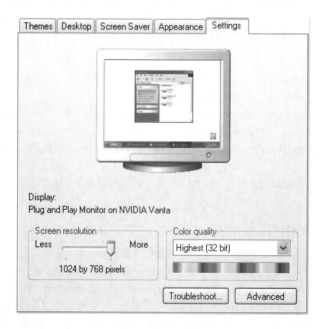

Distortions Created by Zoom Levels

As you increase the size of the pixels, you add distortion to the image display. This distortion does not affect the actual image, just the display of the image. This may seem distracting at first when trying to add detail. In time, however, you will begin to see how the individual pixels pull together to form the image you see on the screen. What appears to be jagged squares of varying colors is actually tiny dots. The more you zoom in, the larger the dots appear.

Advantages of the Overview Palette

When you are using tools other than your Pan tool, the Overview palette becomes invaluable. In Preview mode, you can zoom in and out of your image and change the area of detail you want to see and never loose your big-picture bearings. Click the Info tab to view detailed information regarding your image, including its size and how much memory it takes.

Magnifying the Detail

The Magnifier tool works similarly to a magnifying glass and magnifies only the area your cursor is over. This can be handy when working on small details in your image. To activate the Magnifier tool, open the View menu and click Magnifier, or press CTRL-ALT-M.

To increase the magnification level, press CTRL-+. To decrease the magnification level, press CTRL--.

Capturing Screens

The screen capture function enables you to capture specific elements of an application window. The illustrations in this book were taken with a screen capture utility. Think of screen capturing as a glorified Copy and Paste operation.

Setting Up Screen Capture

To set up screen capture, complete the following steps:

1. Open the File menu and click Import | Screen Capture | Setup. The Capture Setup dialog box will open.

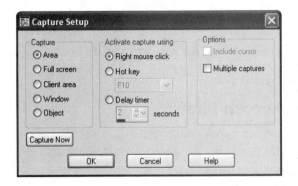

2. In the Capture area, select the type of capture you want to take:

   ■ **Area**   Enables you to draw a rectangle around the area you want
   to capture.

   ■ **Full Screen**   Captures the entire area of the screen.

   ■ **Client Area**   Captures only the active client window.

   ■ **Window**   Captures the active application window.

   ■ **Object**   Captures the selected object, like a button or toolbar.

3. In the Activate Capture Using area, select the method you want to use
   to begin your capture:

   ■ **Right Mouse Click**   Begins the capture when you click your right
   mouse button.

   ■ **Hot Key**   Sets a hot key to begin the capture.

   ■ **Delay Timer**   Sets the number of seconds that must pass before the
   capture begins.

4. In the Options area, select Include Cursor if you want to include the cursor in
   the capture. Select Multiple Captures if you want to take a series of captures
   without returning to the Paint Shop Pro 8 window after each one.

NOTE   *The Include Cursor option is not available for area captures.*

5. Click Capture Now to take a capture right away.

6. If you want to keep your settings and capture your screens at another time, click OK.

Capturing a Screen Shot

Once you have the screen capture feature set up, you are ready to take a screen snapshot. You can do this either from the Capture Setup dialog box, or by opening the File menu and clicking Import | Screen Capture | Start.

 *To start the capture process, you can also press* SHIFT-C.

To capture an area of a screen, complete the following steps:

1. Set up the capture feature to capture an area.

2. If the Capture Setup dialog box is open, click Capture Now. If the dialog box is closed, press SHIFT-C to begin the capture.

3. Open and prepare the area you want to capture. For example, if you want to show a dialog box with certain options set, set those options before beginning your capture.

4. Click your right mouse button or press the hot key you defined in Capture Setup (the default hot key is F10). The cursor will change to a crosshair.

5. Position the cursor to the corner of the area you want to capture and click your left mouse button to begin defining the area by drawing a rectangle. Move your cursor over the area you want to capture, and then click your left mouse button again to end the capture.

6. The image will be brought into Paint Shop Pro 8.

7. Save the file in a format that fits your needs.

To capture a screen element, complete the following steps:

1. Set up the capture feature to capture an element of the screen.

2. If the Capture Setup dialog box is open, click Capture Now. If the dialog box is closed, press SHIFT-C to begin the capture.

3. Open and prepare the area you want to capture. For example, if you want to show a dialog box with certain options set, set those options before beginning your capture.

4. Click the element you want to capture to make it active, and then click your right mouse button or press the hot key you defined in Capture Setup.

5. Unless you chose the Multiple Captures option in Capture Setup, the image will be brought into Paint Shop Pro 8.

NOTE *If you selected the Multiple Captures option in Capture Setup, you can continue to take screen captures one after the other without having to start the capture process each time. When you are done, return to the Paint Shop Pro 8 window to view and save your captures.*

6. Save the file in a format that fits your needs.

Visual References

Sometimes when you are working on an image, it is difficult to keep things in perspective. Paint Shop Pro 8 offers tools such as rulers, grids, and guidelines to offer a level of preciseness to your work. For example, if you are creating an advertisement and need to keep within restraints, it is helpful to use these visual references.

Rulers

To toggle the rulers between Show and Hide, open the View menu and click Rulers.

 *To toggle the rulers between Show and Hide, you can also press* CTRL-ALT-R.

The ruler can be set to display units in inches, pixels, or centimeters. To change this unit of measure, open the File menu and click Preferences | General Program

Preferences. Click the Units tab and select a measurement unit from the Display Units pull-down list.

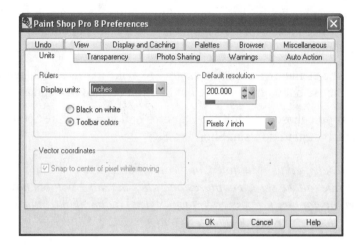

Guides

Guides enable you to mark precise areas of your image so they can be cropped, selected, or modified. To toggle the guides between Show and Hide, open the View menu and click Guides.

Guide handle ———

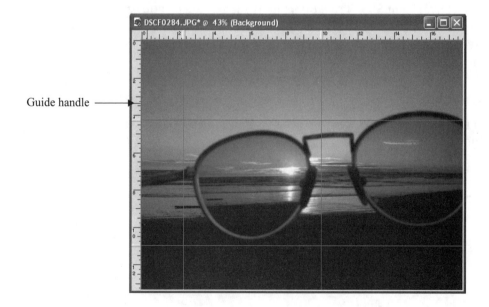

To create a horizontal guide, click the top ruler and drag the guide down to the desired location. To create a vertical guide, click the left ruler and drag the guide over to the desired location. You can place as many guides as you like in an image.

To move a guide, click and drag the guide handle. You can also right-click the guide handle to open the Guide Properties dialog box. From this box, you can specify a precise location for the guide, delete the guide, or specify a new guide color.

TIP *To remove a guideline, click and drag the guide handle beyond the outside border of the rulers.*

Once a guideline is in place, you can use it as a snap point for selection tools or for precise placement of other objects. To do this, open your View menu and click Snap to Guides. The Snap to Guides option will be enabled or shaded.

Then, in the Tools toolbar, click the Selection tool. Click and drag a rectangle over the image from one guideline to another and release your mouse button. Watch how the selection tool snaps to the guidelines you have defined. If this doesn't happen, make certain your Snap to Guides option is selected in the View menu.

Grids

The grid behaves in much the same way as the guidelines do, but there are more lines to contend with. A grid can be very useful when it comes to moving layers or objects in an image. Enable the Snap to Grid option in the View menu to use the gridlines as snap points.

Changing Grid, Guide, and Snap Properties

To fine-tune the way your grid, guide, and snap functions appear and work, open the View menu and click Change Grid, Guide and Snap Properties.

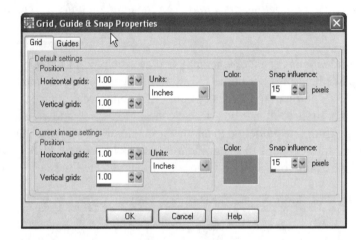

Controlling Your Actions

One of the nice things about Paint Shop Pro 8 is that you can experiment without fear. If you make mistakes, you can easily erase them and return to where you left off, undoing either one action at a time or several actions at once.

Undo and Redo One Action at a Time

To undo and redo your actions one at a time, click either the Undo or Redo button in the Standard toolbar.

Undo   Redo

Using the Command History

To undo several actions at once, open the Edit menu and click Command History. In the Command History dialog box, select the actions you want to undo and click Undo.

If you click Clear, your entire command history will be deleted.

Part II

Basic Image Editing

Chapter 5

Simple Image Editing and Printing

How to...

- Understand the difference between photo correction and enhancement
- Quickly enhance and print a photo
- Improve the composition of a photo through cropping
- Straighten out a crooked photo
- Set up and print photos

In this chapter, you will discover some ways to improve the overall composition of an image, enhance the overall photo quality, straighten out crooked photos, and set up and print photographs from Paint Shop Pro.

Why You Need to Correct and Enhance Photos

Many photo printers on the market today allow you to print pictures without using a computer; you only need to insert the camera's memory card into the printer and you have a photograph. While I can understand the appeal of popping in the media and having the photograph appear, I always want to fiddle with the photo a little (sometimes a lot) before I print it.

It would be nice if there were a single button in Paint Shop Pro that you could click to automatically make all of the necessary adjustments to your picture. But there isn't, because the computer doesn't have any way of knowing what is right or wrong with your photo. However, if you can identify the parts of your photo that need improvement, Paint Shop Pro does provide a large variety of tools to either enhance or fix them. In this chapter, you will discover how easy it is to make a few adjustments so that your photos look better when you print them. However, before going any further, you need to understand the difference between correcting and enhancing a photograph.

Understanding Photo Correction and Enhancement

There is a difference between correction and enhancement. "Correction" refers to adjusting photos to make them appear as they should. If the orange in the photo is green, the color needs to be corrected (adjusted). If a digital image is too large to post on the Web or too small to print, it needs to be corrected. On the other hand, if you want to make a photo look better by making the colors richer, removing a zit from a young face, or blurring a background to emphasize a subject, you're *enhancing* the photo. Now that that's understood, let's look at how to perform some of the most common basic photographic adjustments.

Preparing Your Photos for Printing

Here is the quickest way to get pictures from your camera ready for printing. It only involves four steps.

- Rotate the picture (if necessary)
- Crop the photo (if necessary—and it probably is)
- Apply One Step Photo Fix
- Print the photos

Rotating Your Photos in Paint Shop Pro

This is the first and most common correction you should make with Paint Shop Pro. Anytime you take a photograph with the camera in portrait orientation, it needs to be rotated. For the record, when we talk about the orientation of the camera, we are saying which part of the image is on top: if the wide part is on top, it's in landscape orientation; if the narrow part is, it's portrait. The choice of orientation is usually determined by the subject matter. The columns near the entrance to the Acropolis shown in Figure 5-1 are vertical, so the camera was rotated to make a portrait shot. The Main Street photo of a tiny Texas town had to be photographed in landscape orientation to capture the sign and the dilapidated building.

When you take a photograph in portrait orientation and bring it straight into Paint Shop Pro, it will be oriented in landscape, as shown next.

FIGURE 5-1   Photo in landscape orientation (left) and photo in portrait orientation (right)

From the Image menu, select the rotation that turns your photo so that the top of the photo is pointing up, in this case, 90 degrees counter-clockwise, as shown in Figure 5-2.

Another Way to Rotate Your Photo

You can also rotate your photo by using the Free Rotate command (CTRL-R), which opens the following dialog box. From here, you can select one of the preset rotations or enter a custom value to rotate it at an unusual angle to create an effect (see "The Effects of Rotating a Bitmap Image").

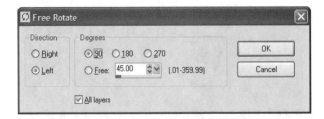

If your photo does not appear to be straight because it was placed crooked in a scanner, you should rescan the photo if possible rather than attempting to rotate it in Paint Shop Pro. If the photo is not a scanned image, you should use the Free Rotate command until it appears straight. As a general rule, when taking action

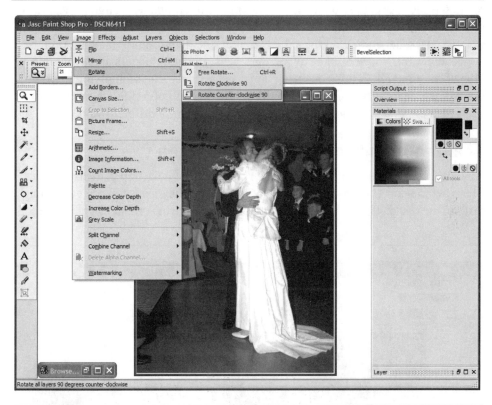

FIGURE 5-2   Use the preset rotation settings to quickly reorient your photos.

photos, the camera doesn't always end up being level with the horizon. There are times when having the photo be at an angle produces a desired effect, but a general rule of composition, the horizon should be level.

TIP   *Action shots should almost always be in a landscape orientation.*

The Effects of Rotating a Bitmap Image

A bitmap (also called raster) image is made up of pixels. When you rotate a bitmap image such as a photograph either 90, 180, or 270 degrees, Paint Shop Pro rearranges the order of the pixels in the image and the image quality remains unaffected because only the order of the pixels changes. However, when you rotate the same bitmap image at any angle, Paint Shop Pro must recreate all of the pixels to create the rotation effect. Anytime you must recreate pixels in an image, it slightly degrades the image. The degradation usually produces a slight softening of the overall image. In most cases, depending on the subject matter, the deterioration may not even be noticeable. Still, you should be aware that the degradation occurs and avoid this type of rotation unless it is necessary. This is especially true of applying multiple non-90 degree rotations. For example, if the first rotation (non-90 degree) doesn't straighten the image, undo the rotation (CTRL-Z) and try a different value.

The Importance of Photo Composition

Now that your photos are all pointed the right way, the next step is to crop them. Many people don't like to crop their photos because they want to keep everything that's in the photo. The truth is that most photographs like the one shown in Figure 5-3

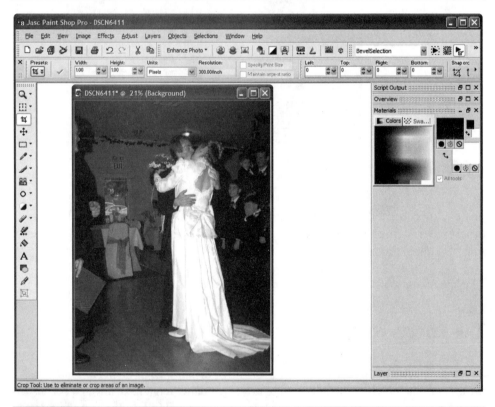

FIGURE 5-3   The Crop tool provides a quick and simple way to improve the composition of most photographs.

are greatly improved by removing parts of the scene that distracts the viewer. Cropping is done using the Crop tool (R) (shown left), and its operation is pretty obvious. The part that requires judgment on your part is what to crop and what to leave.

Why You Should Crop Before Anything Else

You should crop before making any tonal or color correction because the automatic correction features of Paint Shop Pro read the information contained in the entire image to determine what and how much correction to apply.

For example, in the squirt gun mêlée shown in Figure 5-4, the girl on the far right is in deep shadow. While it is possible to recover her from the darkness (so to speak), the focus of the photo is the action in the center. If any of the automatic features of One Step Photo Fix are applied, they will balance out the dark (shadow) and bright (highlight) portions of the photo. The result will be in inaccurate correction applied to the photograph. If you first remove the shadowy subject from the photo, the automatic adjustment will work better.

FIGURE 5-4   The girl in the shadow will affect the automatic tonal correction if not cropped before it is applied.

Cropping a Photo

Operating the Crop tool is pretty simple, but for the record, here is how to use it:

1. Select the Crop tool in the Tools toolbar and place the cursor inside the image.

2. Click and drag a selection rectangle to surround the part of the photo that you want to keep and let go of the mouse button.

3. Adjust the rectangle by clicking and dragging either its sides or corners. You can move the entire selected rectangle around the image by placing the cursor inside it and dragging it around.

4. Double-click inside the rectangle or click the Apply button (looks like a check mark) in the Tool Options palette to crop the photo.

Cropping Your Photos to a Specific Size

If you plan on printing your photograph, you should consider cropping it to one of the predefined photo sizes. This way your printed photograph will fit into picture frames and photo albums that can only accommodate certain sizes. Paint Shop Pro provides several ways to crop to a specific size using either the Crop tool or the Canvas Size command.

Using the Crop tool to create a specific size is similar to the preceding steps:

1. Select the Crop tool in the Tools toolbar.

2. In the Tool Options palette, you can enter the finished size or click the Presets button and pick the desired finished size from the list of preset sizes, shown in Figure 5-5. Click the OK button to place a Crop rectangle on the photo.

3. Move the selection rectangle around the image by placing the cursor inside it and dragging it around.

FIGURE 5-5   Using presets provides an easy way to crop a photo to standard sizes.

4. Double-click inside the rectangle or click the Apply button in the Tool Options palette to complete the crop action. The cropped photo is shown in Figure 5-6.

NOTE   *If the requested crop size is larger than the selected photo, the Crop tool will change the resolution of the image so it fits. The resolution appears in the Tools Options bar.*

FIGURE 5-6   Using presets ensures this cropped photo will be the correct size
when printed.

You can also change the size of the currently selected image with the Canvas
Size command in the Image menu. This command either adds or subtracts pixels
from the edge of the image, so entering a value that is smaller than the currently
selected image will crop it. However, because you cannot visually control where
the cropping occurs on the photo, as you can with the Crop tool, using the Canvas
Size command for cropping is not recommended.

What to Crop

Here are some general cropping rules to consider and some examples. First, decide
what the subject of the photo is and remove anything that distracts from the subject.
The photograph I am going to use to demonstrate the importance of this was taken at
the twenty-fifth anniversary and vow recommitment of some good friends—Brian
and Debbie. The photo shown next doesn't appear to be anything special.

By cropping the photo, as shown next, the couple (and four of their eight children) becomes the focus of the photo. Don't be afraid to remove part of the photo to get in close. No one is going to look at the photo and ask what happened to the pastor or the exit sign.

Cropping the photo focuses the image (Figure 5-7) and draws the viewer's attention to the youngest member of the wedding party who, like most kids, finds mom and dad smooching more than he can bear to watch.

Digital Pictures Have Their Limits

If you watch TV or go to the movies, at some point you will probably have seen the critical scene where someone asks a technician to zoom in on some part of a video or satellite photo, and then says my favorite line: "Now enhance it." Amazingly, the blurred license plate or face suddenly comes into crystal clear focus. Don't believe it. That only happens in the movies. When you crop out everything but a small part of your photo to emphasize it, be careful that you are not left with a photo the size of a postage stamp. If you only want to show the picture on the Web, you can make it pretty small, but if you want to print a photo, you should have enough size to print it at a resolution of 150dpi for most inkjet printers. For digital camera users, it is when you are cropping a photo and using only a small portion of the original that all of those extra megapixels the camera produces come in really handy because the remaining cropped image is still large enough to make an acceptable photos.

FIGURE 5-7   Cropping reveals the youngest son hiding his eyes from mom and dad kissing.

Other Cropping Suggestions

Never feel that you must crop a photo. Sometimes, all of the extra space around a subject can draw attention to it, or it is necessary for the composition. Figure 5-8 shows a young man sitting on the edge of an empty parking lot eating a snow cone on a hot Texas afternoon. The emptiness around him is part of the composition, so I left it.

Our last cropping suggestion applies to taking the photograph as well. Whenever possible, avoid placing your subject in the center of the photo. Placing a photo with the subject in the dead center is what they do for passports and drivers licenses, and we all know how good those photos look.

Applying One Step Photo Fix

The One Step Photo Fix command is a totally automatic feature that applies several tonal and color corrections to the selected photo. When I tested this feature, the majority of the time it did a very good job of getting the most out of the photo without having to open and use other correction tools. The tool is accessed by

FIGURE 5-8   The emptiness around this young man helps the viewer see how that snow cone holds his total attention.

clicking the Enhance Photo button in the Photo toolbar and clicking One Step Photo Fix from the drop-down list that appears, as shown next. It will take a few moments for Paint Shop Pro to apply all of the filters. You can view the progress of each filter in the status bar that appears on the bottom of the screen.

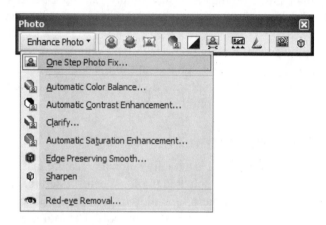

Straightening Out Photos

Paint Shop Pro 8 has a new Straighten tool that will automatically straighten out a photo. I generally don't recommend using this or other features like it because it degrades images. The user can just as easily spend an extra minute and realign the photo in the scanner with no resulting degradation of the image. Of course, if someone else scanned the photo or it was photographed at an angle and you can't rescan or take the photo again, this feature can be a real time saver.

Figure 5-9 shows a photo of Eric and his younger brother at his high school graduation. After the photo was placed in the scanner, the scanner lid was flopped down, which caused the photo to do exactly as predicted: it moved. I noticed this when I did the scan preview. Under normal circumstances, I would lift the lid and reposition the photo, but here is how to straighten out an image using the Straighten tool in Paint Shop Pro 8:

1. In the Tools toolbar, select the Straighten tool from the drop-down list, as shown next.

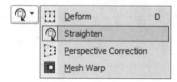

FIGURE 5-9   Here is a classic example of a photo not being aligned correctly on the scanner.

2. When the tool is selected, a reference line appears with squares on each end. Drag each square so the line is on or parallel to either the horizontal or vertical element of the photo. In the image shown below, I placed the reference line parallel with the photo so you can see it more clearly; in actual practice, you would make the line coincide with the edge of the photo.

3. Double-click anywhere in the image, and it will be straightened to the correct vertical or horizontal angle. Figure 5-10 resulted when the Crop image option was not selected in the Tools Options toolbar. Paint Shop Pro added pixels (dark area) creating an image that does not lose any of the original image pixels. Figure 5-11 shows what happens when the Crop image feature is selected.

While there are several other options for the Straighten tool besides the Auto mode, to straighten our photos, you should use the Auto Mode setting with the Crop Image feature enabled. See the Paint Shop Pro online help for detailed information about using the other settings.

Putting Corrections and Enhancements Together

To show how corrections and enhancements work together to prepare your photos for printing, you will take a photo of a really cute child taken during Festival in Athens (when everyone seems to wear a costume) and make it into a nice 4 × 6 photo.

FIGURE 5-10   The straightened photo when the Crop image option is not selected

F05-08* @ 39% (Background)

FIGURE 5-11   The straightened photo when the Crop image option is selected

5

Your first step is to evaluate the photo. Figure 5-12 shows a photo that is already straight but needs to be cropped so it is in portrait orientation. It is also too dark. To fix these problems, follow these steps:

1. Choose the Crop tool and select the 4 × 6 vertical setting from the Presets in the Tools Options toolbar, as shown right. The 4 × 6 crop area appears on the left side of the photo. Use the crop cursor and drag it over the subject. Double-click the cursor, and the image is cropped to a 4 × 6 image.

Presets:
13 x 18 cm horizontal
13 x 18 cm vertical
20 x 30 cm horizontal
20 x 30 cm vertical
3.5 x 5 in horizontal
3.5 x 5 in vertical
4 x 6 in horizontal
4 x 6 in vertical
5 x 7 in horizontal
5 x 7 in vertical

OK   Cancel

FIGURE 5-12   Pretty girl but the overall composition and tonal qualities are poor.

2. Apply the One Step Photo Fix, and the image should look a lot better, as shown here:

3. There is one final adjustment to perform to show off the girl's lovely face: select the Lighten/Darken tool (L) to emphasize her face and make it stand out just a little more. (See the before and after images in the color insert.)

While it is a little beyond basic editing, for a final touch you can use the Soften Brush from the Tools toolbar to soften the background (see Figure 5-13) and make the girl stand out to the viewer. The Soften brush slightly blurs the pixels as the brush is applied. The amount of the blurring that occurs is determined by the opacity setting of the brush in the Options palette.

Printing Photos

Now that you have cropped and otherwise adjusted your photo the way you want it, it's time to print it, maybe for putting in a frame on your desk or making copies to send to friends or family. A few years ago, it would have required a $10,000 printer to get a decent-looking color photograph. Now, with an inkjet printer (costing less than a few hundred dollars) and the new photo papers available, you can produce photographs that look like the real thing.

FIGURE 5-13   The finished photo is ready to print and frame.

Sorting Out Today's Color Printers

With color inkjet printers being the dominant printer in the market today, you can walk into any office or computer store and see a long line of them on the shelves. Most printer manufacturers offer at least five different models of printers ranging in price from $100 to $800. If that wasn't confusing enough, from the output produced by each printer, it appears that they all have roughly the same quality of output. To help simplify the decision making process of which printer to buy, you need to understand the different printer classifications and what they do. The following are the general categories of color printers available in the marketplace today:

- Color inkjet printers
- Photo inkjet printers—dye-based inks
- Photo inkjet printers—pigment-based inks
- Dye sublimation printers

Color Inkjet Printers

Most of the inkjet printers sold in the market today are color inkjet printers. Most print their color using a black ink cartridge and a color cartridge that contains three different colored inks (called a tri-color cartridge). Black is always maintained as a separate color for two reasons: it allows the printing of standard text without wasting any color and, while it is theoretically possible to create black using the three different colored inks together, the black produced by the color cartridge would look more like dark mud than black. These color inkjet printers offer very fast print speeds (for text), and some can print on both sides of the paper (duplex). Hewlett-Packard (HP) even has a printer that can detect what kind of paper is in your printer and automatically select the correct media settings. In short, they are pretty amazing.

Sorting Out the Color Printers

Almost every inkjet printer that you can find uses dye-based inks to print. This is because the colors produced by dye-based inks are more vivid than pigment based inks. On top of that, pigment-based printers cost roughly five times as much a dye-based printers. With these limitations, what is the advantage of pigment-based ink printers? Longevity. Prints produced using a pigment ink-based printer are certified to last over 100 years. How important is this? If you are a professional producing prints for a client, it is very important. If you are printing images for your own

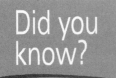

Higher Resolution Doesn't Mean Better Photos

Many inkjet printer manufacturers focus on the printing resolution of their products. Resolutions such as 2400 dots-per-inch (dpi) are common with some companies that advertise resolutions as high as 5,760dpi. While these astronomical numbers sound like they will produce the best possible photos, the truth is that most of them print the stunning sample photos you see in the stores at a resolution of 720dpi. So what happens if you print one your photos at higher resolutions such as 2,440dpi? It will take almost four times as long to print the photo, it will use twice as much ink, and, worst, the shadow areas of the photo may actually appear darker, causing loss of detail. So what is the higher resolution of the printer used for? When printing photos that are 8 × 10 or larger, the higher resolution does improve the fine detail in an image. However, for smaller photo formats such as 5 × 7 or 4 × 6, stay with 720dpi. The bottom line is, when deciding which printer to buy, ignore the resolution figures. Also when printing a photo, don't be tempted to override the factory recommendations for printing at a lower (720dpi) resolution.

personal use and the photo begins to fade (after five to seven years), you can always print another one.

In the category of dye-based printers there is another question: What makes a color inkjet different from a photo inkjet printer?

Most color inkjet printers are described as four-color printers in that they use four inks to produce color output. The four inks used are black (K), Cyan, Magenta, and Yellow (CMY). There are still some three-color printers on the market that create their color output using CMY, and they have a separate black pigment-based ink cartridge that is only used for printing text. Three-color printers do not produce good color, especially for photos, and should be avoided.

What You Need to Know About Printer Ink and Media

It is a poorly kept secret that printer manufacturers make very little profit on the printers they sell. Instead, they look to the sales of the consumables (ink and paper) to make the profits that keep shareowners happy. Because these consumables are so expensive, many third-party companies provide their own ink cartridges and refill kits for existing cartridges while other make photo papers.

Did you know?

Do You Know the Color Symbols?

The major colors used in printing have single-letter abbreviations. Most of these color abbreviations make sense. For example, the primary colors are Red (R), Blue (B), and Green (G), and the complementary colors are Cyan (C), Magenta (M), and Yellow (Y). Then there is Black (K), which seems like it should be B, but that letter is already in use by Blue. There are also two light versions of the colors, Light Cyan (c) and Light Magenta (m), which are used in 6-color printers. These are referred to as light colors not because they have half the calories of regular colors, but because they have half of the color content of the regular color.

Should You Use Third-party Ink Cartridges?

The important question is, are the inks used by the third-party ink cartridge vendors as good as those provided by the manufacturer? I have tested several of them and found their output quality ranges from poor to good. I recommend you use the printer manufacturer's cartridges if you only use a few cartridges each year. If your cartridge demands are heavier, you may want to consider one of the zillion vendors on the Internet.

The only way to find out how good third-party replacement cartridges are is to first print a sample photo using the printer manufacturer's cartridges, then buy a third-party set, print another sample, and compare the results you get. If you are not satisfied with the results, return the cartridges and ask for a refund. If you are satisfied with them, continue to use them and occasionally print another sample print, as the quality assurance of some of these houses varies.

What's at Stake if You Use Third-party Inkjet Cartridges?

Most printer manufacturers state that using these third-party ink supplies voids the printer's warranty. Most users believe this. This is a common misperception by many printer owners. Manufacturers have threatened to void printer warranties when cartridges are refilled by third-party manufacturers, but the brand of supplies you purchase for your printer is your decision. You are not required by any machine manufacturer's warranty to use only its brand. The Magnuson-Moss Warranty Improvement Act prevents manufacturers from doing that.

Print a Photo

Once you have the image ready to print, there are several ways to begin the printing process from Paint Shop Pro 8:

- Click the Print button in the Standard toolbar
- Choose Print from the File menu
- Use the keyboard shortcut (CTRL-P)

Using the Media That Produces the Best Results for You

It used to be paper was just paper, but now it is a specialized media. Each type of paper is made for a specific purpose, such as inkjet paper, photo paper, photo glossy paper—and those are just the ones that you see at retail stores. There are many more unusual types of inkjet papers available on the Internet, such as papers that turn photos into puzzles, a coffee cup, or even canvases. You will be looking at a lot of specialty papers for different scanner projects throughout this book, but first, a few general facts about inkjet papers.

Printing color photos on cheap copy paper produces poor pictures even though it uses the same amount of ink as it would printing on photo paper. Printing a lousy-looking poor photo on very expensive paper won't make the photo look any better. The secret to getting the best printing results for your scanned images is to find a paper that has the texture and finish that you like and then to experiment with your printer settings to get the results that you want.

Adjusting Your Printer Settings for Best Results

Regardless of which printer you are using, you can access the software that controls your printer. To do this, select Print, and you will see the dialog box shown next. The name of the computer's default printer appears near the top of the dialog box.

While the specific details will vary from printer to printer, the following procedure works for most situations:

■ To change the selected printer, click the Printer button. This opens a list of all of the installed printers. To change the properties of a specific printer, click the Properties button alongside the printer name. This launches the printer-specific software that allows you to control many of the printer features.

■ Within the Printer dialog box, you can select the media that is loaded in the printer, as well as the color management that the printer should use to print the scanned image. The choices of media (paper) are limited to the names and types offered by the printer manufacturer. This can cause a bit of head scratching when you are using a paper that is different from the choices shown. See "You Should Match Photo Papers with Printer Settings" at the end of the chapter for information about this.

■ If this is your first time setting up the printer, you should experiment with several different settings. Print the scanned image and write on the back of the photo what settings you used. Once you are satisfied with the results, save the settings with a unique name and use these settings to print your photos.

Set Paint Shop Pro Print Settings

Once you have the printer set to print your photos, you can make any necessary adjustments in the Paint Shop Pro Print dialog box to control how the image is placed on the paper. As you can see by the tabs on the opening dialog box in Figure 5-14, there are two types of settings: Placement and Options.

Most of the controls on this page are fairly obvious: number of copies, making the image placement portrait or landscape. The left side of the Size and Position section allows you to specify how much to scale the image. The right side contains several buttons that control how Paint Shop Pro places the image on the paper:

■ **Fit to Page**   Expands the existing photo so that it fills the page. This is not recommended in most cases, especially if the original image is very small, because the resulting print will be of poor quality.

- **Center on Page**   Places the image (unaltered) smack in the center of the page.

- **Upper Left of Page**   Places the image at the upper-left corner of the original. This is very handy if you are printing the photo on a page that is larger than the photo and it is going to need to be trimmed.

- **Custom Offset**   Positions the photo on a specific part of the page.

The Options tab contains options that are primarily used for prepress work (images that are sent to printers) (Figure 5-15). Check in the Paint Shop Pro User's Manual for details on these options.

5

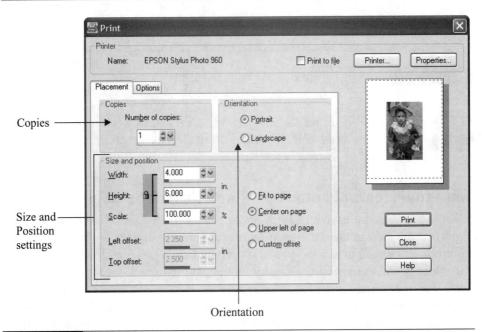

FIGURE 5-14   The Print dialog box for placement of images on a page

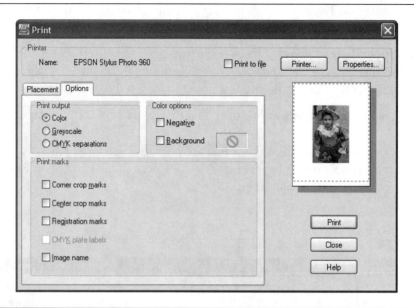

FIGURE 5-15   The Options page of the Print dialog box

Even if your inkjet printer is referred to as a CMYK printer (and many are), do not use the CMYK option. All of these printers expect the color information to be in RGB format.

You Should Match Photo Papers with Printer Settings

What happens if you have an Epson Photo printer loaded with Kodak photo paper? If you look at the Paper pop-up menu, you will not see anything but Epson papers listed, so how do you know which Epson paper matches the Kodak paper that you have installed? First, try looking at the printed information that came with the paper. Most of the papers vendors list the best paper settings for most major printer manufacturers. If your printer is too new to be listed, check the paper manufacturer's website to see if they give setting recommendations for your printer. If both of these don't pan out, try to match the type of paper (glossy, matte, and so on) with one that is closest on the printer's paper list.

Chapter 6

Correcting Photographic Problems

How to...

- Perform basic color correction
- Remove color cast from photos
- Revive dull or lifeless photographs
- Correct over- and underexposed photographs
- Remove red-eye
- Correct lens distortion

With film photography, you take your photos during vacations or special events and hold your breath when you get the envelope of photographs back from the developer. Once the picture is taken there isn't much you can do. With digital photography and Paint Shop Pro, that's all changed. While you can still take bad photos with even the most expensive camera, now you have the ability to correct, enhance, and otherwise play with the photos on your computer before printing them.

Fine-Tuning Your Color

One of the biggest disappointments people experience with digital cameras is color that appears lifeless or seems a little off from what it should be. In this chapter, you will discover that adjusting the color isn't rocket science. In fact, with the tools built in to Paint Shop Pro 8, it is pretty easy to get the color right. Because most of the discussion in this section involves color, I recommend that you put a bookmark in the color insert section so you can easily get to it from here.

Color Casts and Their Causes

Outdoor photographs taken with a digital camera often have a color cast, a subtle but dominant color that is introduced into the photo. The most common color cast produced by a sunny cloudless day is blue. This is because the automatic white balance (AWB) in most digital cameras gets tricked by large amounts of blue sky and bright daylight.

More than Just the Blues

If blue was the only color cast that affected digital cameras, we would all be a lot happier. Unfortunately, there are several sources of light that affect the color balance

Did you know?

The Difference Between Accurate Color and Desired Color

When working with color photos it is important to determine what you want from the finished print. Do you want the color to be accurate, or do you want the colors to look good? It may surprise you to know that colors that are accurate don't always look as good. For example, once I was enjoying one of the many impressionist collections at the Musée d'Orsay in Paris. In the museum gift shop, I purchased one of those large (and heavy) coffee table books that included prints of all the works of the collection. I wondered how the reproduction in the book compared with the originals I was currently viewing. To my great amazement, I discovered the images in the book had more vibrant colors and, overall, appeared much more vivid than the original paintings I was viewing.

Were the colors in the book accurate? No. The colors in the reproduction matched the original but not accurately. Which image looked better? The reproduction. When correcting color, you must keep in mind who the intended audience is. If the purpose of the book was to preserve for all posterity an accurate record of the original, the reproduction should have matched the original perfectly. In this case, however, the publisher wanted to sell books and so, within reason, they boosted the overall appearance so the reproductions looked better, while being relatively faithful to the original. So, before you begin making color correction you must ask yourself this question: What is more important to you, color accuracy or the overall appearance of the finished work? In 99.9 percent of the cases, it will be making the color look good.

of your photos. A photo taken in a windowless office lit entirely by fluorescent lights, produces a sickly green color cast. Applying magenta (the opposite of green) using Color Balance corrects the color cast.

Some light sources introduce a desirable color cast. When your subject is illuminated by incandescent light or a sunset, the resulting colors shift toward the warm colors, which are always more appealing. This is why colors in photos taken in the morning and the late afternoon are more appealing than those taken when the sun is high overhead.

Before You Begin Any Correction

There are some fundamental rules concerning raster images and Paint Shop Pro that need to be made crystal clear before attempting any correction or enhancement.

The first rule is that nearly all of the adjustment and correction tools that I cover in this chapter will not work on 256-color (8-bit) images. If you attempt to do so, Paint Shop Pro will post an Auto Action message box like the one shown next allowing you to increase it to 16 million colors (24-bit). Clicking OK increases the color depth of the currently selected image.

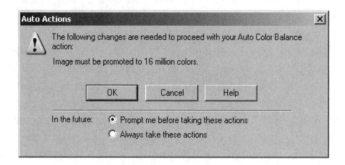

 *If you want an Auto Action to occur without notifying you, select the Always Take These Actions button at the bottom of the message box. If not, it will always prompt you before taking the action.*

The second rule applies to images with layers (other than background). The tools and effects work only on the layer of the photo that is currently active. The exception to this is a few adjustment dialog boxes that have an option that allows the tool or effect to be applied to all layers.

Discover the Photo Toolbar

Most of the photo correction work you do in this chapter will use a tool in the Photo toolbar; when enabled, as shown in Figure 6-1, it allows an effect or tool to be used with the click of a button rather than having to go through several levels of menus. To enable the Photo toolbar, choose View | Toolbars | Photo Toolbar.

The Photo toolbar in Figure 6-1 is undocked. You can drag the toolbar toward the top of the screen and dock it with the other toolbars, as shown next.

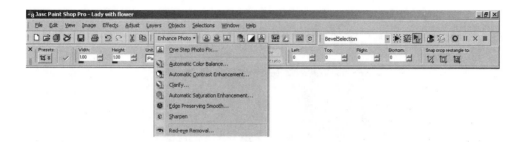

Using Adjustment Dialog Boxes

The controls in the adjustment dialog boxes in Paint Shop Pro operate in a similar manner. I've used the Automatic Color Balance dialog box (Figure 6-2) to demonstrate their different parts and operation.

6

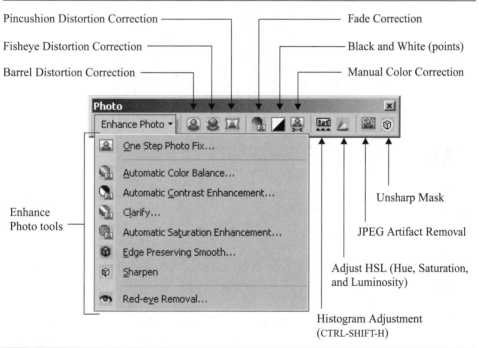

Pincushion Distortion Correction

Fisheye Distortion Correction

Barrel Distortion Correction

Fade Correction

Black and White (points)

Manual Color Correction

Enhance Photo tools

Unsharp Mask

JPEG Artifact Removal

Adjust HSL (Hue, Saturation, and Luminosity)

Histogram Adjustment (CTRL-SHIFT-H)

FIGURE 6-1   The Photo Toolbar

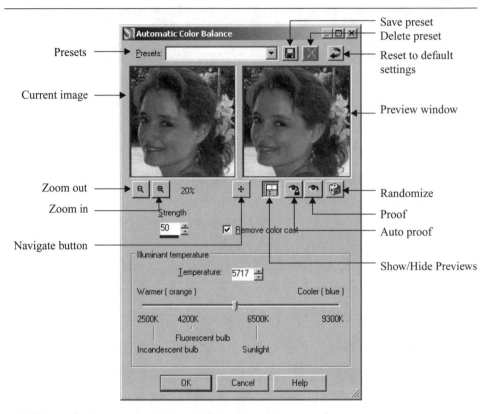

Presets

Current image

Zoom out

Zoom in

Navigate button

Save preset

Delete preset

Reset to default settings

Preview window

Randomize

Proof

Auto proof

Show/Hide Previews

FIGURE 6-2   The Automatic Color dialog box

Dialog Box with a View

Six of the seven buttons under the current image and proof windows are used to control the windows above them. Obviously, the zoom buttons zoom in and out of the image in the windows. Clicking and holding the Navigate button opens another window containing a small version of the photo with the zoomed area indicated by a rectangle, as shown next. Drag the rectangle to a different part of the image you want to preview and release the mouse button.

Changing How Your Preview Operates

If this is your first time working with Paint Shop Pro, you might be wondering how effective such a small preview window is. Often it is difficult to see the "big picture" in such a tiny window, and you may want to preview the effects on the actual image. To make the image bigger, you can click the Show/Hide Previews button to hide the preview windows, as shown next.

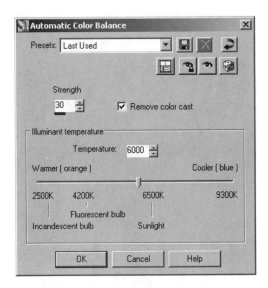

The Proof Is in the Preview

Whenever you make a change to one of the adjustments in the dialog box, the change always appears in the preview window. To preview the effect the adjustment is having on the image, press the Proof button. Depending on size of the photo and the complexity of the effect, it may take a few moments for the change to appear. None of the changes that you see in the image are applied until you click the OK button. When the preview appears in the image, changing any of the settings will toggle the Preview button off. To continuously view the changes in the image, click the Auto Proof button on. This may sound like a good option, but when you are working with a large image or applying complex effects, Auto Proof can really slow things down.

Were you wondering about the Randomize button? Each time you click the dice button, it will randomly change all of the settings in the dialog box. While I don't recommend using this feature with standard photo adjustments, there are some effect filters that have a multitude of settings, and the randomizer feature provides a quick way to discover some great and not so great settings for those.

Toggling the Preview button on and off is a quick way to compare the before and after results of an effect on an image.

Saving Your Settings

Once you have fine-tuned a setting for the dialog box it is possible to save it for use again on another image, and in fact, that is the purpose of the buttons across the top of the dialog box. For example, if you were taking a lot of digital photos around the same time of day with the same camera, you could save the settings for the filter you used to correct the color cast and apply to all of the other images. Doing this is quite simple. You can save, load, and delete the settings or restore to the factory defaults by clicking the appropriate button.

Now that you know how to use adjustment dialog boxes, let's move on. Next, you'll learn how the Automatic Color Balance is used to correct color in an image.

The Automatic Adjustment Tools

In Chapter 5 you learned about One Step Photo Fix, which does a great job of fixing an image by applying several of the automatic adjustment tools at the same time. However, if you just want to remove color casts or make slight adjustments to the amount of lighting in a photo, then application of the individual automatic tools is the best choice. Let's begin with how to remove color casts using the Automatic Color Balance tool.

Removing Color Casts with Automatic Color Balance

There are two ways to open this tool. From the menu, choose Adjust | Color Balance | Automatic Color Balance or, from the Photo toolbar, click the Enhance Photo button and pick it from the list. Figure 6-3 (in the color insert) is a photo of Renee taken as she was leaving church on Easter Sunday. She was under the shade of the porch, but the parking lot was brightly lit (this is Texas, after all). The result of this combination produced a slightly underexposed photo of her with a noticeable blue cast to it.

The Automatic Color Balance dialog, shown next, provides a single adjustment slider measured in color temperatures and a check box for enabling the Remove Color Cast feature. Even though you want to remove a color cast, the most important setting is the color temperature slider. For more information on color temperature, see the section "How Color Temperature Works." Moving the slider to the left makes the colors in the photo warmer (more red) and moving it toward the right makes the colors cooler (bluish). The markers on the slider for Incandescent Bulb, Fluorescent Bulb, and Sunlight are references to the general color temperatures of these light

FIGURE 6-3   This color photo has a slight bluish cast.

sources. Just because a photo is taken outdoors in the sunlight doesn't mean you need to move the slider to that point on the scale.

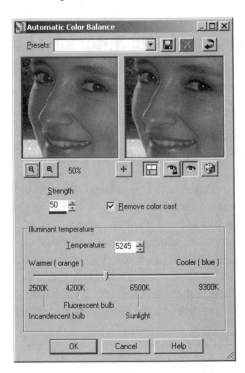

To correct the blue color cast of the photo, move the slider to the left toward the warmer colors. Toggling the Proof button on and off displays anything in the photo that should be white. In this case, a good white reference point is the white flowers in Renee's hair. If you cannot find anything white in the image (although in most cases you will be able to), look for a light neutral color and adjust the slider until the cast color disappears. It's difficult to remember what the image looks like for more than a few seconds, so toggle back and forth with the Proof button to achieve the best setting. After that looks correct, check the Remove Color Cast check box and change it to a higher setting, such as 50. Again, toggle back and forth between the preview and original settings. Note that enabling the Remove Color Cast feature will slow down the preview, and the difference produced by it will be subtle.

Once you are satisfied with the settings, click OK, and the finished image will look like Figure 6-4 in the color insert. Upon studying the resulting photo carefully, you may notice that Renee looks a lot like Donna Reed.

How Color Temperature Works

To understand why the Automatic Color Balance works the way it does, it helps to understand some basics of color temperature. Even though the light from the sun

FIGURE 6-4   Using the Automatic Color Balance removes the cast improving the photo.

or a light bulb looks white to us, it contains a mixture of all colors in varying proportions. The color of a light source is described by its color temperature. The color temperature scale is calibrated in degrees Kelvin, much like a thermometer that reads heat in degrees Fahrenheit. The color temperature scale operates in a manner opposite from what you might expect. That is, the lower color temperatures (reddish light) are considered warmer and the higher color temperatures (bluish light) are cooler. For example, daylight contains proportionately more light at the blue end of the spectrum, while incandescent light is made up with more light from the red end. Hence, daylight photos appear cooler and candlelight shots seem warmer.

Helping Automatic Tools Do a Better Job

When any automatic adjustment tool is applied to a photo, the contents of the entire image is evaluated by Paint Shop Pro 8 and the correction action is applied based on the information that was extracted from the photograph. In some cases, this may result in a poor automatic adjustment. In other situations, the proper application of color correction to one range of colors may cause another range of colors to look worse. In both cases, it sometimes is necessary to isolate one part of a photograph from the other using a selection. A selection allows you to edit a particular area of your image without affecting other areas.

Bringing a Little Light into a Darkened Image

For all of my years taking photos, I still now and again change a setting that either prevents the camera's flash from firing or fires the flash at a reduced setting. With film photography, the flashless photo is a goner—unless you have your own darkroom, and even then, success is not guaranteed. With digital images and Paint Shop Pro, there is a much better chance of saving photos from this dark fate.

The flash was set to a low-power setting when this photo of Stephanie and her son, shown in Figure 6-5, was taken.

Here is a quick way to fix this photo using a seemingly unlikely feature: the Automatic Contrast Enhancement (ACE) effect.

1. Open the photo in Paint Shop Pro.

2. Choose Automatic Contrast Enhancement from the Photo toolbar or select Adjust | Brightness and Contrast. This opens the dialog box shown next.

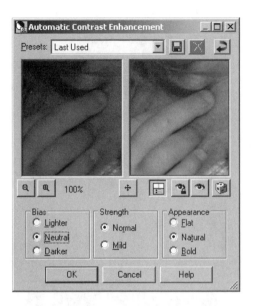

3. Change the photo's lighting by setting a combination of Bias, Strength, and Appearance. This feature controls several different tonal attributes, so toggle the Proof button often to determine the best settings and then click the OK button. The result is shown in Figure 6-6.

FIGURE 6-5   She smiled but the flash didn't fire at full power.

FIGURE 6-6   Automatic Contrast Enhancement corrects more than contrast.

 *While you are concentrating on improving the lighting, be careful not to be seduced by the extra contrast of the Bold setting—it may blow out detail in the light areas and cause details in the shadows to turn to pure black.*

In addition to correcting lighting problems, the ACE is an excellent choice for making otherwise drab photos look better. The photograph of the geese shown in Figure 6-7 (left) was taken on an overcast day, resulting in a photograph that was too dark.

Using ACE to correct the lighting may result in colors appearing a little washed out, but the good news is that there is an automatic tool to correct this, too.

Making Images More Vivid with Automatic Saturation

One of the more common problems faced by photographers is photos with colors that are dull, appear washed out, or both. The classic example of this problem is something most of us have experienced. You stand on the brink of some geological wonder like the Grand Canyon with your camera taking photos with great expectations in the resulting photographs. But when the photos of the Grand Canyon come back, the colors don't look anything like what you remember. There is a reason for this.

FIGURE 6-7   Original photo (left); after applying Automatic Contrast Enhancement (right)

When you are on location, your eyes dynamically adjust and allow you to see a greater range of colors, but your camera records only a fixed amount of Red, Green, and Blue (RGB). This color problem, and others like it, can easily be corrected with the Automatic Saturation Enhancement feature.

Using this feature, like the other automatic correction effects, is pretty simple and self-explanatory. Automatic Saturation Enhancement can be accessed either from the Photo toolbar or by choosing Adjust | Hue and Saturation | Automatic Saturation Enhancement, which opens the dialog box shown here:

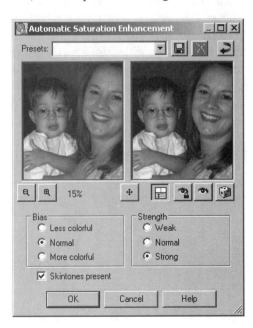

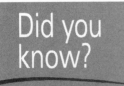

What Is Saturation?

An image with good color saturation can display subtle color changes distinctly so that the human eye perceives them as being different from one another. If similar colors blend together or if colors appear dark, they are oversaturated. Colors that appear washed out and faded are undersaturated. If a color image is completely desaturated, it appears to be a grayscale image.

One suggestion about using auto saturation: if there are people in the photo, make sure that the Skintones Present check box is checked. This prevents colors in the range of colors associated with lighter skin color from becoming oversaturated and looking red and blotchy.

Fixing Red-Eye

Red-eye is a major problem for anyone who takes photos with a flash. Everyone has taken at least one photo that was ruined by red-eye rearing it ugly eyes—a problem that's even more frustrating when you use a camera with an anti-red-eye feature that rarely works as advertised. The red-eye effect is caused by the flash reflecting off of the retina of the person you are photographing. For the record, a couple things that help reduce red-eye are using an external flash or taking the photo in a well lit room. Also, it helps if the subject is sober (no kidding!).

Some people are prone to red-eye, though, and no matter what you do, you get the "demon eye." However, you can get rid of red-eye like the one shown in Figure 6-8, with Paint Shop Pro's Red-eye Removal feature. (As a side note, I work with most of the popular photo editors, and the red-eye removal tools in Paint Shop Pro are quite simply the best around.)

Choose Red-eye Removal from the Adjust menu to open the dialog box shown next.

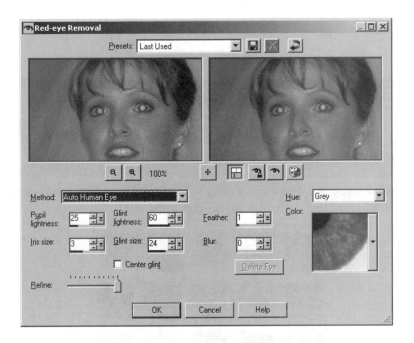

6

FIGURE 6-8   Here is a classic red-eye photo that is easily corrected with Paint Shop Pro.

The dialog box looks a little intimidating, but it's very easy to use this feature:

1. Make sure the Method is set to Auto Human Eye (if the eyes are human). Use the Navigate button in the middle of the dialog box to position the red-eyes you want to remove in the Preview window on the left.

2. On the right side of the dialog box, select the general eye color from the drop-down list labeled Hue. Try and pick the person's actual eye color. Amanda's (the bride's) eyes are brown. In most cases this is all you need to do. If you really want to get an exact color match (which no one will ever notice), click on the eye color in the Color box, and a large number of variations of that color appear, as shown next.

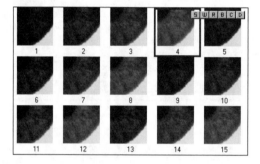

3. Place the crosshair cursor in the left window directly over the red-eye reflection and click. After a moment, the preview window on the right will show the corrected eye, as shown next.

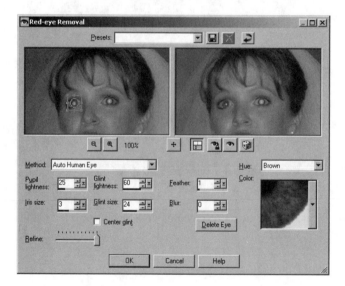

FIGURE 6-9   In a few moments, the red-eye is gone.

4. Repeat for the other eyes. In the example photo, the bride has brown eyes
    and Jim's, the dad's, are gray. When you finish with the brown eyes, use
    the Navigate button to select Jim's eyes and they will be corrected as well.
    The Redeye Removal tool remembers each eye color assigned. Click OK,
    and the red-eye is a thing of the past, as shown in Figure 6-9.

TIP   *This is not the time to change the subject's eye color. You should always do
your best to match the eye color correctly. If you don't, viewers who know
the subject will look at the photo and think (they never say) that something's
not quite right about the photo, though they won't be able to tell you
what it is.*

Other Touch-ups You Can Do

After you finish removing the red-eye, it is a good time to use the Lighten tool (L)
and whiten both the whites of the subjects' eyes and their teeth (don't go overboard,
or the subject will appear to have glowing eyes):

1. Select the Lighten/Darken tool from the Tool palette and change the
    Opacity to a low value (around 5).

2. Use a small brush size (only a few pixels) and lightly apply it to the white around the eyes and the teeth (if showing).

Removing Defects from Photos

Paint Shop Pro includes a lot of tools that help remove defects from images. Most of these are covered in Chapter 8 on repairing and restoring photographs, but there is a specific tool in Paint Shop Pro that is very handy with images that have been made into JPEG files and, as a result of heavy compression, have visible artifacts.

To remove the artifacts caused by JPEG compression, choose Adjust | Add/ Remove Noise | JPEG Artifact Removal, which opens the dialog box shown next.

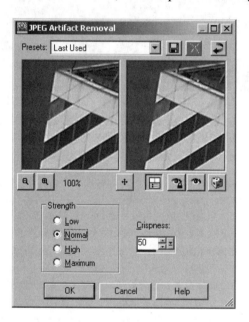

Why You Need Sharpening

No matter how crisp your original photograph is and how great your scanner is, you will always lose some sharpness when an image is digitized. An image also loses sharpness when it is sent to an output device or when it is compressed. As a result, most images will appear "soft" when printed unless some degree of sharpening is applied. Paint Shop Pro contains several sharpening filers that can help make your images as sharp as possible.

Did you know?

What Are JPEG Artifacts?

The JPG format was designed by the Joint Photographic Experts Group (JPEG). Any fuzziness or noise (random colored pixels) introduced into an image when it is compressed is called an artifact. High-compression ratios result in images with blockiness in the blue and red channels. These blocks are especially obvious in the flat areas of an image containing a single color. In areas with lots of detail, artifacts called "mosquito noise" become noticeable. (This term comes from the ripple effect that mosquitoes make when their legs touch water.)

What Is Sharpening?

Sharpening adds edges. The human eye is influenced by the presence of edges in an image. Without edges, an image appears dull. By increasing the difference (contrast) between neighboring pixels, Paint Shop Pro enhances the edges, thus making the image appear sharper, whether it is or not. However, while sharpening filters help compensate for images or image elements that are out of focus, don't expect sharpening to bring a blurred photograph into sharp focus.

TIP   *Sharpening is one of the last effects you should apply. Apply it after tonal and color correction, as it will affect the results of both.*

How Sharpening Affects Noise

All computer images include noise. Noise consists of pixels that may produce a grainy pattern or the odd dark or light spot. Images from photographs will always have noise. Actually, any image, including those captured with digital cameras, will have noise of some sort. Even the most pristine photo in your stock photo collection that was scanned on a ten-zillion dollar drum scanner will exhibit some noise.

What does noise have to do with the Sharpen filters? When you sharpen an image, you sharpen the noise as well. In fact, the noise generally sharpens up much better and faster than the rest of the image because noise pixels (like the tiny white specks in a black background) contain the one component that sharpening filters look for: the differences between adjoining pixels. Since the act of sharpening seeks out the differences (edges) and increases the contrast, the edges of the noise are enhanced and enlarged more than the rest of the pixels in the image.

This means that if you have an image containing a lot of noise, you should avoid applying any sharpening to it, as it will enhance the noise producing white or rainbow-speckled pixels over all of the image.

Lens Distortion and Correction

Since the sensors in a digital camera are physically smaller than a standard 35mm negative, digital camera lenses must be wider than their film counterparts to capture the same area. As a result, pictures taken with digital cameras can suffer from one of two forms of lens distortion: barrel (lines bowing out) and pincushion (lines bowing in), as shown next.

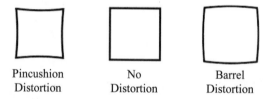

Pincushion   No   Barrel
Distortion   Distortion   Distortion

Normally, wide-angle lenses exhibit barrel distortion. Barrel distortion is clearly shown near the edges of the photo. Pincushion distortion is a lens effect that causes images to be pinched at their center. Pincushion distortion is associated with zoom lenses or telephoto adapters and only occurs at the telephoto end of a zoom lens. The distortion is most noticeable when you have a very straight edge near the side of the image frame.

Correcting Barrel Distortion

Barrel distortion is a lens effect that causes images to appear sphere-like at their center. Barrel distortion is associated with wide-angle lenses and only occurs at the wide end of a zoom lens. This distortion is most noticeable when you have vertical or horizontal elements in the photo such as in the photograph of the Texas flag (Figure 6-10). If you attempt to make a panorama using images that have any lens distortion, it will make stitching the photos together more difficult.

To remove barrel distortion in an image:

1. With the distorted image open, turn the Grid on (View | Grid) for a point of reference when correcting the distortion.

2. Select Adjust | Lens Correction | Barrel Distortion to display the Barrel Distortion Correction dialog, shown next.

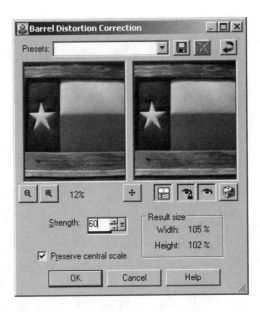

3. Change the Strength setting until the horizontal or vertical elements no longer appear bent outward. Use the Proof button to see the effect on the image against the grid. Click OK. The result is shown in Figure 6-11.

FIGURE 6-10   Barrel distortion causes the lines in the flag to bend.

FIGURE 6-11   The flag looks better with the barrel distortion removed.

Correcting Other Distortions in Photos

When you take a photo of a building, or anything large for that matter, a certain amount of distortion is introduced. The photograph shown in Figure 6-12 was taken on Wacker Drive in Chicago with a wide-angle lens. The buildings look as if they are bending inward, especially on the edges of the photos.

Even though this distortion was created by a wide-angle lens and as such is a form of barrel distortion, you resolve this distortion with the Perspective Correction tool. In Figure 6-13, the tops of the buildings appear smaller than the bottoms, a form of distortion called Keystoning. Here is the procedure to correct it:

1. Open the photograph and select the Perspective Correction tool.

2. A four-sided polygon appears on the photo. Grab the points and move them so that the vertical lines align with the vertical lines of the buildings near the edge of the photo, as shown in Figure 6-13.

3. With the Crop Image option unchecked, double-click the photo. The resulting image is shown in Figure 6-14.

FIGURE 6-12   Wide-angle lenses distort the shapes of buildings.

FIGURE 6-13   The Perspective correction polygon handles are used to establish the degree of distortion.

FIGURE 6-14   The perspective correction applied without cropping creates angular sides.

4. Using the Crop tool, remove the edges. As with all distortion corrections, material at the edge of the photograph will be lost. The corrected image, shown in Figure 6-15, has the vertical elements of the buildings corrected. The odd thing about it being perfectly vertical is that it doesn't look natural *because* of the lack of keystoning.

Pincushion Distortion

Pincushion distortion is the opposite of barrel distortion. Whereas the edges of a photo push outward with barrel distortion, they push inward with pincushion distortion. Wide-angle lenses produce barrel distortion, and telephoto lenses create pincushion distortion. The image shown lower right (on the next page) was taken of the architectural detail of a building in Chicago using a 200mm telephoto lens; the grid view was turned to make it easier to see the distortion.

FIGURE 6-15   Correct wide-angle lens distortion with the Perspective Control tool.

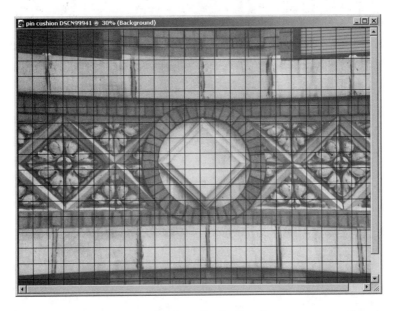

Like the barrel distortion described earlier in the chapter, you use the pincushion distortion to restore the image to what it looked like before it was distorted by the effect of the lens.

Chapter 7

Add Text to Your Images

How to...

- Use the Text tool
- Add basic text to a photograph
- Create a cartoon text balloon
- Map text to a path
- Create simple but great text effects

Pictures may speak a thousand words, but there is no replacement for a clever bit of verbiage to add impact. In this chapter, you'll discover how fun it is to add text to your images and create an effect that even the most diligent scrap-booker would envy. So, gather your favorite images, and let's have some fun.

Text, Plain and Simple

Think of the Text tool as nothing more than a simplified word processor without all the fancy tools such as spell check, tables, and complex formatting. This tool is not designed to help you write your next novel or magazine article; it is merely designed to add small amounts of text to an image.

Text Tool Options

When you click the Text tool in the Tools toolbar, several options appear in the Tool Options palette shown next. Many of them are familiar options found in word processors but a few are unique to Paint Shop Pro.

Choosing Text Properties

The Create As option enables you to define the one of three different types of text—Vector, Selection, or Floating.

- **Vector**   Creates the text on a vector layer as opposed to a raster layer. Unlike raster layers, vector layers can be edited, resized, and deformed without affecting the quality. With vector layers, however, you cannot apply any of the Paint Shop Pro effects. An example of what can be done with vector text is shown in Figure 7-1. After the text was applied, it was rotated and reshaped using the Object Selection tool (O).

■ **Selection**   Creates an empty text selection that behaves very much like a stencil in the shape of the text and properties you choose. The selection becomes part of the layer (or background) that is currently active. When

FIGURE 7-1   Vector text can be reshaped for added emphasis.

you select the text selection and move it, the pixels within the text selection move too, leaving the color of the background in its place. This type of text cannot be edited, but there is a wealth of things that you can do with it. The text selection in Figure 7-2 was left empty and the Outer Bevel filter (Effects | 3D Effects | Outer Bevel) was applied at the default settings.

TIP   *If you want to move the text marquee and not portions of the layer underneath, select the Move tool (*M*) and right-click and drag the selection to another location. See Chapter 10 for detailed information about working with selections.*

FIGURE 7-2   Effects filters can also be applied to text selections.

■ **Floating** Similar to vector except that it creates a floating selection that hovers over the layer and maintains its own style and texture. When you move the selected text, the layer underneath is not affected. This type of text cannot be edited, but you can apply brushes and other tools without first converting it to a raster layer. In Figure 7-3, the Picture Tube tool (using the Old Glory picture tube) was applied to the floating selection to create a patriotic image. You can learn how to make this image at the end of the chapter and discover more about using the Picture Tube in Chapter 11.

Some of the following choices in the Tool Options palette are common choices that you have encountered in other Windows applications or are unique to Paint Shop Pro 8.

■ **Font** Lists the available fonts installed on your system.

■ **Size** Enables you to either choose a font size (in points) from the drop-down list or enter in your own size.

FIGURE 7-3 Applying the Picture Tube tool to a floating text selection creates impressive effects.

- **Stroke Width (Pixels)** Applies an outline around the text when set to a value other than 0.0. The current foreground color in the Materials palette defines the color of the outline. Use the stroke width to create outlined text like the one shown right. While applying an outline works well on block shaped text (called sans serif), it doesn't do well with fancy display text.

- **Anti-alias** Smoothes the jagged edges of letters by blending them with the background color. Unless you are working with a 256-color grayscale or 24-bit color image, you won't see the true effects of this feature. The best practice is to leave it selected.

- **Warp Text** Available when text characters follow a path and enable you to warp the characters to a specific shape.

When the curve of the path to which you are aligning the text is not gradual (that is, it's a sharp angle) the Warp Text option may cause the individual characters to overlap each other and may introduce distortion in the individual characters.

- **Alignment** Aligns the text to the left or right edge of the insertion point or centers it.

- **Font Style** Sets the way the font appears. Select B for bold, I for italic, U for underline, or A to insert a horizontal line through the text (commonly referred to as Strikethrough).

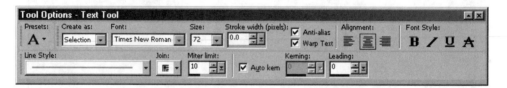

- **Line Style** If you have defined a stroke width greater than 0.0, this tool enables you to select the type of line to use for the outline of each character. The color for the line style is determined by the current background color.

- **Join** Defines the way the corners of each letter appear. Your choices are Miter, which forms a very square look; Round, which offers a smoother look; or Beveled, which creates a semi-round look. If you select Miter as a choice, it will produce mitered (pointed) corners if the width of the corner is within the value that you set in the Miter Limit box and produces beveled corners when the corner width exceeds the value of the limit.

- **Auto Kern**   Automatically defines the spacing between each adjacent character based on the font type and size.

- **Kerning**   Increases or decreases the space between each adjacent character if Auto Kern is turned off. This is handy when placing text along a path and you need to shorten or lengthen the text string without changing the font size.

- **Leading**   Increases or decreases the space between text lines. When left at 0, the spacing is determined automatically based on the font type and size.

Using the Text Tool

Now that you are familiar with the settings of the text tool, you are ready to have some fun and get creative.

Add Text to an Image

In this project, you will use your own photo and possibly your own text so as to be similar to the one shown here:

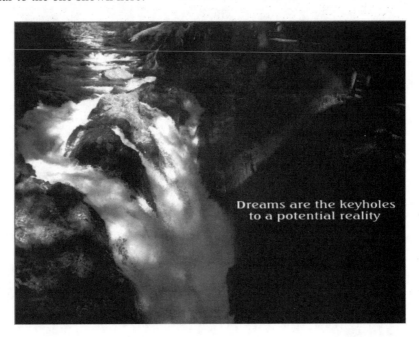

To add text to an image, complete the following steps:

1. Open the photo to which you want to add text.

2. Save the image as a native Paint Shop Pro 8 file so you won't overwrite your original image file.

3. In the Tools toolbar, click the Text tool (T).

4. In the Tool Options palette, make the following choices:

   ■ **Create As** Vector

   ■ **Font** Your favorite font

   ■ **Size** 22 (the size of the image will determine the font size that you actually use)

   ■ **Stroke Width** 0.0

   ■ **Anti-alias** Checked

   ■ **Alignment** Centered

5. On the Materials palette, click the background color swatch. From the Color dialog box, select the color you want your text to be, and then click OK.

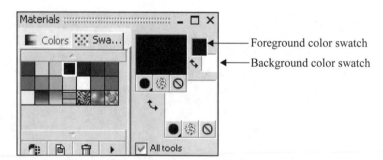

6. Click where you want to place your text in the image.

7. In the Text Entry dialog, type your text. Press ENTER when you want to start another line. The Text tool does not automatically wrap. If you want this text to appear in the Text Entry box each time it opens, select the Remember Text check box.

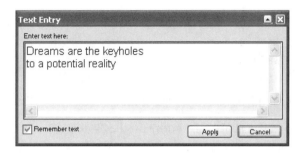

8. Click Apply.

9. To position the text, click the Object Selection tool (O) located at the bottom of the Tools toolbar and then click the selected text. When the cursor changes to crossed double-headed arrows, click and drag the text to the desired location and the text appears in the desired part of the image.

Add a Cartoon Text Balloon to an Image

On those photos that simply scream for dialog, it is fun to add cartoon captions. Figure 7-4 is an example of what can be created.

FIGURE 7-4   The addition of a cartoon caption balloon to a photo can be just plain fun.

To add a cartoon thought balloon, complete the following steps:

1. Open the photo to which you want to add text and save the image as a native Paint Shop Pro 8 file as in the preceding step 2.

2. In the Tools toolbar, click the Preset Shape tool.

3. Click to open the Shape List button in the Tool Options palette to view the available shapes.

4. Choose a shape for your text balloon. There are several cartoon caption balloons (which Jasc calls Callouts) to pick from—I used Callout 4 for the sample photo at the beginning of this procedure.

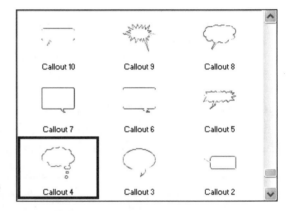

5. Click inside the image and click and drag the cursor to define the size of the new text balloon shape.

6. If you need to flip the balloon so that it faces the right direction, open the Image menu and select Mirror, or press CTRL-M.

7. Click and drag a corner handle to size the balloon proportionately, or click and drag one of the side, top, or bottom handles to stretch the balloon tall or wide.

8. To move the image, position your cursor near the center of the balloon image until the cursor changes to a crossed double-headed arrow. Click and drag the image to the desired location.

9. Press CTRL-D to deselect the balloon image.

10. Click the Text tool on the Tools toolbar, and then select the Create As Vector option in the Tool Options palette. You can select your favorite font,

but I recommend the Comic Sans for this style of caption. Change the size so the caption fits in the balloon.

11. Change the background color to the color you want your text to be. Pick a color that offers good contrast to make it easier for your viewer to read.

12. Click the balloon you just created.

13. In the Text Entry box, type the text you want to place in the balloon and click Apply.

14. To position the text, click the Object Selection tool and then click the selected text. When the cursor changes to crossed double-headed arrows, click and drag the text inside of the balloon. With the text in place you have a caption that adds a little humor to a photo. The use of balloon captions isn't limited to adding humorous comments; you can also use it to point out reference points on a photo or provide instructions like the one shown right.

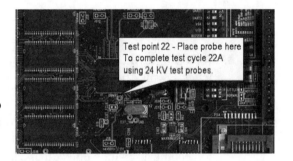

Editing Text

If you created vector text, you can edit the text with the Text tool. If you want to alter the actual shape of individual characters at the vector level, you can convert the text to curves.

To edit vector text, complete the following steps:

1. Select the Text tool (T).

2. In the Layers palette, right-click the text layer you want to edit and then click Edit Text from the pop-up menu.

3. Edit your text and click Apply.

 *If you want to change the font type, size, or alignment, highlight the text in the Text Entry dialog and change the attributes in the Tool Options palette.*

Convert Text to Curves

When you convert vector text to curves, you essentially turn them into individual objects that can be manipulated. As with any curve, you can add nodes, change the angles of line segments, or use the Node Edit or Line tool to create some very interesting effects. Once the text is converted to curves, however, you can no longer edit the text with the Text tool.

To convert text to curves, complete the following steps:

1. Click the Object Selection tool (O) and select the text you want to convert.

2. Open the Objects menu, click Convert Text to Curves, and select one of the following options:

   ■ **As a Single Shape**   To produce one path containing a contour for each letter. By making the text string into a single shape you can apply any effects to all of the characters in the text string as a single object.

   ■ **As Character Shapes**   To convert each letter into a separate vector object. The advantage to this is that it allows each character in the text to become a separate object that can be twisted, turned, and reshaped as required.

The text in Figure 7-5 was converted to curves as Character Shapes after which the initial letter C of Chicago was selected, enlarged, and repositioned. Then all of the text was selected, and the Object Selection tool was used to skew it to the right.

Saving Your Text Styles

Presets are text attributes you can save and recall to achieve a consistent look and feel. This is handy when you are creating calendar images and want the text on each image to look the same.

To create a preset, complete the following steps:

1. Click the Text tool (T) and set the text tool options you want to save as a preset.

2. Click the Presets button in the Tool Options palette.

FIGURE 7-5   Text converted as character shapes gives more creative choices.

3. In the Presets dialog box, click the Save button.

Text styles you have saved

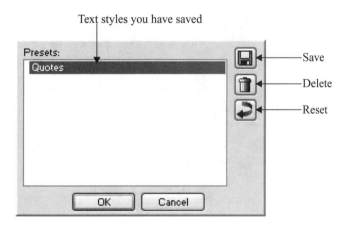

4. In the Preset Name text box, type a name for your preset.

5. If you want to define additional options, click Options.

6. Attributes that do not have a red X over them are saved with your preset. If there is an attribute that you do not want associated with the preset, click that attribute to place a red X over the top of that attribute's Save button.

7. Click OK.

Text That Follows a Shape

A fun little feature of Paint Shop Pro 8 is Fit Text to Path, which offers the ability to create text that rides along a vector object that defines a shape—called a path. Figure 7-6 shows text that follows a path drawn with the Pen tool.

Figure 7-7 is an example of using the Fit Text to Path to flow the text with the path hidden.

> **TIP** *If you don't want the line to show, select the path (called a shape layer) in the Layers palette and turn off the visibility by clicking the icon that looks like an eye.*

FIGURE 7-6   Making text follow a path creates additional creative possibilities.

FIGURE 7-7   Hiding the path makes the text appear to flow around the cup.

How Text on a Path Works

You can either create the path you want your text to follow first, or you can convert existing text to follow a vector shape. Prior to experimenting with this fun feature, you might want to take time to learn how Paint Shop Pro determines where to start and stop the text.

Alignment

Before writing your text, you determine if it is going to be justified left, right, or centered. Where you click on the vector object determines where your text begins. The click point can either be the left, right, or center position for your text, depending on how you have it justified.

If you are fitting existing text to a path, the start and end nodes of the path determine how the text aligns. For example, if you have the text centered, the text will be centered between the start and end nodes of the path. Likewise, left-justified text will start at the start node, while right-justified text will end at the end node.

Orientation

The direction of the path determines whether the text aligns above or below the path, right-side up, or upside-down. To change the direction of the text, click

Objects | Edit | Reverse Path. To change the distance between the path and the text, adjust the leading value for the text. The higher the value, the greater the space between the text and the path will be.

Open Paths and Closed Paths

An open path is a line where the start and end points aren't joined, while closed paths form an enclosed shape of some kind. If the text on an open path hangs past the end nodes, the angle of the last line segment determines the direction the text will take. If text goes beyond a closed path, the text will wrap around on top of itself.

Place Text on a Line That Isn't Straight

In this example, you will learn how to create text that conforms to a shape. Having text flow around an object in a circular shape is a very popular graphic design technique.

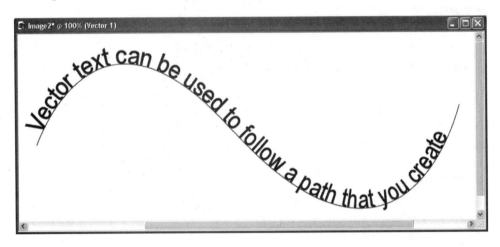

To align text to a shape, complete the following steps:

1. Click the Text tool on the Tools toolbar and select the following options in the Tool Options palette:

   ■ **Create As**   Vector

   ■ **Font**   Your choice

◀ There are a lot of things wrong with this photo besides the plastic bag and the sunflower pointing the wrong direction.

▶ With the help of the Clone tool and a replacement sky, we can turn this photo into something Van Gogh would have loved.

This is a lovely photograph of a rose.

Using the artistic effects of Paint Shop Pro filters, we can make it into an even lovelier work of art.

Photo Fun

- **Size**   Your choice
- **Stroke Width**   0.0
- **Anti-alias**   Checked
- **Alignment**   Left

2. Change the background color to Black.

3. Click where you want to begin your text.

4. In the Text Entry dialog, type your text and click Apply.

5. Click the Preset Shape tool, and then click the Shape List button in the Tool Options palette.

6. From the Shape List, select the Circle shape.

7. Click your canvas where you want to begin drawing your shape and click and drag your cursor to draw your shape. In this example I dragged it around the photograph of the film reel.

TIP   *To constrain drawing of a new shape to equal width and height, hold* SHIFT *while drawing the shape.*

8. Click the Object Selection tool (O) and click and drag the shape so it is centered over the object that you want the text to flow around. In this example it is the film reel.

9. In the Layers palette, expand the vector layer by clicking the plus (+) sign. There should be two objects listed; one for your text and one for the shape you just drew.

10. Hold SHIFT down, click the text layer in the Layers palette, and click the shape layer to select both. Release your SHIFT key.

11. Right-click the selected layers and click Fit Text to Path.

12. Click the visibility icon (looks like an eye) and the circle you used for a path becomes invisible.

Rotation
handle

FIGURE 7-8 Text following the edge of a strong graphic is a real attention grabber

13. After the text fits to the path, you can adjust the rotation to get your words
aligned with the top of the shape. Click the rotation handle and rotate the
objects until they are aligned they way you expect, as shown in Figure 7-8.

14. When you have everything aligned the way you want, click CTRL-D to
deselect the objects.

Here is another example of applying the text around a different object.

7

TIP *If you want your text to be inside the shape, instead of outside, select the shape layer and click the Pen tool. Press CTRL-SHIFT-R to reverse the shape, or choose Objects | Edit | Reverse Path.*

Creating Special Text Effects

Creating special text effects gives your text a little attitude and offers a bit of a punch to your message. Use a combination of textures and effects to build your own unique look and feel. The following examples show only a snippet of what you can do with different textures, fills, and effects.

Transparent Text

If you have a photo with a lot of solid color in it, such as all the blue sky in Figure 7-2, and you need to add just few words of text, you can use transparent text to create a professional-looking title.

Follow these steps to create transparent text:

1. Open the image and select the Text tool (T).

2. Change the Create as setting to Selection in the Tool Options palette.

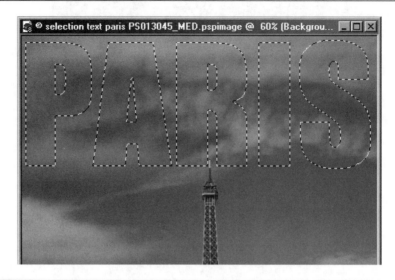

FIGURE 7-9   The selection marquee is placed where the text effect will be applied.

3. Enter the text you want to add. As you type, actual text appears in the image. Adjust the other type settings (font, kerning, etc.) so it fits the image as desired. When finished, click the Apply button and the text is replaced by a selection marquee (see Figure 7-9).

4. Choose Effects | 3D Effects | Outer Bevel and choose the default settings as shown right.

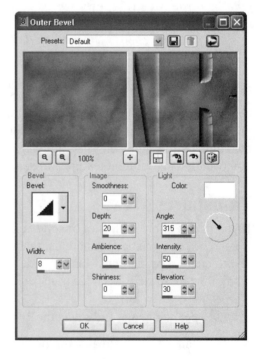

5. Click the OK button and remove the selection (CTRL-D).

TIP   *This technique doesn't work well over complex backgrounds.*

Adding Picture Tubes and Text

By using the Picture Tube tool to fill the selection, you can really get creative. This technique is so much fun and so easy it should be illegal.

1. Follow the first three steps in the previous technique. For this example, I used "USA" as the text, for obvious reasons.

2. Select the Picture Tube tool in the Tools toolbar. Select the Old Glory picture tube (you can download this for free from the Jasc website—it's part of the set called Summer). Apply the Picture Tube to the selection, as shown next.

3. Choose Effects | 3D Effects | Inner Bevel and change the settings in the dialog box, as shown here:

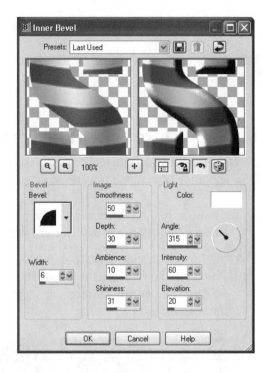

4. Click the OK button and remove the selection (CTRL-D).

5. As an extra touch you can add a photo edge.

Part III

Advanced Image Editing

Chapter 8

Repairing and Restoring Photographs

How to...

- Repair tears and creases in photos
- Restore faded photos
- Clean up dirty photos

All of the features and power of Paint Shop Pro 8 make the job of converting old, torn, and otherwise damaged photos easy. In this chapter, you will discover how you can use Paint Shop Pro to reverse the damage done by time and mishandling. You will also learn the best ways to scan images for preservation and restoration.

Preparing Your Image or Document

Unlike digital camera photo goofs (leaving the flash off, putting a finger in front of the lens, etc.), older damaged images and other important documents must first be scanned before you can repair them. In most cases, you will need to remove the photo from its frame before scanning. If you cannot remove it from the frame without damaging it, then you will need to scan the entire photo or document (frame and all). Be aware that when you scan the entire photo, frame and all, there is a chance that the color of the frame will influence the scanner's auto exposure feature during the scan. To solve this problem, you should either select only the photo and try the automatic setting again, or manually adjust the tonal settings. Just remember to perform the evaluation of the scan with Paint Shop Pro and not from the preview window in the scanner software, which is a poor representation of the image.

Laying Image Flat on the Glass

It will be difficult to scan a document or image that has been rolled up for a long time because it will curl up. If the image is not laying flat on the glass, it will create highlights and shadows, especially along the creases. Figure 8-1 is part of a photo panorama taken of my navy boot camp company over 35 years ago that was kept rolled up for most of that time. When I placed it on the scanner, the weight of the scanner lid wasn't enough to keep the photo flat to the glass and it lifted slightly, causing the white reflections.

When I scanned it the second time, I held the scanner lid down tightly on the scanner (be careful: the scanner glass can break), and the resulting scan appears in Figure 8-2. While the crease remains, the bright reflections are now gone. There are still creases and tears (none of these defects were on me—ha!) and you will discover how to repair damage like this later in the chapter.

FIGURE 8-1   Capturing rolled photos can be a challenge.

FIGURE 8-2   Keeping the photo flat reduces unwanted reflections.

How to Handle Old Photos

Always hold prints or negatives by their edges. Do not touch the surface if you're not wearing cotton gloves; even clean fingers can leave natural secretions that can damage a photo over time. You can get cotton gloves specially made for handling photos at your local camera store.

Never mark the back of your photo permanently in any way. The chemicals in some markers (especially a Sharpie) will eventually find its way to the other side of the photograph and ruin it. If you must make a temporary identification, write brief information gently with only a very soft 2B or 4B pencil.

Never repair a photograph by applying adhesive tape to it. I saw the Dead Sea scrolls last year and, after talking to one of the archivists, I discovered that one of their major restoration tasks of the past five years has been removing the Scotch tape that the original curators used to piece it together. If you have a photo that is in several pieces, keep all of the pieces in a clean, chemically inert polyester bag or sleeve.

Preparing to Restore Photos

When you are scanning an image for the purpose of restoring it, you will need to make a few adjustments to your normal scanning routine. First, if the photo or image that you are scanning is really old (and most of the examples in this chapter are), they are fragile, and therefore you should exercise caution when handling and preparing them for scanning.

Scanning for Restoration

This section contains guidelines for scanning photographs and other documents specifically for restoration and preservation. In several ways they differ from normal scanning guidelines.

Enlarging the Original

When repairing or otherwise restoring, make it a general rule to scan images at 200 percent. By doubling the size of the original, you force the scanner to capture the maximum amount of detail in the original photo and give yourself more material to work with. Some exceptions to this rule are when the original is really small.

In such cases, you should consider using an even larger resize factor (such as 300 percent through 500 percent). If the original image is large enough to cover the entire scanner glass, don't enlarge it. The default setting of your scanner (100 percent) will probably be sufficient.

Using the Highest Quality Scan Setting

When you are scanning for repair, restoration, or preservation you want to get as much image detail from the scanned image as possible without having to worry about how big the final file will be. For photos and memorabilia that you want to preserve, scan the original using RGB (24-bit) color. Black-and-white photos in most cases should be scanned in grayscale—the exception being if they have been hand colored or have a colored stain on them. Preserving the color in such cases allows isolation of the stain using color-sensitive selection tools.

Scanning All of the Original, Warts and All

When scanning for preservation, you should not be selective and scan only part of the original. For example, Figure 8-3 is an old photo taken near the turn of the

FIGURE 8-3   Even though the paper frame is in poor shape, you should always scan it all when preserving photos.

century that was glued to a stained paper frame. To preserve this image, you should scan the photo, the frame, and in most cases even include a little extra around the edges. When you get around to restoring the photo, you can crop out the frame from a copy of the scanned photo, but I recommend you preserve all of the original and how it appeared when it was photographed.

Saving Photos Using a Lossless File Format

Do not save the original as a JPEG file. For restoration work, you should not save the images you are working with using any file format that uses lossy file compression. This includes Wavelet, JPEG, and JPEG 2000. Lossy file compression degrades the image. Probably the most popular lossless graphic format is TIFF, and you can choose one of several lossless compression options, meaning they do not degrade the image. Be careful not to choose the JPEG compression option that is now available as a choice for TIFF.

Repairing Tears and Creases

One of the more common problems with old photos is that they have not usually received museum quality care and storage. Unprotected, the important images can easily become bent, folded, and otherwise damaged. Physically, there isn't anything that can be done for the original (with the exception of work done by a restoration specialist), but it's relatively easy to repair an electronic version and then to print it.

How much damage was caused by folding a photograph depends on its age and the material it was printed on. Photos from the past 30 years are printed on a flexible Mylar that can stand almost any degree of contortion, while photos printed around the turn of the twentieth century through the late 1950s were printed on stiff material. In most cases, even a slight bend produces a hard, raised crease from which the image may flake off, as in the example shown in Figure 8-1.

Here is the step-by-step procedure to repair a crease from an old photograph; the example photo was taken in 1896.

1. After ensuring the scanner glass is clean, position the original photo on the center of the scanner glass. Run a preview scan and change the output size so the resulting scan is twice as large (200 percent) as the original.

2. Save the original scan and then save a copy to work on using the Save As command. The original scanned photo (shown next) doesn't appear to be in terrible shape.

3. When you open the copy, make sure that the Paint Shop Pro 8 view is set to 100 percent, called Actual Size. Because of the large size of the image, only a portion of it will be visible in the image window. When doing retouching and restoration work, it is often necessary to get in quite close—200 percent through 400 percent—to fix the image, but you must always return to 100 percent to accurately evaluate the changes made (see Figure 8-4).

4. Select the Clone brush (not the Scratch Remover) from the Tools toolbar, as shown next. This tear is too wide to use the Scratch Remover effectively.

5. Change the brush settings to a soft-edged brush. In Figure 8-5, I start with the most distracting part of the defect, the crease that is running across the man's face. Right-click to select a spot near the crease to use as the sample point for the Clone brush. Next, dab along the crease rather than holding down the mouse button and dragging the brush along the crease.

8

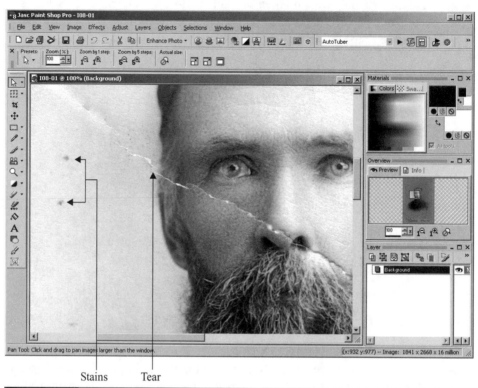

Stains   Tear

FIGURE 8-4   At 100 percent, the image doesn't fit in the image window but it accurately shows the damage that must be repaired.

TIP   *Dragging the Clone brush makes a visually apparent line. It isn't as bad as the original crease, but it still looks like someone has been tinkering with the photo. Changing the sample point often (using either side of the crease) prevents repeating patterns.*

6. When working on critical areas (like the crease across his face) zoom in as much as necessary so you can use the smallest, soft-edged Clone brush to get the small areas. In the image shown in Figure 8-6, I am working at a magnification of 200 percent and using a smaller brush to get in and around the tear that went through the nostril.

TIP   *To quickly move around an image (especially at high zoom levels) use the Preview window (shown in the previous illustration) by dragging the rectangle.*

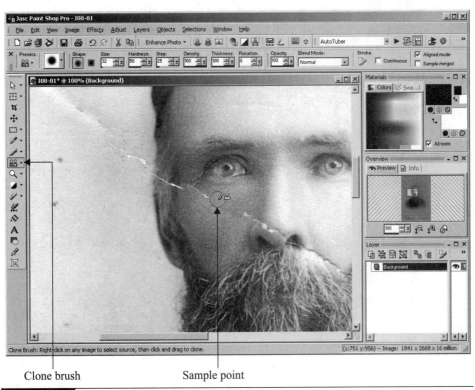

Clone brush   Sample point

FIGURE 8-5   The selection of the Clone brush source is important.

7. Use the Clone brush to remove the remaining parts of the crease and some of the dark spots on the background.

8. Return to either 100 percent or Fit to Window zoom level to see how the entire image looks.

9. This particular photo has lost some of its quality over the years. Using the One Step Photo Fix feature makes the photo look even better by applying over six different auto enhancements to the image. The finished image is shown in Figure 8-7.

10. To complete the work, resize the image to return it to its correct size. There is a natural softening of the image that is the result of making it smaller. This can sometimes make a harsh image look better. If it softens it too much, apply the Unsharp Mask filter at a low setting.

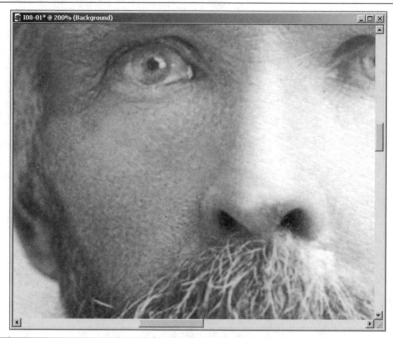

FIGURE 8-6   It is important to zoom in and out to achieve the best photo touching results.

Did you know?

What's the Clone Tool?

The Clone tool takes a sample from part of an image, which can then be painted onto another image or different part of the same image. The user selects a sample point (source) on the image and then moves the Clone brush to the desired area of the image and begins applying copies of pixels from the sample point to the area under the Clone brush. The position of the source in relationship to the Clone brush is controlled by the mode of operation selected. When Aligned in the Options toolbar is checked, the position of the source relative to the Clone brush remains fixed at what it was when the Clone tool is applied. If it's not aligned, the source point snaps back to the original starting point each time the mouse button is let go. This nonaligned mode is a handy way to clone the pixels in a smaller area to a larger area without having to constantly reset the source point.

FIGURE 8-7   Using the Clone tool, it is a simple matter to remove even the worst damage.

Restoring a Paper Frame

While the Clone tool and Clone brush are great tools, there are other solutions available for repairing and restoring a scanned image. In the example photo, the paper frame (shown next) in which the photo was mounted has seen more than its share of use and abuse.

In this restoration, you are going to use portions of one part of the frame to cover another. With the image loaded in Paint Shop Pro 8, change the view to 100 percent (actual pixels). As shown next, in the lower-left corner there are two serious stains, so that's where we'll start.

1. Select an area of the frame that is clean, create a rectangle selection, and put a feathered edge on the selection, like the one shown next. The feathering of the selection produces gradual transitions so your patch work isn't visually apparent. Because this is a large image, the 6-pixel feather I chose will produce a very small transition area.

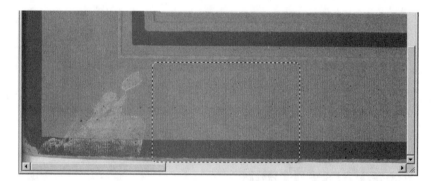

2. While holding down the ALT key, drag the selection to the left until it covers the bad spot on the corner, as shown in Figure 8-8. By ALT-dragging, you copy the pixels inside the selection marquee.

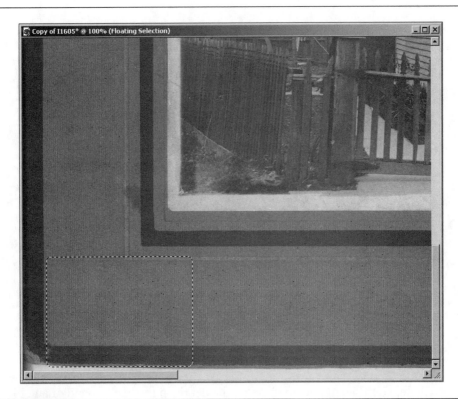

FIGURE 8-8   Moving a selection over the paint stain easily and quickly covers it.

3. There are several ways to defloat the selection. The easiest is to right-click inside the selection or remove the selection (CTRL-D). Continue making more selections to repair all of the stains on the paper frame.

4. The final step is to make a hard-edged selection (no feather) of the dark-edged border to rebuild the worn corner of the print. The finished corner is shown in Figure 8-9.

Cleaning Up Dirty Backgrounds

Just as with the frame you repaired in the previous section, a dirty background can be repaired with a Clone tool or brush, but it would take too much time. Instead of

FIGURE 8-9   Using floating selections removes the stains in just a few minutes.

using Clone, you'll learn how to clean up the debris in the background of an old photo—the example was taken way back in 1897 (Figure 8-10).

Here is how to clean up the dirty sky in the sample photo:

1. Open the image. Using the Freehand Selection tool, select part or all of the background that you want to clean. Use the Smart Edge of the Freehand Selection tool to quickly create a rough selection composed of the background of the image, as shown in Figure 8-11.

2. With the background selected, there are several ways to remove the dust and debris. You could just press DELETE, and the background will become pure white (assuming your background color is set to white). However, this produces an artificial-looking backdrop that can be distracting. Instead, use

the Salt and Pepper filter (Adjust | Add/Remove Noise | Salt and Pepper
Filter) at a high setting to remove the debris and leave a background that
appears to be part of the original print. If the remaining background is too
dark, use the Gamma Correction (CTRL-G) to lighten it up. This will remove
the dirty look of the sky but leave it looking uneven so it appears to be part
of the original photo, as shown in Figure 8-12.

To be honest, there is as much debris on the house walls in this photo as there
was in the sky. However, because the dust and scratches are dark, they don't stand
out, so I left them.

To finish repairing the photo, I did a few things in addition to cleaning up the
background. First, I inverted the selection that was made and used Paint Shop
Pro's Darken brush to make the chimney and the right side of the roof darker.
Then I used the Burn tool, set to mid-tones and a light opacity (10 to 15 percent).
Figure 8-13 shows the final image, which is—as we say in Texas—all dressed up
and ready for church.

FIGURE 8-10   This photo is over 100 years old and looks like it has a hundred years of
dirt and scratches on it.

FIGURE 8-11   The use of a selection isolates the background for effective debris removal.

How to ... **Fine-Tune a Selection**

As useful as Paint Shop Pro's automated selection tools are, sometimes you finish making a rough selection and realize some parts of it need adjustment. Jasc included a neat feature in Paint Shop Pro 8 called Edit Selection. When you select this feature (Selections | Edit Selection), the area of the photo that is protected is covered with a red tint. Selecting the Paintbrush (B) and painting the image with black subtracts from the existing selection; painting with white adds to the selection.

FIGURE 8-12   The Salt and Pepper filter removes debris from the background.

FIGURE 8-13   Another photograph that has been rescued before it suffered anymore damage.

Another Way to Remove Stains

With all of this advice on stain and dirt removal, I wonder if I can get a guest spot on the Martha Stewart show!

The image shown in Figure 8-14 has a stain on it caused by a clear oil such as mineral oil or sewing machine oil. What makes this type of stain unique is that it darkens the color, but the stain is, for all intents and purposes, transparent. The placement of the stain on the oval paper frame pattern precludes placing a selection over it, as you did earlier in the chapter. In this case you will isolate the stain with a selection and tweak the hue, saturation, and lightness. Here is how it is done:

1. Use the Magic Wand tool set to a low tolerance and select the stain. You will need to play with the tolerance until you get the correct setting. If

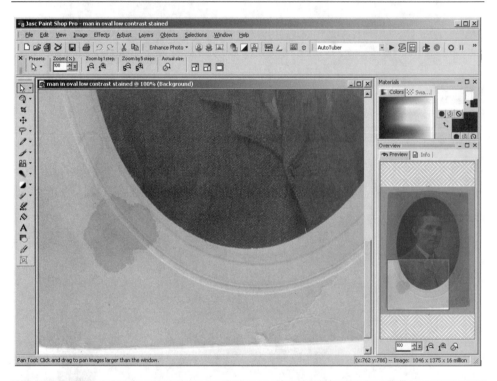

FIGURE 8-14   A stain can easily be removed using Paint Shop Pro 8.

your selection includes areas isolated from the stain, check the settings
for your Magic Wand tool. With a little tweaking, you should end up
with a selection like the one shown in Figure 8-15, which accurately
outlines the stain.

NOTE *Don't put a feather on your stain selection; if you do, you will see a faint
outline of the stain when you are done.*

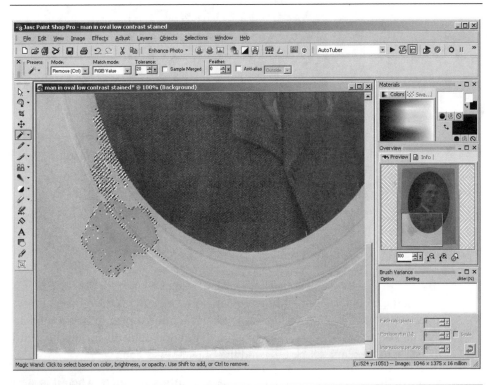

FIGURE 8-15   Selecting a stain is the first step to remove it.

2. Once you have the selection the way you want it, hide the marquee (CTRL-SHIFT-M) and open the Hue, Saturation, and Lightness dialog box (SHIFT-H), as shown next.

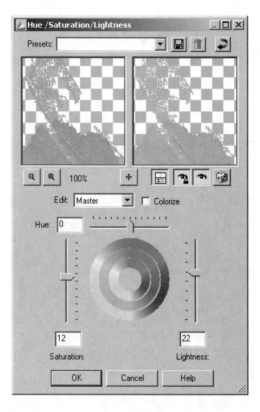

3. Adjust the Lightness first until it appears to be as light as the surrounding area. Note that the color inside the section does not appear to be as vivid as the outside area. No problem: move the Saturation controls up slightly until the stain disappears. Click OK, and the big stain is gone.

4. Remove the selection (CTRL-D)—it's easy to forget it's there when it is hidden. Use the Clone tool to clean up any remaining dirt or stains. The cleaned up paper frame is shown in Figure 8-16. Now all I need to do is call Martha!

FIGURE 8-16   In less than 2 minutes, you and Paint Shop Pro 8 can remove a stubborn
stain from any object.

If time and page count allowed, I could go on for another 30 pages on this
topic—it is so much fun to restore old photos and see what things used to look
like! However, I have covered some of the basics of image restoration in this
chapter.

Chapter 9

Automating Paint Shop Pro 8

How to…

- Automatically rename batches of images
- Create scripts to perform repetitive tasks
- Combine the power of scripts with batch processing

Paint Shop Pro 8 includes powerful tools that can automate repetitive tasks. This can be a real time saver; especially when you are processing the over-400 digital photos you took on your vacation to Mule Shoe, Texas. Called Batch Process and Scripting, these features provide you with a quick and easy way to apply conversions, effects, or just about any other command to multiple images.

Using the Batch Command

The Batch Process command automates the process of saving and renaming multiple images simultaneously. Batch processing was available in previous releases of Paint Shop Pro and has been updated in Paint Shop Pro 8 so you can now rename files and apply a script to a series of images in a folder. In the following sections, you will learn how to use Batch Process to change the format, location, and names of a group of files. The Batch command also allows you to apply scripts to files while doing this. Scripts are covered later in this chapter.

Using batch processing is simple, but because of the way some of the features are configured the way they operate may not be immediately apparent and you might get a little frustrated the first time you use them if you don't pay close attention.

Saving Multiple Image Files to a Different Format

If you take a large number of photos with your digital camera at an event (wedding, vacation, graduation, etc.), you need a way to move the images from your camera into the computer. I covered several ways to move the images from your camera's digital memory card into your computer in Chapter 3. But what happens when you want to convert all of the photos into a different format? That is when you will want to process them as a group using the Batch Conversion feature. (See also "Did You Know? The Advantages of Changing File Formats," later in this chapter.)

Batch processing works by making copies of original files, called source files. Paint Shop Pro converts the images to the new format and saves them in the output folder you select. It's important to note that the original images are not changed.

To change multiple files to a different format:

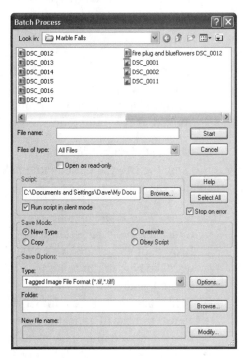

1. Open the Batch Process dialog shown right by choosing File | Batch | Process.

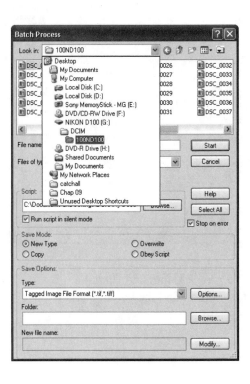

2. Use the Look In drop-down list to navigate to the folder containing the source (original) files. In the illustration shown left, the memory card for my digital camera is selected. Select the files you want converted by holding down CTRL and individually selecting them, or click the first file in a series, hold down the SHIFT key, and select the last file.

Even if you want to select all of the files in a folder, don't use the Select All button unless you have finished all of the other Batch Process selections. Select All not only selects all of the files, but it also starts the Batch process.

3. In the Save As Group box, click the Type drop-down list to select a new file format for the images. If the new format itself has options that must also be selected, the Options button is not grayed out. Click it to open the Save Options dialog. From here you can choose options that will be applied to every file processed.

4. Choose the output (destination) folder for the new files. This can be done using the Browse button and clicking the folder into which you want to save the converted files.

5. If you want to create a new folder for the images, click the Browse button, select where you want the new folder to be located, and click the New Folder button. The new folder, shown right, will appear ready for you to type in its new name. Double-click the new folder or press ENTER to finish the job of making the new folder. Don't forget to select the new folder you just made after creating it. After the folder is selected or created, click Start to return to the Batch Process dialog box.

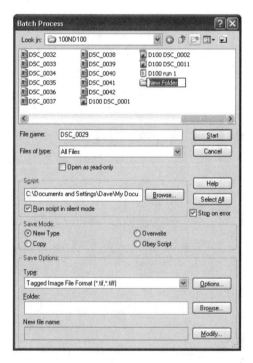

6. After you have selected the source folder/files and the destination folder, click the Start (or Select All) button to begin the process. A dialog box with a progress indicator like the one shown next appears. Click the OK button, and the batch process is complete.

If you cannot close the Batch Progress dialog box after the batch job is complete, check the Windows status bar and make sure that an error message has not been generated. If one has, clear it by clicking the OK button; you must do this before any other actions in Paint Shop Pro can proceed.

If you do not select an output folder, Paint Shop Pro saves the converted files in the same folder as the source files. This will cause errors if the source folder is a digital camera memory card that is already full.

Did you know?

The Advantages of Changing File Formats

By default, digital cameras save their images using JPEG compression because it allows them to get more photos onto the digital memory card. If you are shooting with your camera set to get a large number of photos into a relatively small memory card, your compression setting is pretty heavy, and the process of opening and resaving an image at the same compression setting will produce defects in the photos called artifacts. One way to prevent this is to change the photos from JPEG to a nonlossy format like Tagged Image Format File (TIFF) or Paint Shop Pro's native format (PSP). While the images will increase in size, they will not deteriorate no matter how many times you open and save them.

If your Batch Process dialog is already set up the way you want it, you can double-click a filename in the source file and it will process the image immediately.

Files That Won't Work Using Batch Process

It's a good idea to check the Stop on Error check box in the Batch Process dialog box. That way, if you select a file that Paint Shop Pro cannot normally open, it will stop and display an error message like the one shown next. If you don't select this check box, the program processes all the images without stopping.

Renaming Multiple Files

Every digital camera I am aware of assigns a number to each image taken, usually a sequential number. My Nikon uses a file naming format of DSC_*nnnn* where the *nnnn* represents a four-digit number. When you are managing hundreds of photographs, a file named DSC_0235 doesn't tell you much. One of my favorite Batch Processing features is modifying all the names of the files you are copying. For example, yesterday I was taking photographs in Johnson City, Texas with my Nikon D-100. When I transferred all of the images into a folder on my computer, I used Batch Processing to modify all of the filenames. So photos starting with names like DSC_0235 end up in the Johnson City folder as D100 DSC_0235.TIF, DSC_0236, DSC_0237, etc. or Exterior D100 flowers DSC_0235.TIF, 0236—you get the idea.

The Batch Rename function is similar to the Saving Multiple Image Files to a Different Format procedure shown previously, except that the renamed files are not copied to a different folder. Here is how it is done:

1. Open the Batch Rename dialog shown next by choosing File | Batch | Rename.

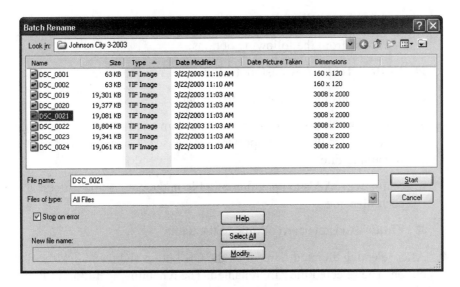

2. Click the Modify button to display the choices for renaming your files, as shown here:

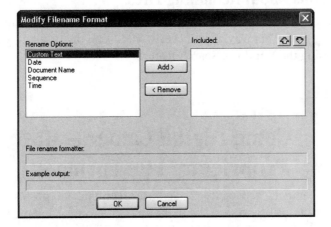

3. From this dialog box you can select the predefined filename modifiers to replace or add to the original filename. Click Add to move the highlighted

Rename Options choice into the Included list. You can add as many as you want. Choose from the following options:

- **Custom Text**   Any custom text that you want to add.

- **Date**   Adds the current date to the name.

- **Document Name**   Ensures that each converted file retains its original name. This is the most important choice; see "Considerations about Renaming Files."

- **Sequence**   Adds the position of a file in the conversion process to each filename.

- **Time**   Adds the current time to the name.

4. After selecting the modifiers, click the OK button and then click the Start button. The selected files are renamed. The renaming operation is almost instantaneous.

Considerations About Renaming Files

I strongly recommend always including the original filename (Document Name) when renaming files. This way, if you ever want to find the original, you can search for it using the Windows Search feature.

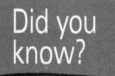

Some Digital Cameras Have Proprietary File Formats

Some digital cameras (especially the semi-professional and professional models) offer the ability to save the photos in a file format that preserves the sensor data without converting it to a JPEG or TIFF file. This format is typically called Raw (the name refers to the raw sensor data contained in the file). The file format used is dependent on the camera you are using. For example, my Nikon saves these files as NEF (Nikon Electronic Format) files. There are many advantages to using Raw sensor format, but you need software made by your camera manufacturer if you want to open, adjust, and save the images in standard graphic formats that can be used by Paint Shop Pro or any other photo editor.

If you only select Custom Text or Date as a modifier (and not Document Name) Paint Shop Pro will try and rename all of the files to the same name, which Windows will not allow. If the Stop on Error check box is selected, it will stop and ask you if you want to continue; if it's not selected, it will process the first file selected and ignore the rest.

Using Scripting

Scripting is a powerful new feature in Paint Shop Pro 8 that can be utilized at several levels. You may have already run some scripts without being aware of it; for example, if you have used the One Step Photo Fix feature, you were actually running one of the scripts in the scripts folder. There are several different kinds of scripts that can be run, including the predefined scripts that shipped with Paint Shop Pro 8. You can also use the script recording feature or the Python scripting language to write your own scripts. In the remainder of this chapter, you will learn about the basics of running and recording scripts. You will also discover what resources are available for those of you brave souls that want to plumb the depths of writing scripts.

9

Displaying the Script Toolbar

Although all of the script commands are available though the menu (shown right), it is much easier and faster to work with scripts using the Script toolbar. If the Script toolbar (Figure 9-1) is not already displayed on your monitor, choose View | Toolbars | Script.

TIP   *Most of the Script toolbar buttons have equivalent menu commands that can be accessed by choosing File | Script.*

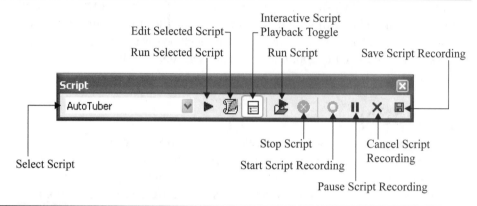

Interactive Script
Playback Toggle
Edit Selected Script
Run Selected Script   Run Script   Save Script Recording

Select Script

Stop Script   Cancel Script
Start Script Recording   Recording

Pause Script Recording

FIGURE 9-1   The Script toolbar

The Script Toolbar Buttons

The buttons in the Script toolbar fall into two general categories. The first four buttons (from the left) are used to select, run, and edit previously saved scripts. The remaining four are used to record, pause, delete, and save scripts. The remaining two buttons are related to writing scripts and are generally not available (grayed out).

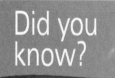

What's the Difference Between Trusted and Restricted Scripts?

Scripts in Paint Shop Pro 8 use a popular programming language called Python (www.python.org), which is discussed at the end of this chapter. Because there is always the possibility that someone will use this powerful tool to create malicious scripts, Paint Shop Pro provides a restricted execution mode. In this mode, which is on by default, scripts have restricted access to other parts of the Paint Shop Pro program and your computer operating system. Restricted execution mode does not affect scripts you record in Paint Shop Pro. To toggle execution mode on and off, click the Interactive Script Playback Toggle button on the Script toolbar. When execution mode is on, the button will have a border around it. Scripts that cannot run in restricted mode should be saved in the Trusted Scripts folder. Jasc recommends that you exercise caution when running scripts from unknown users.

Selecting and Running an Existing Script

Paint Shop Pro ships with a variety of scripts. While some script names describe what the script does, such as OneStepPhotoFix, others do not. To discover what they do and how to use them, you will need to click the Edit Selected Script button on the Scripts toolbar. This opens the script in Notepad or the Script Editor dialog box, as shown in Figure 9-2. There you will (I hope) find a description of what the script does and, in some cases, specific requirements of using the script.

To run one of the scripts provided with Paint Shop Pro do the following:

1. On the Scripts toolbar, click the drop-down button to display the list of scripts currently stored in the Scripts folder, shown next. The actual content of your list may vary from the one shown here.

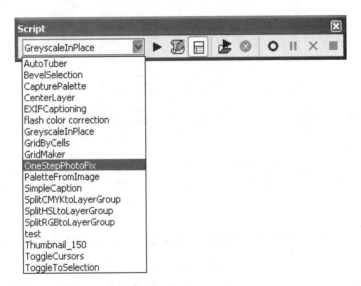

2. Click the script you want to run.

3. To run the script, click the Run Selected Script button in the Script toolbar. It may take a few moments for the script to run, so keep an eye on the status bar at the bottom of your screen to make sure it has finished.

Script Requirements

Regardless of which script you are using, you will need to have an image open before you can play the script. For some scripts, additional conditions are required, such as certain layers needing to be open or, in some cases, multiple images needing

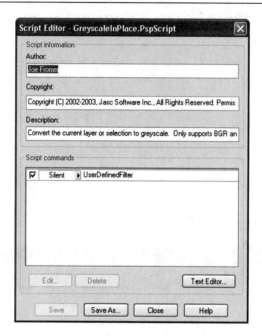

FIGURE 9-2   Here is where you can find what the script does.

to be open. If the necessary conditions don't exist, you will usually receive an error message telling you what is missing or an auto action box that offers to create the missing component for you.

Running a Script not Listed in the Scripts Toolbar

When you want to run a script that doesn't appear on the drop-down list in the Scripts toolbar (that is, a script that wasn't saved in the Scripts folder), you need to use the Run Script button instead of the Run Selected Script button:

1. Click the Run Script button on the Scripts toolbar. This opens the Run Script dialog box shown right.

2. Navigate to the folder containing the script you want to run.

3. Select the script and click Open to execute the script.

 Regardless of how complicated a script is, every action that happens when a script is run is undone by the single use of the Undo (CTRL-Z) command.

Recording a Script

Now that you know how to play prerecorded scripts, the next step is for you to learn how to record your own scripts. Recording a script is very simple. All of the script actions can be controlled from the buttons on the Script toolbar. To record and save a script use the following procedure:

1. Decide on the actions you intend to record before you start recording a script. While it is possible to edit the script after you have recorded the script, it is much easier to get it correct the first time.

2. To begin recording, click the Start Script Recording button in the Scripts toolbar. All actions you make will now be recorded and added to the script until you click the Pause, Save Script, or Cancel Recording button.

If you make a mistake while recording a script, don't use Undo (CTRL-Z) to correct it, or you will record both the mistake and the Undo action. I recommend canceling the recording and starting over again.

3. Perform the actions you want included in the script. At any point while recording a script, you can pause the script recording by clicking the Pause button on the Scripts toolbar.

4. When you have finished recording, click the Save Script Recording which opens the Save As dialog box. Enter a name for the script and click Save. The script will now appear in the Scripts toolbar drop-down, assuming you saved it in the Scripts folder. There is also a button that allows you to save pertinent information about your script such as the author name, the copyright, and most importantly, a description of what the script does.

9

Watching Scripts in Action

You may want to see exactly what your script is doing—while it is doing what it's doing. Jasc has included a window called the Output Window that displays the actions that occur when a script is running. This window displays a lot of information including commands that are currently running (although not all the commands), script error information such as Python syntax, and Python statements that are output from hand-written scripts containing print command errors or runtime errors.

To display this window, choose F3 or select View | Palettes | Script Output from the menu.

 *To clear the Output Window, use the Clear Output Window command, which is only available through the menu File | Script | Clear Output Window.*

Source Code Programming

To create scripts that can make decisions, use data from an open document, or that prompt the user for data, it is necessary to create scripts using the Python programming language. This is a powerful language that requires learning the Python language before writing or editing any script. For more information on this language, go to http://www.python.org.

Part IV

Create Original Images Using Paint Shop Pro 8

Chapter 10

Create a Photo Montage

How to...

- Use selections like a professional
- Make photos wider
- Create photo montages
- Add objects and people to photos using masks

One of the coolest things you can do with Paint Shop Pro is adding or removing people or objects from a photo. We all have some favorite photo of ourselves or a loved one that also includes someone we wish wasn't in the picture. Before digital photo editing, removing the jerk from the photo was crudely resolved with a pair of scissors. Figure 10-1 is a classic example I created almost six years ago, my first experience using the Clone tool. When I was able to seamlessly (well, almost seamlessly) eliminate the guy from the photo, I was hooked. I have been removing, adding, and generally rearranging people and objects in photographs ever since. In this chapter, you will discover how to use the many Paint Shop Pro selection tools to isolate the part of the photograph that needs to be removed or moved. You will also discover how to use layers to manage your photographic montages.

FIGURE 10-1   Breaking up may be hard to do in real life, but with Paint Shop Pro it's not that hard to make people go away.

The Power of Selections

The secret of putting parts from different photos together in the same image is in selections. Selections can range from the very simple, such as the rectangular shapes of a building, to complex shapes, such as a person or a pet. Because these complex selections require more precision, Paint Shop Pro provides a large assortment of tools that allow you to precisely select that portion of the image that you want to work on while still protecting the other parts of the image. To be able to use these tools effectively, you are going to spend a little time learning just how selections work and how to use them.

Understanding Selections

Paint Shop Pro has a number of different tools whose only purpose is to define the part of the image you want to work on. The area that is defined is called a selection, and all of the tools that are used to make the selections are know as selection tools. If this is your first time using Paint Shop Pro, don't let the large number of selection tools with their strange-sounding names overwhelm you. You are going to learn this one step at a time, beginning with a look at what a selection is.

Isolating and protecting something using selections is a concept we all have used at one time or another in our lives. I have heard many analogies to selections and their uses; here are a few of the more popular ones: If you have ever used a stencil, you have used a selection. The stencil allows you to apply paint to part of the material and it protects the rest. Another example of a selection that is closer to home (literally) is using masking tape to block off the parts of a room on which you don't want to get paint (which for me would be just about everything in the room!). Selections in Paint Shop Pro act just like a stencil or masking tape when it comes to either isolating or applying any effect to part of an image.

10

Rounding Up the Selection Tools

There are three different types of selection tools in the Tools toolbar that can be accessed by clicking the tiny black icon next to the Selection tool (S). These three tools are

- Selection
- Freehand Selection
- Magic Wand

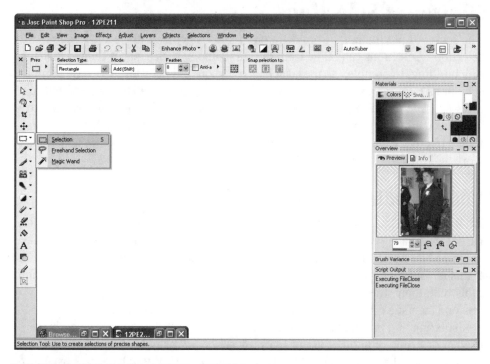

FIGURE 10-2   Selection tools are the basic building blocks for isolating and protecting parts of an image.

While I have mentioned these tools in previous chapters, I'm going to tell you how selection tools can be used to create some cool stuff. First, let's look at the most basic of the tools: the Selection tool.

Expanding a Photograph Using Selection

Using the Selection tool shown in Figure 10-2, you can create selections in the shapes of rectangles and ellipses; if you access the Tool Options palette, you can also create unique selections in fixed shapes.

Using a floating selection is a great trick if you want to expand the photograph shown in Figure 10-3.

1. Use the Canvas Size feature (Image | Canvas Size) to add additional area to the edge of the image, as shown next.

FIGURE 10-3   Make your photo wider using a floating selection.

2. Choose the Selection tool (S) and choose Rectangle as your selection type in the Tool Options palette. Drag a selection over the part of the photo you want to duplicate to add on the edge of the photo. The edge of the selection is marked by flashing black and white marquee that has come to be called "marching ants," as shown here:

3. Holding down the ALT key, drag the selection (it becomes a floating selection) over the new extension of the image shown next. Holding down the ALT key makes a copy of the current selection. If you don't hold it down, the contents of the selection is removed and replaced with the current background color.

4. Promote the Floating Selection to a Layer (CTRL-SHIFT-P) and remove the
selection (CTRL-D).

5. At this point, there are some obvious edges that must be removed to make
the transition seamless. You can use the Eraser tool (X) to remove edges of
the top layer, exposing the original background underneath. Be careful not
to expose the new background, but if you do, use the Undo command (CTRL-Z).

6. Another way to smooth over the transition is to flatten the layers (Layers |
Merge | Merge All (Flatten)) and use the Clone tool to copy parts of the
photo over the seam to match the edges, as shown in Figure 10-4.

TIP   *You can hide the selection marquee through the Selections menu
(Selections | Hide Marquee) or by using the shortcut key (CTRL-SHIFT-M).*

10

FIGURE 10-4   The floating selection is used to expand a photo.

The Selection Tool Options Palette

If this is the first time you have worked with Paint Shop Pro, the Selection tools might seem quite limited. After all, how often will you need to select a rectangle? Jasc has included many more shapes which are selected in the Tool Options palette. In fact, you can create about any shape imaginable using these tools if you learn how to use some of the features found in the Options bar shown in Figure 10-5.

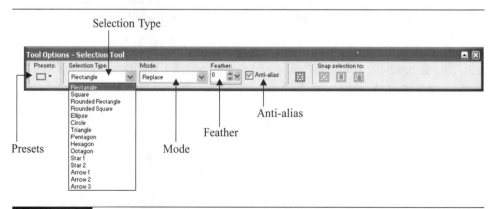

FIGURE 10-5   The Options bar gives more capability to the Selection tools.

Making Photo Shapes

Paint Shop Pro provides 15 different selection shapes, giving you a great way to create unusual photo shapes. Here is how to use the predefined selection shapes to create some fun photo shapes:

1. Pick the Selection tool (S) in the Tools toolbar and then choose the desired shape from the Tool Options palette.

2. After selecting one of the shapes, click and drag over the image to select an area, like the star shape dragged over the photograph shown right.

3. Copy the contents of the selection to the Clipboard (CTRL-C).

4. Open an image that you want to add to the selection. I used a photo of a barn door with a star (not uncommon in Texas). Paste the selection as a new layer (CTRL-L), as shown here:

5. Use the Text tool (T) to add appropriate text. Choose Effects | 3D Effects | Drop Shadow and put drop shadows under the new layer and the text as shown in Figure 10-6.

There are three different ways that the Selection tools interact with existing selections. The default setting for the Selection tools is Replace. With this setting, any time you make a selection, it replaces the current selection (if one exists). The ones you will use most often are the Add To and Remove settings. See the section "Adding Some and Taking Some" later in this chapter. Their operation is obvious (I hope). By using the Selection tools in combination with these modes, it is possible to make almost any irregular shape imaginable.

Feathering the Selections

Up until now I have been discussing selections that have a hard and defined edge. However, there are many times that you want to make a selection that has a soft edge, for example, when you are removing someone or something from one photograph into another. Using a feathered selection blends the subject being moved into the picture more smoothly. You need to be careful with the amount

FIGURE 10-6   Selections and layers can be used to create composites.

of feathering you apply to the selection, however. Usually, just a few pixels are sufficient. If you put in a large amount of feathering, the object looks like it has a glow or is furry.

There are two ways to feather a selection: you can enter a value in the Feather box of the Tool Options palette and the feathering will be applied to the selection as it is drawn. The value you enter is the distance from the selection (in pixels) that the feathering will be applied. You can also add feathering to an existing selection by using the keyboard shortcut (CTRL-H) and entering in a value.

Figure 10-7 was created with a Paint Shop Pro selection. After making the selection, I applied three different settings of Feathering and copied the image to the Clipboard with each of the three different settings from the original photograph. Of the three copies of Michelle, the one on the left was not feathered, the middle one used a feather of 3 pixels, and the one on the right had a feathering value of 9. The feather effect produced by any particular setting is controlled by the size of the image. For example, the original photograph of Michelle was taken with a Nikon Coolpix 990; as a result, the image is pretty large. On a larger image like this a 3-pixel feather will have less of an effect than the same feather setting would have on a much smaller image. While the higher feathering setting in the image on the right loses tiny detail in her hair, it gives it a desirable softening effect—just remember that this smoothing effect on the hair isn't always a good thing.

10

FIGURE 10-7   Feathering produces much softer edges when a subject is copied out of a photograph.

While there are many things that can be done with the Selection tools, they are essentially basic tools. When you need to create an irregular-shaped selection, it is time to consider the Lasso tools.

Rounding Up the Selection Tools

There are three different types of selection tools in the Tools toolbar which can be accessed by clicking on the tiny black icon next to the Selection tool (S). These three tools are:

- Selection tool
- Freehand Selection tools
- Magic Wand

Unlike the Selection tool that we looked at previously, which only produces closed shapes, the Freehand Selection tool lets you draw a meandering path around a subject. When you are done you either let go of the mouse button or double-click it (depending on which tool you are using), and Paint Shop Pro will make a straight line back to the starting point to complete the selection.

The Freehand Selection Tool

The Freehand Selection tool has four methods (called types) for creating a selection: Freehand, Point to Point, Smart Edge, and Edge Seeker. Each type of selection mode is chosen from the Tool Options toolbar. While they all produce the same results, each uses a different method to produce a freehand selection.

Freehand Selection

The simplest selection type is Freehand. Using this method, you simply draw around the edge of the area you want to select or protect by clicking and dragging your mouse or stylus. As soon as you release the mouse button (or lift your stylus if you are using one), Paint Shop Pro completes the selection by closing the shape to the original starting point of the selection. This type of selection is a good choice for creating simple or rough shapes like the one shown next. This tool should not be used to draw complex or large freehand selections because you cannot rest your hand (by letting go of the mouse button or stylus) while creating a selection as you can with the other types of selection.

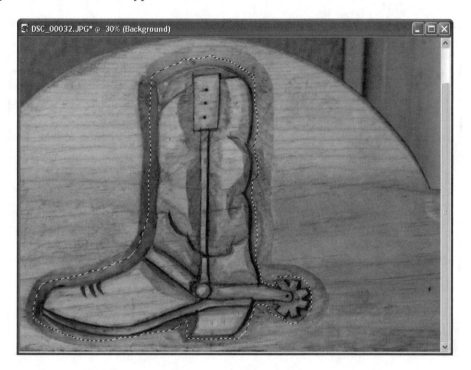

Point to Point Selection

The Point to Point method creates a selection made out of a lot of straight lines. A common misconception about this tool is that it is only for creating a selection containing straight lines. Nothing could be further from the truth. To prove the point, I offer a definition of a circle I had to learn in high school geometry: a circle is a polygon composed of an infinite number of sides. As with the Freehand selection type, clicking once on the image produces the starting point of your selection, and clicking at points along the edge of the subject creates straight lines between each point. You continue adding these points to the selection as you continue clicking until your selection nears the starting point. To complete the selection, double-click the left mouse button or right-click, as shown next. If you accidentally put a point in the wrong spot, you can delete the point by pressing the DEL key. Each time you press the DEL key, the last point of the selection is removed.

CAUTION *When making Point to Point selections, don't click your mouse button too fast when adding points to the selection. Paint Shop Pro might mistake it for a double-click and complete your selection.*

Using Edge Seeker and Smart Edge

These selection types are similar to the Freehand tool except they have the ability to automatically detect the edge (in most cases) as you move it along the edge of the subject you want to isolate, which can save you a lot of work. Both of these tools work by examining the pixels surrounding the area being selected and attempting to detect an edge based on the difference between the color or brightness of adjacent pixels. What makes the two tools different is how they operate.

The Edge Seeker performs its edge detection beginning where you start the selection with your first click, and then you click around the edge of the area you want to select. In this manner it works similarly to Point to Point selection except Paint Shop Pro automatically detects the edge along a line between the points.

The Smart Edge detects the edge of a subject by creating a long rectangle as you drag the cursor over a portion of the edge you want to select. When you release the mouse button, the edge inside the rectangle is evaluated and the edge detected. With both types, you continue to do this until you get back to the starting point.

> **TIP** *If you have ever worked with Adobe Photoshop or Photoshop Elements, the Edge Seeker Freehand tool in Paint Shop Pro is very similar to their Magnetic Lasso selection tool.*

Magic Wand Tool Magic

The Magic Wand tool is a great tool for making selections of areas containing similar colors or levels of brightness. The problem with using this tool is the fact that many users have no idea how it works and are disappointed when the magic doesn't work. So, I'll tell you how it works and then we'll do some cool stuff with it.

The first fact about the Magic Wand tool: no magic (were you surprised?). Up until now, all of the selection tools you have used involved either closed shapes or lassos that surrounded the subject to be selected. The Magic Wand tool, however, acts a little like dropping a stone in a calm pool of water. The selection, like ripples of water, spreads outward from the starting point. It continues radiating outward, selecting similar (and adjacent) colored pixels until it reaches pixels whose color or shade is so different from the starting point that they can't be included.

Making Selections with Stylus or Mouse?

Most of you use selections to isolate a part of a photograph so you can copy it into another image. Because you are essentially drawing an outline, you may find that creating a complex outline using a mouse is a challenge. Why? Ask yourself this simple question: Can I sign my name with a mouse? If your answer is yes, you need to date more. Seriously, for most of us the answer is no; if you are going to be creating a lot of selections, you should consider getting a graphics tablet. The industry standard for graphic tablets is Wacom Technology (www.wacom.com). These tablets used to be quite expensive, but now some models like the one shown in Figure 10-8 can be purchased for less than $100. Does this mean you can't use selection tools without a graphics tablet? Of course not—it's just a lot easier if you have one. With that matter settled, let's consider some ideas on how to make better selections.

FIGURE 10-8 Using a stylus makes creating selections much easier.

Getting the Best Selections (in the Least Amount of Time)

Whether I was doing art layout for work or for community projects (read: free), I have spent the past ten years making selections and the resulting composite images. In that time I have come up with a short list of tips that I'm going to share with you to help you make great selections.

Making a First Rough Cut Selection

If the image is so large that it does not fit on the screen when viewing at 100 percent (Actual Size), you should shift the zoom level to Fit on Screen in the Tool Options palette and make a rough selection. It doesn't matter which selection tool you use. You just want to get as close as you can without spending a lot of time doing it. This selection gets you in the ballpark.

TIP *You can quickly zoom in and out using the scroll wheel on your mouse (if your mouse has one).*

Zoom and Move

On some areas you may need to zoom in at levels even greater than 100 percent (Paint Shop Pro goes up to 5000 percent, which must allow you to select microbes and stray electrons). Now and again you should return to Fit to Screen just to keep a perspective on the whole image. This is done easily if your mouse has a scroll wheel that allows you to easily move in and out.

When you set the Zoom to Actual Size (CTRL-ALT-N), in most cases the image no longer fits inside the image window. Normally when you are zoomed in this close, you can press the A key and the currently selected tool turns into the Pan tool. The exception is if a selection tool is active making this feature disabled. Another way to move around an image without using the Pan tool is to use the Overview palette (F9). The problem with this approach is it requires you to move the cursor off the screen, thereby interrupting the selection you are creating. There is a way to make a selection at a high zoom level, however: while drawing a selection, Paint Shop Pro automatically pans the image as you approach the edge of the image window, so Paint Shop Pro keeps moving the image around, allowing you to reach any part of the photo.

Adding Some and Taking Some

10

You can add or subtract parts from your rough cut selection using the Add to Selection and Subtract from Selection modes to shape the selection to fit the subject you are trying to isolate. Here is a trick that will save time when doing this part. First, rather than changing modes in the Options bar, use the key modifiers. Pressing the SHIFT key changes the selection mode to Add (for adding to the current selection), and the CTRL key changes it to Remove (to subtract from). Just remember that these modifier keys must be pressed before you click the mouse.

TIP   *Change the mode to Add or Subtract before you start. For example, if you select Add to in the Tool Options palette as the Selection mode, you need to use the* CTRL *key only when you want to subtract from the selection.*

Fine-Tuning Your Selections

After you have created a selection and used the Add and Remove modes to make the marquee fit the area you want to select as much as possible, you can then use the Edit Selection mode to make the selection even more precise. By choosing Selections | Edit Selection, all of the selected area on the image will appear to be covered in a red tint, a carryover from the olden days when we did work like this with using ruby lithe.

How to ... Paint a Selection

To make changes to the selection in the Edit Selection mode is very simple:

1. Choose Selections | Edit Selection. The existing selection marquee disappears and the protected area appears covered by a red tint.

2. Select the Paint Brush tool (B) from the Tools toolbar.

3. Paint the red (selected) area with black to remove the selection, or paint it with white to restore or add it to the selection.

4. To ensure a smooth nonjaggy edge to your selection, you should use a soft-edged brush (set hardness to 30 or less). For areas that need a tight selection, use a hard edge brush (set the hardness to 0).

5. When you finish editing your selection, choose Selections | Edit Selection again to toggle the mode off. When Edit Selection is toggled off, the selection marquee reappears.

TIP   *If the Selection Marquee (marching ants) doesn't appear after you make a selection, make sure Hide Marquee (CTRL-SHIFT-M) isn't enabled.*

Keeping Your Final Objective in Mind

While you are fine-tuning and improving a selection, you should keep at the forefront of your mind the ultimate destination of the image you are selecting. Here are some questions that will help you decide on the degree of exactness you want to invest in your selection.

- How close are the background colors of the image you are selecting and the current background colors? If they are roughly the same colors, then investing a lot of time producing a detailed selection doesn't make much sense because a feathered edge will work just fine.

- Will the final image be larger, smaller, or the same size as the original? If you are going to be making the current image larger, every detail will stick out like the proverbial sore thumb, so any extra time you spend to make the selection as exact as possible will pay big benefits. If you are going to reduce the size of the subject, a lot of tiny detail will become lost when it is resized, so don't invest a lot of time in the selection.

- Is this a paid job (a priority) or a freebee? Creating a complex selection is a time-consuming process. I once spent nearly half a day on a single selection for a project that wasn't as important as others I should have been working on. Don't let projects get away from you. Consider what you are going to do, keep you efforts and time within the allotted time, and don't get lost in the job.

Finding the Edge in the Dark

Before leaving the subject of selection options, there is one last situation which needs to be addressed. On some images, the edge and the background are in the shadows, which makes it difficult to see the edge you want to select. If it is difficult for you to see the edge, there is little chance of the Smart Edge or Edge Seeker selection modes detecting the edge either. The most common example of a darkened edge and background is in portraits of someone in a dark business suit or with dark hair (or both) against a dark background, like the partial view of one shown in Figure 10-9.

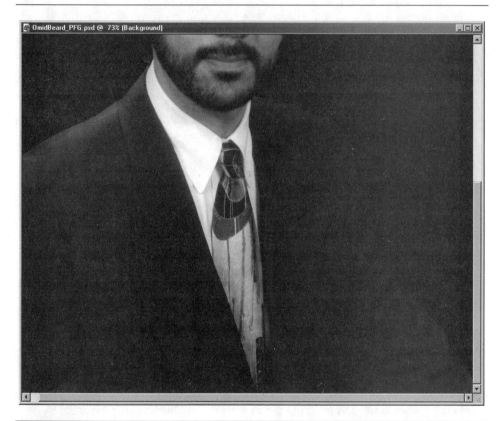

FIGURE 10-9   A dark business suit against a dark background can be difficult to select.

Because publications don't like to print dark images like this, it is often necessary to select the individual from the image and place him or her on a different background.

Here is a slick trick that will make it much easier to select such a difficult subject almost every time:

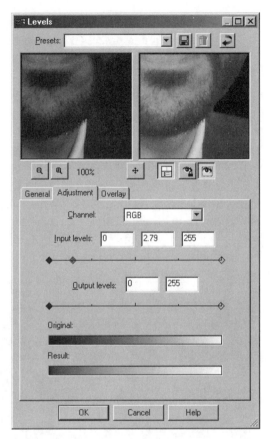

1. Choose Layers | New Adjustment Layer | Levels, which opens the Levels dialog box.

2. Drag the middle slider (gamma) of the Input Levels to the left until the edge becomes light enough to detect, as shown right. The image may appear pretty ugly at this point but that doesn't matter because an adjustment layer doesn't make changes to the image. Click OK to close the dialog.

3. In the Layers palette (F8), select the Background, choose your favorite selection tool, and create the selection.

4. After the selection is complete, right-click the Levels adjustment layer in the Layers palette and from the pop-up menu select Delete. A message box will ask you if you want to delete this layer; click Yes. With the Adjustment layer gone, the image returns to its former darkness, and the selection you created remains.

Let's Select Somebody

I can run on about these tools for many more pages but I won't. I am going to get some coffee while you make what is possibly your first freehand selection. This involves a groomsman named Jonathan in a cluttered church office wearing a ridiculously overpriced rental tuxedo. If his mother is going to frame this photograph, the background must be replaced with something a little less cluttered. If you want to give this exercise a try, you can download the files from the book's site at www.Osborne.com.

1. Download and open the picture labeled TuxedoJon.pspimage. (I made this sample image a lot smaller than the original so it wouldn't gag your system.)

2. Choose the Edge Seeker tool and getting as close as you can to the edge of the tuxedo, click and drag a line around Jonathan until it looks like the one shown in Figure 10-10. When you finish, you will have selected Jon but because you really need to select the background, invert the selection using SHIFT-CTRL-I.

10

FIGURE 10-10   Using the Smart Edge tool you can quickly select Jon from the background.

3. If you don't want to make the selection yourself, you can use the selection I made inside the PSP image. To load my selection, choose Selections | Load/Save Selections | Load Selection from Alpha. When the dialog box appears, change the values to match those shown in Figure 10-11, making sure to check the Invert Image check box.

4. One way to emphasize the subject is to blur the background using Gaussian blur. The problem with this approach is the background in this photo is so cluttered that by the time that you get it blurred enough to do the job, it looks sort of surreal. On top of that, Jon and the couch on his right are the same distance from the camera, so it doesn't look right. Try replacing the background with a different one. Download and open the file Background.JPG. When it is open, select the entire image (CTRL-A), copy the image to the Clipboard (CTRL-C), and close the image (don't save the changes).

5. With Jon's photo selected, choose Edit | Paste Into Selection (CTRL-SHIFT-L). Wow! A well-composed photograph has now replaced the previous cluttered one, as shown in Figure 10-12.

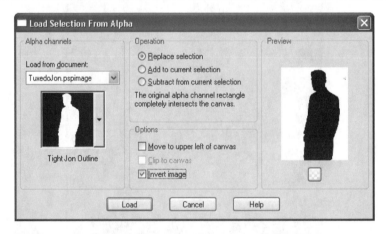

FIGURE 10-11   You can load a saved selection and save a lot of time.

FIGURE 10-12   The new background is much less cluttered than the original.

Saving and Loading Selections

After spending a lot of time creating a selection, you'll want to save it. If a selection is not saved as a Paint Shop Pro file, it will be lost as soon as the file is closed. There are two ways to save your selections. You can save it as a pspselection file to your hard disk, or you can save it with the image in an alpha channel.

The Alpha Channel

Before you learn how to save a selection, I must introduce a term that you may have heard before: the alpha channel. The alpha channel is not a channel at all, but is the name assigned by Apple (who invented it) for additional storage space that was added to the graphics file format called TIFF (Tagged Image Format File). Why is it called alpha channel? The truth be known, when they created the concept of the channel, Apple wasn't sure what it was going to be used for until Adobe latched on to it, made it into the general purpose storage for selections, and is the storage area for many other application specific features as well. While it is still technically referred to as an alpha channel to differentiate it from the red, green, and blue channels, Adobe and the rest of those working in the graphics industry just call it a channel. How many alpha channels can fit into a Paint Shop Pro file? Good question—how big of a file can you live with? For all practical purposes, there is no limit to the number of additional channels that can be included in a TIFF, Paint Shop Pro, or even a Photoshop file.

Saving a Selection to the Alpha Channel

Here is how to save your selection to the alpha channel:

1. Choose Selections | Load/Save Selection | Save Selection to Alpha. This opens the dialog box shown in Figure 10-13.

2. If the image already has an existing channel, you can add your new selection to replace an existing one, but you will probably be saving to a new channel. Choose New and give the channel a descriptive name.

3. Click OK, and the selection will be safely tucked into the image, increasing its file size.

When you open a file containing a selection in the alpha channel, the selection won't appear on the image. To load the saved selection, choose Selections | Load/Save

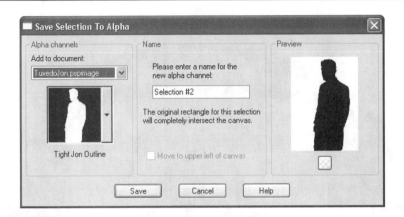

FIGURE 10-13   The Save Selection dialog box

Selection | Open Selection to Alpha and pick the name of the stored selection (if there is more than one) that you or someone else tucked away into the image.

You must save the image as a Paint Shop Pro (PSP, pspimage), TIFF (TIF), or Photoshop (PSD) file to preserve the selection you just saved.

Using Other Sources of Selections

It may surprise you, but many stock photography companies offer selections in their photos. Two different companies that offer photographs with selections are PhotoSpin (www.photospin.com), which is a great online photo subscription service, and Hemera (www.hemera.com), which offers large collections of photo objects on CDs (lots and lots of CDs). The image shown in Figure 10-14 is a photograph of a diving mask that was downloaded from Photospin.com. Like many of their images, it contains a selection.

Many stock photo agencies give you a choice of formats when downloading photos. If you are planning on using a selection saved in an image, remember that JPEG images cannot contain a selection.

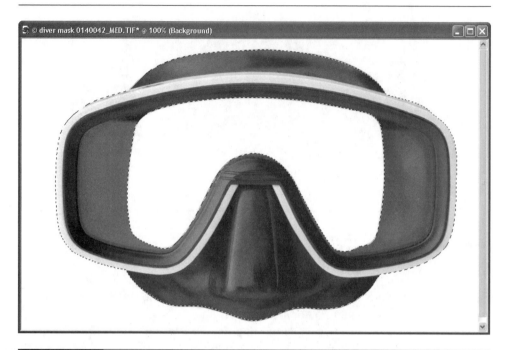

FIGURE 10-14   This photo of a diver's mask comes with a selection.

Creating Photo Montages

Using a selection, you can take an object in one photograph and place it in another. The following sections give you ideas on how to experiment to make different types of photo montages.

Making New Objects Appear Like They Belong

Sometimes the object being placed is not the right size. Fortunately, Paint Shop Pro has a Deform tool that allows you to resize the new object. Here is how to do it:

1. Select the object you want to copy into another photo and then copy it to the Clipboard (CTRL-C). To demonstrate this technique, the selection that was saved with the photograph of a diver's mask shown in Figure 10-14 is loaded and used to isolate the mask.

2. Open the image into which you want to place the diving mask and paste the contents of the Clipboard as a raster layer (CTRL-L). The result is the original photograph of Kelly (she is showing off her snow cone blue tongue) and the mask (which is too large), shown here:

3. Select the raster layer containing the object (the diver's mask) in the Layers Palette (F8) and use the Move tool (M) to position the object where you want it placed on the image.

4. Select the Deform tool (D) in the Tools toolbar. Control handles appear around the object. Click and drag the handles to change both its size and shape, as shown next.

TIP *If you right-click and drag one of the Deform corner handles, you can scale an object to a desired size while keeping the aspect ratio locked to prevent distortion.*

10

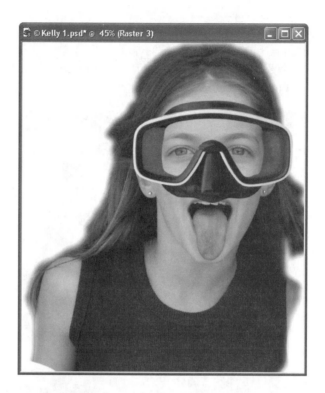

5. Even with the mask resized, the nose piece is still too large. By selecting the Warp Brush in the Tools toolbar and picking the Push Warp Mode in the Tool Options palette, you can push up the nose piece so it is out of the way. For a final touch, add a drop shadow (Effects | 3D Effects | Drop Shadow) under the mask and add a beach photo to the background. The result is shown in Figure 10-15.

Recipes for Surrealism

The only limitation you will face with Paint Shop Pro when it comes to creating images both real and surreal is your imagination. In this section, I want to whet your appetite for making your own creations by including some examples that were made using selections.

The image in Figure 10-16 was created in parts. The background was created using a pattern made from a photograph of wooden shutters using the Kaleidoscope filter. Then the Planar filter (Kai Power Tools 3) made the pattern that appears to fade into the horizon. The glass ball was an object I made at another time, and I

FIGURE 10-15   Using a variety of tools makes it easy to make this into a great beach scene.

made it appear as if it were half sunk into the floor by erasing the lower half with the Eraser tool. The sky on the horizon came from another photograph that was pasted into the back. Then, using a photograph I took of an ornate wood door in the Texas capitol, I created a selection around it and pasted it as a layer in the image.

By using the Deform tool it is possible to resize and reshape any object you place in a photo. Figure 10-17 shows what happens when the Deform tool is used to twist and distort the door.

Figure 10-18 (also shown in the color insert) is a project that was made to demonstrate layers with selective transparency. The background is an actual photograph of a checkered tile floor. Applying the Eraser tool at a low opacity setting to the raster layer containing the glass ball and the capitol door glass allows the background to be seen through these objects, creating a greater sense of realism in this surrealistic scene.

FIGURE 10-16   This surreal image was created using selections and layers.

FIGURE 10-17   The Deform tool was used to twist and distort the doorframe.

FIGURE 10-18   The checkered floor can be seen through the partial transparency of the glass ball, creating greater realism.

Did you know?

Changing Objects with the Deform Tool and Warp Brush

The Deform tool (D) is used to resize (called scale), distort, rotate, and apply perspective to either entire images or to layers on an image. Without this tool and its ability to change the size and shape of photographic objects you have imported from other photos, it would almost be impossible to create realistic-looking photo montages. By moving the different handles on the image when the tool is selected, you can change the perspective and size of almost any photo object. Remember when applying perspective that everything is actually in two dimensions (2D), so there are limits as to how much perspective you can realistically apply.

The Warp Brush is new to Paint Shop Pro 8 and, while this tool is great fun for producing gross distortions, it is also an essential tool for reshaping objects so they appear to fit seamlessly into a photo montage. This is such a great and powerful tool, I have devoted part of the next chapter to showing what you can do with it.

Did you know?

Removing Holes and Specks from Your Selections

10

One of the first problems you may run into when working with the Magic Wand tool is clicking in an area that will not produce a uniform selection but instead creates a bunch of little selections. These tiny selections develop at points in the image where the difference between the color value of the starting point is too great to be included in the overall selection. These unwanted selections can range in size from very tiny ones that contain a few pixels, called specks, to much larger ones, called holes. In earlier releases, removing these specks and holes, which could number in the hundreds, was a laborious process. Paint Shop Pro has added a command that can, in most cases, clean this up automatically. Choose Selections | Modify | Remove Specks and Holes to open a dialog box that offers you the choice of removing specks, holes, or both. Many times, selecting the specks only will clean up a selection without having to include holes. Some selections have large areas intruding into the selection, which the program could mistake for a hole. So make sure that your settings are just enough to select the tiny holes, but don't delete the part of the selection that you want to keep.

Photo Montages without Selections: Masks

Selections provide an excellent way to create photo montages, but in this section, you will learn that there are other ways to combine photos: you can use a mask to produce even cooler results. For starters, let's cover some basics about masks.

The concept of a mask is simple. It's a grayscale image that sits on its own layer. The mask controls the transparency of the layer below it. Masks act like regular layers in that their visibility can be turned on or off, and the opacity of the mask layer can be adjusted or linked to other layers. Masks can be created, edited, and saved in alpha channels just as selections can be. That was a lot of facts crammed into a few sentences. Jasc has a wealth of details on the subject of masks in their help files and in the users manual. Now, let's discuss the incredible things you can do using masks.

Using a Mask to Make a Photo Montage

Here is a simple trick that allows you to quickly make a photo montage from two photos:

1. Open the first image. The example photo is the Texas capitol, as shown next. Select the entire image (CTRL-A), copy it to the Clipboard (CTRL-C), and close the photo.

2. Open the second image (the example is a photo of a glass door in the capitol, as shown next).

3. With the top layer selected, choose Layers | Load / Save Mask | Load Mask from Disk, which opens the dialog box shown next. In this example, one of the sample masks (Edge Canvas 01) was loaded.

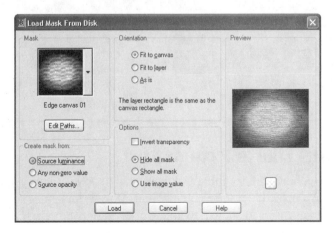

FIGURE 10-19   A mask allows portions of one layer to be seen through another.

4. A new layer called Mask Raster appears in the Layers palette and is grouped with the top raster layer shown next. The effect of the mask is the photo montage shown in Figure 10-19.

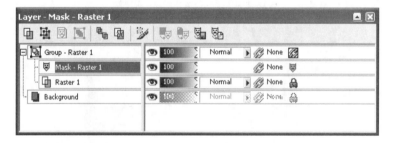

Using Masks Like Selections

In the previous technique, a sample mask was used to create an effect. Now you'll learn how to use a mask layer to selectively add and subtract areas of a layer from viewing. It is much easier to show how this works than to explain it.

1. Open the image you want to put into another, select the part of the image you want to place in the other, and copy it to the clipboard. You probably recognize the young lady in the photograph shown next. If you think it is my daughter's roommate, you're correct. If you thought it was a movie star, you aren't the first.

2. Open the second image (shown next).

10

3. Paste the contents of the Clipboard as a new layer (CTRL-L), shown right.

4. Choose Layers | New Mask Layer | Show All. This creates a mask layer that is grouped with the raster layer that was pasted onto the image.

5. In the Layers palette, select the Mask layer. Choose the Brush tool and ensure the foreground color is black and the background color is white. Paint away the areas that you want to become transparent using the left mouse button. Every place on the mask painted black becomes 100 percent transparent. If you accidentally remove too much, you need to paint only the area using the right mouse button; this paints it white and restores it to 100 percent opaque. The finished result is the silly composite shown in Figure 10-20.

FIGURE 10-20   Use mask layers to create a photo composite image like this one.

Rearranging a Photo with the Clone Brush

The last way to add or subtract objects from your photos is to use the Clone brush (C). In Chapter 8, you learned how the Clone brush could be used to repair damaged images; in this section, you will look at how you can use the Clone brush to remove, replace, or rearrange objects, people, or even parts of people from a photo.

Figure 10-21 shows a photograph that at first appearance doesn't appear to be all that good. By using the Clone brush and other tools you learned about earlier

10

FIGURE 10-21   Using the Clone brush will make this photo look much better.

in the chapter, however, you can remove and replace parts of it to make it a much better photo. Here is how it is done.

1. First, you need to remove the clutter on the horizon. Use the Edge seeker Selection tool, to create the selection shown next, which preserves the foliage on the horizon but removes the buildings, signs, and light poles. To fine-tune the selection, use Edit Selection.

2. Open a photo containing a replacement sky like the one shown here. Because you will only be using the top part of the photo, the bottom of the photo doesn't concern you.

3. Select the Clone brush and right-click the part of the clouds that you want to copy. Paint Shop Pro will beep, indicating it has set the source point. Now select the original photo and place the Clone brush in it. Using the left mouse button, paint the clouds into the selection. Continue until it is finished and looks like the image shown right.

4. The next step is to remove the sunflower that is pointing the wrong direction. Change the size of the Clone brush so it is large enough to remove the sunflower in just a few passes. Right-click the area on either side of the part you want to remove, then clone it out, as shown here. Change the source point several times while doing this to prevent a visual pattern from developing.

5. Zoom in at the bottom of the photo and use the Clone brush to remove the plastic bag that was at the bottom of the photo, as shown next.

6. Lastly, use the Clone brush to replace the part of the lower sunflower that is covered by the leaf. The trick to doing this is to use a small soft brush (hardness 60) and to use as a source point a small spot on the yellow petal where the edges are clear and defined. Apply it in short strokes over the leaf (or the part of the image that you want to remove) and then go pick another source point. It is time consuming to do it right. Figure 10-22 shows the down and dirty I did in less than five minutes.

Switching Faces

For most of us in photo editing, the most common task is replacing faces of people in group shots who blinked when the flash went off. This is why when you take a group shot you should always take several photos (at least four) before letting anyone move. In the example you are going to look at, a co-worker had a photo taken of his family in a field of bluebonnets (a Texas Hill Country tradition). In the first photo the wife blinked, and in the second the baby blinked.

1. Because these were photographs, I had them pick out which of the two photos they liked the best and scanned in the entire photograph (Figure 10-23).

FIGURE 10-22   Using the Clone brush and another photo made this into a nice outdoor photo.

FIGURE 10-23   Great photo except the baby blinked when the flash went off.

2. Next, I scanned in the portion of the second photo I wanted to copy to the first photo, as shown next.

3. Making the Clone brush very soft (hardness 0) and a little smaller than the child's face, I right-clicked in the middle of the face and then selected the full photograph and painted the face over the blinking one. That's all there is to it. The finished photo is shown in Figure 10-24.

FIGURE 10-24   Using parts of the second photo to keep everyone's eyes open.

Chapter 11

Add Dazzling Effects to Your Photos

How to...

- Frame your photos in Picture Frame
- Create effects with Picture Frame
- Use picture tubes to create fantastic effects
- Combine picture tubes and Picture Frame
- Use built-in effects and third-party plug-ins
- Create great distortion effects with the Warp brush

Many of the earlier chapters of this book focus on the important subject of correcting and enhancing images. In this chapter, I let it all out and discuss some of the cool and outrageous things that you can do to photos and other images using Paint Shop Pro.

Photo Frames

When you want to display a photo, document, or work of art, whether it is in your home or office, you naturally think of using a frame. Paint Shop Pro 8 has a built-in feature called Picture Frame that allows you to quickly add a wide variety of frames and edges to your photos like those shown in Figure 11-1. Using the Picture Frame feature you can quickly select an edge pattern, matting, and style of frame and (this is the best part), if you don't like the combination you have selected, you can undo it and try another combination.

When you think of frames for your images, you probably think of wooden or metallic rectangles. Another type of frame included in this version of Paint Shop Pro is an edge, which can give photos a more organic, hand-created look. The photo edges included in Paint Shop Pro 8 have rough irregular edges which gives the impression that the image being framed was applied using a brush. An example of a photo edge is shown in Figure 11-2.

FIGURE 11-1   Frames created with Picture Frame

11

FIGURE 11-2   Photo edges add a hand-crafted appearance to your photos.

Putting Your Photo into a Picture Frame

Using the Picture Frame feature of Paint Shop Pro 8 you can create a picture frame around your image very quickly:

1. Open the image you want to frame.

2. From the Image menu, choose Picture Frame.

3. In the Picture Frame dialog box, click Picture Frame to bring up a collection of frames, as shown next. Pick the frame you want to use from the drop-down list by clicking it. The actual frames that appear on your list may differ from the ones shown depending on which frames you have installed.

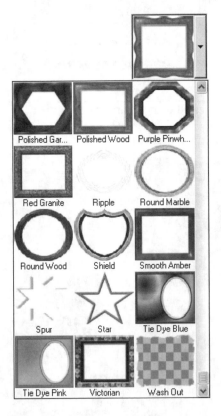

4. There are several choices made in this dialog box about the placement of the photo in the frame.

   ■ Choose Frame Inside of the Image if you want the entire photo inside the frame (the photo will be cropped as a result), or choose Frame

Outside of the Image if you want to increase the size of the overall image so that the entire image fits inside the frame.

■ Select the orientation that matches the orientation of the photo using the Rotate Frame 90° CW (clockwise) check box. With frames that use edge effects like those shown in Figure 11-2, rotating the frame can change its appearance. In this same area you can also choose to flip the frame or make a mirror of it. Because many frames are symmetrical, these options are not often used.

■ Some of the frames do not go to the edge of the image area, such as Corners Tape. The areas between the edge of the frame and the edge of the image can either be made transparent or opaque. Check Keep Transparent to keep the area transparent so that when a framed image is placed on top of another image, the background will be seen through the transparent area. If you choose not to check this option, you can change the fill color by clicking Color Swatch and picking a color to match the background color on which the frame will be displayed. On the frame shown next, the area between the curved portion of the frame and the edge was made white.

5. After making your choices, click OK button, and your framed image appears (Figure 11-3).

11

Did you know?

How Photos Fit in Frames

If the subject of your photo fills the entire image, you should choose to frame the outside of your image as opposed to the inside. If you choose to frame inside the image, Paint Shop Pro 8 crops the photo so that the frame fits within the original photo. If you choose to place the frame outside the image, Paint Shop Pro 8 resizes the canvas (adds more area on the edge of the original, thereby making it larger) so it fits the entire original and the frame.

You can also choose to flip the frame on its horizontal axis, or mirror the frame. Rotating it 90 degrees clockwise changes the look and feel of the frame. It's sometimes fun to experiment with this one. If the height and width of the image vary considerably, the frame will appear thicker along the shorter sides.

FIGURE 11-3   One of the many frames available to enhance photos

Adding Depth to Your Photo Frame with Shadows

When you add a photo frame, Paint Shop Pro adds the frame to the image as a layer, which allows you to do even more cool stuff with your newly framed photo. As you are aware, a real frame has depth and therefore will produce shadows around and along the interior. Adding a small amount of shadow gives a sense of depth to the frame and makes the framed photo look even more realistic. Here is how to do it:

1. Frame a photo using the Photo Frame feature described previously. Open the newly framed photo, and open the Layers palette (F8) to select the background.

2. Choose the Selection tool (S), ensure that the Selection type is Rectangle and the Feather set to a high enough value to make a soft shadow (the value depends on the size of your image, but a value between 20 and 30 should be sufficient). The larger the feather value, the larger and softer the resulting shadow. Check the Anti-alias feature.

3. Click and drag a rectangle on the original image, leaving a small border on the inside of the frame. The feathering will make the selection appear rounded, like the one shown in Figure 11-4.

Feathered selection

Feathered selection

FIGURE 11-4   A feathered rectangle has rounded corners

4. Invert the selection (CTRL-SHIFT-I). Make sure the Foreground color is set to black.

5. Choose the Fill tool (F) and, in the Tool Options palette, change the Tolerance setting to the maximum (200) and set an Opacity value between 60 and 80. Setting the Tolerance at maximum ensures it will flood all of the selected area. The Opacity value controls how dark or light the resulting shadow is—the greater the value, the darker the shadow. Click the image anywhere near the frame and the resulting shadow is shown in Figure 11-5.

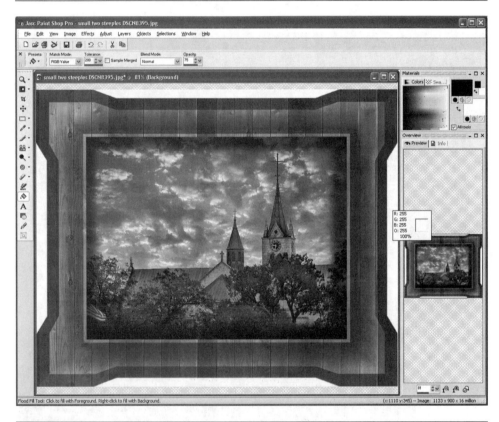

FIGURE 11-5   A shadow inside the frame creates the illusion of depth.

Creating More Realistic Shadows

The shadow created in the previous image creates the illusion of depth. An even more realistic shadow can be created by making the shadow appear on only two edges inside and outside the frame, which is what would occur naturally if the light source were illuminating the frame from some point other than the viewer's viewpoint. While this additional shadow realism isn't critical for most applications, there may be times you will want to place a framed photo in an image that has a strong apparent light source. To accomplish this more realistic shadow effect, do the following:

1. Frame a photo like the one shown in Figure 11-6, using the Photo Frame feature. With the newly framed photo selected, open the Layers palette (F8) and select the Picture Frame layer.

2. Choose Effects | 3D Effects | Drop Shadow. Looking at the frame, the lower-right corner appears slightly darker so the light source appears to be coming from the opposite (upper-left) side of the frame. From the Drop Shadow dialog box, shown in Figure 11-7, adjust the settings to create a subtle shadow. The white box in the lower-left allows you to interactively control the direction and the distance of the shadow by dragging the x point. When the shadow is the way you want it, click the OK button.

11

FIGURE 11-6 This newly framed photo has no shadows to create the illusion of depth.

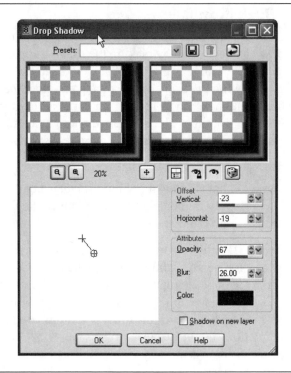

FIGURE 11-7   The Drop Shadow effect can be used to create depth.

3. To complete the illusion, add a drop shadow to the outside of the frame. First, flatten the image (Layers | Merge | Merge All). In the Layers palette, right-click the background and choose Promote Background Layer.

4. Make the image larger using the Canvas Size (Image | Canvas Size). Reapply the drop shadow to the entire frame, as shown in Figure 11-8.

5. Flatten the image and you are finished, as shown in Figure 11-9.

FIGURE 11-8   The drop shadow is applied to both the inside and outside of the frame.

FIGURE 11-9   The completed shadows make the framed photo appear to be a real framed image.

11

Shadow Rules

Shadows have rules—break those rules, and the shadows you create look fake and can become a distraction. The first rule is the longer the shadow (the greater the length), the softer it should appear. Shadow softness is controlled by blur and opacity settings. Another rule is that the length of the shadow produces the illusion of apparent depth. Longer shadows make objects appear to be higher above the background. Keep the shadows you create subtle and not the focus of attention.

More Effects with Photo Frames

Earlier in this chapter I mentioned that when you talk about photo frames, most people usually visualize the rectangular ones that hang on walls or adorn our desks like the one shown in Figure 11-10.

One of my favorite frames that Jasc includes with Paint Shop Pro 8 is the one that looks like a film positive as shown in Figure 11-11.

FIGURE 11-10   A traditional frame for a traditional photo

FIGURE 11-11   Make your photos look like a film negative.

Making Your Frames Float

Here is another idea using the negative photo frames that's just plain fun. Here is how to do it:

1. After applying the film negative Photo Frame to the original photo, select the entire image (CTRL-A).

2. Copy the image to the Clipboard (CTRL-C). You can close the framed photo at this point.

3. After opening or creating an image that is larger than the original framed photo, choose Paste as a new layer (CTRL-L). The image now appears on the new image as a raster layer, as shown in Figure 11-12.

4. With the new layer selected in the Layers palette, select the Magic Wand tool in the Tools toolbar. SHIFT-click inside all 16 of the square sprocket holes—it will only take a moment. Press the DELETE key and the selected areas of the raster layer become transparent (although the change isn't visible yet). You will put these sprocket holes to good use in the next step. Remove the selections (CTRL-D).

11

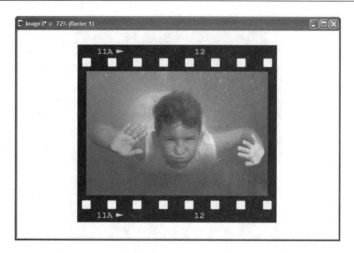

FIGURE 11-12 One of the more imaginative frames provides a unique presentation of a photo.

5. Choose Effects | 3D Effects | Drop Shadow and add a drop shadow. Because the sprocket holes areas are transparent, the Drop Shadow effect produces realistic shadows, as shown next.

6. Make additional film strips and put them on a single image, as shown in Figure 11-13. For more information on how to combine multiple images see Chapter 10.

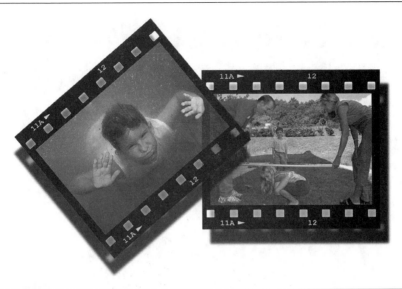

FIGURE 11-13   Photo Frame and Paint Shop Pro make your photos really stand out.

Because filmstrips are transparent, you can use the Eraser tool (at a very low opacity setting) to increase the transparency of the slide. If you look carefully at Figure 11-13 you can see the other filmstrip under the boy's hand.

11

Creative Fun with Picture Tubes

The Picture Tube tool paints by applying a collection of photo objects as the brush is applied to the image. You can add multiple pictures of almost anything you can create or imagine, Picture tubes contain a wide variety of photo objects from painted Easter eggs to ice cream cones.

Picture tubes are a collection of small images or icons, usually related to a specific theme, such as spring, Easter, vacation, and so on, stored in a unique file. Each picture tube file may have any number of images. These images can be real photographs, vector images (saved as raster images), or both. The Picture Tube tool (I) is located in the Tools toolbar and operates as a brush. As you drag it, the images stored in the picture tube are repeatedly applied. These can be used to create individual images or a continuous string of images, such as the one shown in Figure 11-14.

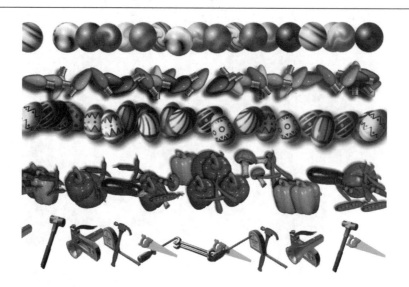

FIGURE 11-14   These are only a few of the many Picture Tubes available.

NOTE   *You cannot use the Picture Tube tool on vector layers. It paints only raster objects on raster layers. Painting picture tube objects on a separate layer makes them easier to modify and move around within an image and also enables you to add special effects to the objects you paint without affecting the entire image.*

There are many ways to use the Picture Tube tool to enhance existing photos. The photo shown in Figure 11-15 (left) is 12-week old Cooper who is celebrating his first Easter, complete with Easter basket. While the overall composition is fine, I thought the addition of a few painted eggs would make it even better, as shown in Figure 11-15 (right).

Making Borders with Picture Tubes

The key to doing really interesting work with the Picture Tube tool is to learn to control it with the Tool Options palette. From this palette you select sets of images called picture tubes. The Picture Tube tool is a brush that paints the images from the selected tube.

Making borders is a classic use for the Picture Tube tool. In the example shown in Figure 11-16, I created a border using some Picture Tube files I downloaded from Jasc. First I selected the pine cone file, and then I used the Text Tool to create a selection which was later filled using another picture tube image called Spruce.

FIGURE 11-15   The composition of the original photo (left) is improved by the addition of some Picture Tube painted Easter eggs (right).

FIGURE 11-16   The Picture Tube tool can create borders and fill text.

The key to successfully making borders is applying the picture tube images in a straight line. Do this by clicking the Picture Tube tool on the starting point and then SHIFT-click the end point to apply the objects from the Picture Tube tool in a straight line between the two points. How the resulting line of images appears on the line depends on the Tool Options settings.

Picture Tube Tool Options

Picture Tube tool's Tool Options palette enables you to control how the objects are placed on the canvas as you paint. The following illustration shows the options you can set for each picture tube object.

Settings

Select Picture Tube

- **Presets**   Enables you to save your current Picture Tube Tool Options settings or open a previously saved one.

- **Select Picture Tube**   Opens the Picture Tube library from which you can select one of the installed tubes. Each picture tube appears on the visual list in alphabetical order with a thumbnail example, as shown next. Keep the View option set to Large Icons to display the name of the Picture Tube. Many of the thumbnails are so small that it would be impossible to determine what they are without the filename.

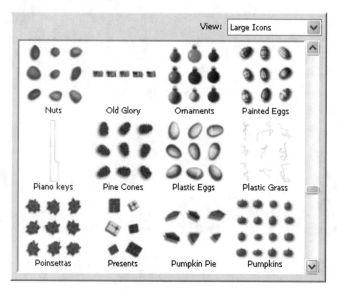

- **Settings**   Each picture tube contains its own default Tool Options settings when it is opened. Open the Settings dialog box to change the default setting for the selected picture tube.

- **Scale**   Determines the size of the objects the Picture Tube tool applies to the image. You can select any value between 1 and 250 percent. Using a setting of 100 percent paints the image at its original size. The appearance of some image types, such as vector images that have been converted to raster to save in the Picture Tube, deteriorates when they are scaled upward.

- **Step**   Defines the spacing between objects painted by the picture tube by controlling the number of pixels to leave between each object in the brush stroke. To paint the objects closer together, decrease this number. To paint the objects further from one another, increase this number.

- **Placement Mode**   This is related to the Step setting. Selecting Random applies the objects randomly between the current step size and 0. This offers a more natural look for objects that paint grass or water drops. The Continuous setting uses the size defined in Step to apply the objects.

- **Selection Mode**   Determines the order the objects are applied in a single stroke:

  - **Angular**   Selects the order that the tube objects are applied based on the direction of the stroke.

  - **Incremental**   Applies the tube objects in the order they are stored in the Picture Tube file.

  - **Pressure**   If you are using a pressure-sensitive stylus, controls the order the objects are placed in each stroke by changing the applied pressure.

  - **Random**   Selects the objects randomly—usually the best choice.

  - **Velocity**   Uses the speed at which you drag your stroke.

Convert Picture Tubes Between Versions

There are a lot of websites out there that have many picture tubes available for download. Because the Picture Tube format changed with the release of Paint Shop Pro 7, tubes made for Paint Shop Pro 5 or 6 must be converted before they can be used. This is easily done with the Jasc tubes converter (which can be downloaded from Jasc's website at www.jasc.com):

1. Open the Tubes Converter (Start | Programs | Jasc Software | Utilities | Jasc Tubes Converter).

2. Browse to the location of your older tubes.

3. In the Paint Shop Pro 8 Tubes Directory field, browse to the location of your Paint Shop Pro 8 tubes directory. This is usually filled by default.

4. Click OK, and the conversion will begin.

After converting your earlier tube versions, the next time you click your Picture Tubes tool it will take a few moments for Paint Shop Pro to refresh its tube list as it displays the following message box.

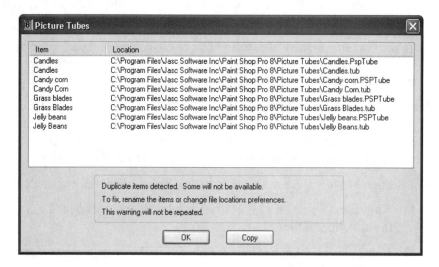

If you are using Paint Shop Pro 7 tubes, just drag them into the Paint Shop Pro 8 Picture Tubes directory, and the next time you open the Picture Tube tool in Paint Shop Pro 8 it will convert them automatically.

Because the Tube Converter doesn't work backward, if you want to use Paint Shop Pro 8 picture tubes with Paint Shop Pro 7, you'll need to copy the version 8 tubes (with their PSPTUBE extension) to the Picture Tube directory for version 7 and then rename the files with a TUB extension.

Making a Christmas Card with Picture Tubes

There are many cool picture tubes available from Jasc and other online sites. One fun way to use them is to make cards for special occasions. The card shown in Figure 11-17 was made using the Holidays tube library I downloaded from Jasc. Making the card is pretty simple:

1. Create an image the size of the finished card (I used 5 × 7), select the Text tool (T), and change the options to Create as Selection.

2. Enter the text you want. When you're finished, it appears as a selection on a raster layer.

3. Select the Picture Tube tool (I), and apply the picture tool (Christmas Ornaments) inside the selection. Adjust the settings in the Tool Options settings until it appears to be the correct size and spacing for the desired effect. Be careful when filling a selection not to overlap the Picture Tube objects so much that the viewer cannot identify it. In the Christmas card example, I had to leave a lot of white space so it was clear the picture tube was made up of ornaments.

4. After applying the Picture Tube objects to the selected areas, copy the contents of the selection to the Clipboard (CTRL-C), and paste it back as a layer (CTRL-L).

5. Use Effects | 3D Effects | Drop Shadow to create a drop shadow. This is important because it prevents the white space in the text from disappearing into the background.

6. Select the background. Use the garland picture tube to make the garland on the top and bottom by dragging the Picture Tool brush horizontally (no need for a perfectly straight line). Next, select the same ornaments picture tube used for the interior of the text and click the garland to place individual ornaments on it. Do the same with the two candles. Note that in the example (Figure 11-17) the ornaments are semi-transparent (you can barely see the garland behind them) and that both the candles and the ornament objects have their own shadows.

TIP
When using individual Picture Tube objects, each time you click the Picture Tube brush, a single object is applied, and it is usually not the one you want. When this happens, click Undo (CTRL-Z) and apply again. Continue until the one you want is applied.

Creating Your Own Picture Tubes

If you have a series of objects that you would like to use in a picture tube, you can save the objects as a new picture tube. It is not a complicated process, and I have not included it in this book because you can find detailed instructions in both the online help and the Paint Shop Pro 8 users manual.

11

FIGURE 11-17   Picture tubes help you make great Christmas cards.

> **TIP**   *If you are looking for more picture tubes, there are several free ones available on the Internet. Start with http://www.jasc.com and go to their Learning Center. In it you will find many links to other PSP sites that provide Picture Tubes for download. You can also search for "free picture tubes."*

Using the Power of Effect Filters

Paint Shop Pro 8 has a large number of effect filters built into it that you can use to create some pretty awesome effects. (The name filters is a term that was originally used by Adobe Photoshop, and it stuck.)

When you open the Effects menu, a large drop-down list, organized into three general areas, appears, as shown in Figure 11-18. At the top of the list is the Effect Browser which can used to preview all of the Effects in a single window. Below that are ten groups or categories of filters. When one of the categories is selected another pop-up menu appears showing the filters it contains. At the bottom of the list there is a horizontal line below which is a User Defined filter and any plug-in filters installed.

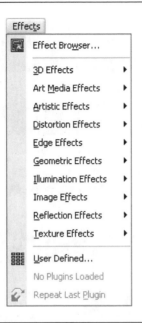

FIGURE 11-18   The Effects menu displays all of the built-in and installed effects.

This is a good time for me to confess that as a digital photographer and photo editor, I have little use for many of the distortion effects in Effects. Still, there are some jewels in there so here are the Effects basics.

First, the Effect Browser is a good idea, but there are so many built-in effects it is difficult to preview them, as shown in Figure 11-19. There's an option to turn off the Quick Render feature, but turning it off is not recommended as it can take a long time to render the preview.

There are a larger number of effect filters available, and this can be a little intimidating. Many of them produce special effects that distort images beyond recognition; others apply geometric distortions, which can also produce interesting effects. Every one of these filters is someone's favorite so just because I don't use one, doesn't mean that it's useless.

Here are a few examples of some of the things that you can do with the built-in effects.

FIGURE 11-19   The Effect Browser gives a preview of many built-in effects.

The image shown in Figure 11-20 is a photograph of a storm grate.

Applying the Polar Coordinates filter (Effects | Distortion Effects | Polar Coordinates) at its default setting creates a really cool distortion like the one shown in Figure 11-21. This is one of over 100 built-in effects, and here is the scary part: you can add more, as you will discover in the next section.

Plug-in Filters

The concept of plug-in filters is simple. A company (such as Jasc) provides access to programs that can be used by programmers to control parts of Paint Shop Pro. These programs, known as plug-in filters, can be called from within an application (like Paint Shop Pro) to provide a wide variety of functions and effects. The plug-in concept first appeared in Adobe Photoshop many moons ago, and it's now used in many applications, including page-layout and vector-drawing programs.

FIGURE 11-20   A photograph of a storm grate

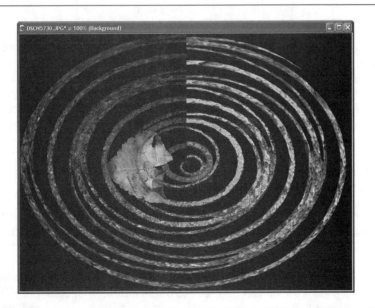

FIGURE 11-21   The Polar Coordinates filter twists the image to produce an unusual effect.

There are many companies that make third-party filters. Traditionally, buyers of these filters install them in Adobe Photoshop—hence, they are often called Photoshop plug-ins. Most of these filters also work with Paint Shop Pro 8. However, you should be aware that some of the really cool plug-ins cost several times more than Paint Shop Pro 8. Another point of consideration is some plug-ins only work with Photoshop. When in doubt, always check the plug-in manufacturer's web page. The plug-in vendors are typically small companies that want to sell as many copies of their product as they can, so if their product works with Paint Shop Pro, they will tell you so.

Installing Third-Party Plug-in Filters

The procedure for installing plug-in filters is a breeze. First, follow the manufacturer's directions to install the filter. Some plug-in filters give you the choice of where to install the filters. If this choice is offered, the filters should be installed in the Program Files/Jasc Software Inc/Paint Shop Pro 8/PlugIns folder. After it's installed, the new plug-in will appear at the bottom of the Effects list.

Finding Third-party Plug-ins

Plug-in filters are rarely sold in retail stores. In most cases, evaluation copies can be downloaded and purchased online. Here are some of the companies that sell these plug-ins:

- **www.jasc.com**   In addition to selling Paint Shop Pro, Jasc also sells a fantastic plug-in called Virtual Painter that allows you to turn photos into paintings. They also sell plug-in filters made by Flaming Pear Software.

- **www.flamingpear.com**   While this company has a strange-sounding name, it has a large collection of some really unusual plug-in filters that can do such things as create images of planets, create the illusion of floods, and create other impressive effects.

- **www.alienskin.com**   One of the early plug-in vendors, Alien Skin sells a variety of plug-in collections at reasonable price.

- **www.andromeda.com**   Another established pioneer of plug-ins, Andromeda makes some of the more useful plug-ins for photographic correction and adjustment.

- **www.procreate.com**   The original "wow" plug-in filter set was called Kai's Power Tools 3 (KPT3). These filters and their successors KPT 5, KPT 6, and Effects are now owned by Procreate. The original KPT3 is included in KPT 5.

Considerations About Buying Plug-ins

Plug-in filters are great and can produce some fantastic effects, but before you buy one, ask yourself an important question: Will you ever need to use this cool effect? For example, Flaming Pear Software has a wonderful plug-in called LunarCell that allows you to create images of planets, like the one shown next. It does a great job creating the planet image, but how often do you need to do this?

Getting Crazy with the Warp Brush

One of the new additions to Paint Shop Pro 8 is the Warp brush. Located in the Tools toolbar, this brush moves pixels around in an image as if they were wet paint and you were finger-painting. There are two types of the effects that you can achieve with the Warp brush: wild and crazy distortions to existing images, or minor image retouching (such as making ears or noses smaller, or changing body shapes). Figure 11-22 is a rare photograph of me in a field of bluebonnets. Figure 11-23 is me after using the Warp brush to prepare me for a part in the next *Lord of the Rings* installment or maybe even a Harry Potter movie.

The Warp brush can produce some incredible distortions, but you should be careful of what you do to photos of people. What you consider funny may be seen as hurtful (possibly liable) by someone else—this is why I used my own photo and one of the Statue of Liberty to demonstrate some of the warp effects.

The best way to learn how to use the Warp brush is to use it. There are eight different Warp modes that can be selected from the Tool Options palette.

The Push mode smears the underlying pixels as you drag the brush.

11

FIGURE 11-22   A photo of me before the Warp brush

FIGURE 11-23   The Warp brush provides elfin qualities.

FIGURE 11-24   The Warp brush's Push mode changes the shape of her arm.

TIP   *When using the Push mode, using a larger brush tends to make the resulting pixel movement less apparent to the viewer.*

Using the Push mode (Figure 11-24) allowed the grand old Statue of Liberty to wave hello to visitors—I also made a few changes to the spikes on her crown.

The Expand mode makes the underlying pixels push out from the center of the brush. Unlike the Push mode, you can place the brush on part of the image, hold it down, and it will push out the pixels as long as you hold it down. To demonstrate this effect, in Figure 11-25 the brush using Expand mode was applied to the arms to "pump her up" and to the spikes to turn them into flower petals.

The Contract mode is the opposite of the Expand mode: when applied, it pulls pixels in toward the center of the brush. Placing a large Warp brush over the entire head of Lady Liberty gives her a shrunken head and makes the spikes longer (see Figure 11-26).

FIGURE 11-25   The Expand mode makes her look like she pumps iron (even though she's made of copper).

FIGURE 11-26   Using the Contract mode produces both a shrunken head and an expanded crown.

FIGURE 11-27   Using the Warp brush Twirl modes adds a new twist to an old crown.

The Right Twirl and Left Twirl modes rotate the pixels whether you drag the brush or just place it on part of the image. This time, I placed the Right and then Left mode brushes on the spikes to create the wiggle effect, as shown in Figure 11-27.

The Noise and Iron Out modes are related. Noise applies random Warp distortion, which produces a rippled bumpy effect, and Iron Out (like a real steam iron) removes the effect. To selectively remove the other warp actions, you need to use the Unwarp tool—effectively a Warp Undo tool. This is a critical tool for removing unwanted warp actions that may occur to pixels that are adjacent to the area you are working on.

The last item in the Warp Brush's Tool Options palette is Deformation Maps, which applies warping based on the deformation map that you select—Paint Shop Pro 8 ships with a set of maps with great names like Jitters and Fun House Mirror.

To use this part of the Warp brush, click the Folder icon in the Deformation Map section of the Tool Options palette. From the Load Deformation Map dialog box that opens (shown next), select a deformation map. In the Preview window, change the size of the map (to small, medium, or large) to control the degree of deformation.

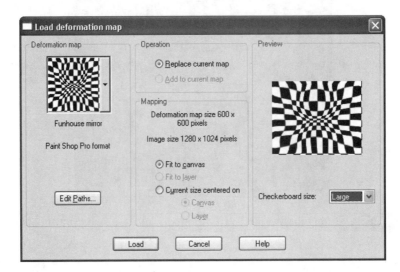

Using Deformation Maps applies the warp effects to the entire image at once. Figure 11-28 is the result of applying the Fun House Mirror map. You can apply

FIGURE 11-28   Applying Deformation Maps to photos

a second deformation map—or more—to compound the effect. Just change the setting in the dialog box to Add to Current map. However, usually applying more than one map to an image makes it unrecognizable.

Even with as much information on effects as we have covered in this chapter, we have only touched the surface. Consider that all of the combinations of built-in effects total over one million. Be afraid—be very afraid. Having done this for many years, my advice for putting some dazzling effects in your photos is to experiment, experiment, and experiment some more.

11

Part V

Create Web Graphics

Chapter 12

Create Images for the Web

How to...

- Create buttons
- Create navigation bars
- Produce a rollover effect
- Define an image map
- Slice an image
- Test and preview web elements

The best part about creating a web page is making all the elements that help your visitors navigate through your site. Paint Shop Pro 8 offers several features that enable you to create some pretty impressive buttons, navigation bars, image maps, and more.

Creating Buttons

Buttons have become quite popular in both applications and web pages. When you click a button, you are either taken to another Web page, or options for the page you are viewing appear. Because buttons offer an area, opposed to a link to click, they are favored over traditional text links. Keeping this in mind, you should create buttons that are both functional and intuitive. There is a variety of button styles, as shown in the following illustration.

Buttons can be simple, or they can be dynamic, meaning they change depending on a given circumstance. For example, when the cursor hovers over the button, the button can change using a rollover effect. Textured buttons offer interesting looks, but be careful not to overwhelm your visitors with too much visual "noise." If you have a textured background, it is best to stick with nontextured buttons. Use your artistic discretion.

Simple Buttons

There is something to be said for simplicity. It allows the mind to rest. In today's world of endless noise and stimulation overload, simplicity can be a very welcome element to a website. Here are a few examples of simple buttons:

Create a Simple Button

In this project, you are going to create a simple rectangular Home button.

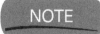 *You can also place text beside the button, rather than on it. An advantage to doing this is that you can use the button for other links without having to later resize it to accommodate longer text.*

To create a simple button, complete the following steps:

1. Open the File menu and select New.

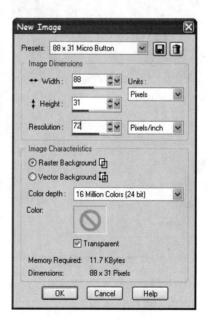

2. In the New Image dialog box, select 88 × 31 Micro Button from the Presets list.

3. Change the resolution to 72 pixels per inch. This is a common resolution for on-screen graphics such as a web page, although 96 pixels per inch is also used.

4. Click OK.

12

5. Click the Flood Fill (F) tool in the Tools toolbar. Make sure your foreground color is set to black. Click inside the button area to flood it with black.

6. Open the Effects menu, select 3D Effects, and click Buttonize. Alternatively, you can click the Buttonize button in the Web toolbar.

To view the Web toolbar, open the View menu, click Toolbars, and then click Web.

7. In the Buttonize dialog box, set Height to 15, Width to 20, and Opacity to 75; click OK.

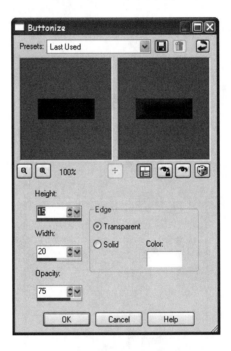

8. Now you are ready to add your text. Click the Text tool (T) in the Tools toolbar and click inside the button image.

9. In the Text box, type **Home**. You may need to adjust the font and size of the text to fit the button. Adjust these settings in the Tools toolbar. When you are satisfied with the way the text looks on the button, click Apply.

10. Use the Move tool (M) to adjust the placement of the text over the button. Your button should now look like this:

11. Save the button as a Paint Shop Pro file.

 To associate the button with the home page, you need to create an image slice. You will learn how to do that in the "Slicing an Image" section later in this chapter.

3D Textured Buttons

Three-dimensional textured buttons add spark to your web page. These buttons can also match your background to offer a sense of conformity. For example, if you own a masonry business, you may want to make the buttons look like they were carved from stone.

Create a 3D Textured Button

In this project, you are going to make a textured button with a three-dimensional look and feel. The end product should resemble something like the following illustration:

12

To create a textured button, complete the following steps:

1. Open the File menu and select New.

2. Change the Height and Width settings to 100 pixels, and the Resolution setting to 72 pixels per inch, and then click OK.

3. Click the New Raster Layer button in the Layers palette and name it Button.

4. Click the arrow for the Selection tool, and then click the Freehand Selection tool.

5. Draw the shape of your button—try to make it resemble a shard of stone.

6. In the Materials palette, click the foreground properties tile, as shown here:

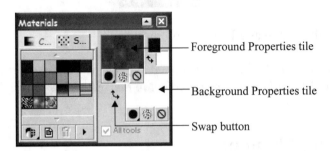

Foreground Properties tile

Background Properties tile

Swap button

7. Click the Flood tool, and then click inside the button area. This will fill the area with a solid color.

8. Click the foreground swatch in the Materials palette to open the Material dialog box. Select the Texture check box, and then select the Granite 1 texture tile as shown in the following illustration. Click OK to accept your new texture selection.

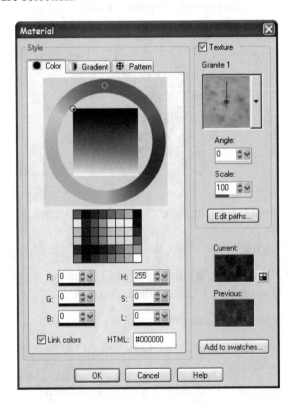

9. Click the Swap button again and click inside your button shape to fill the area with the textured fill.

10. Now you are ready to give your button a little dimension. Open the Effects menu, select 3D Effects, and then click Inner Bevel. Set the options as shown in the following illustration and click OK.

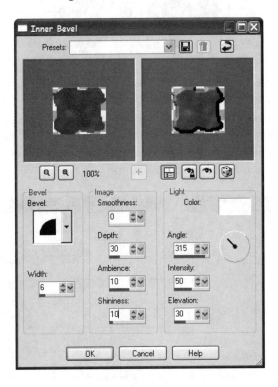

11. To add some text, click the Text tool, and type **Home** in the text entry box. Adjust the settings as needed, and then click Apply.

12. To make the text look as if it is engraved in the stone, you are going to use the embossed effect. Open the Effects menu, select Texture Effects, and then click Emboss.

13. Use the Move tool to adjust the text over the button, and then save the button as a Paint Shop Pro file.

Rollover Buttons

Rollover buttons change their appearance based on certain mouse actions. In the following illustration, the left button displays when the page opens. When the cursor

12

hovers over it, the button changes to the right button. This mouse action is called "mouse over." When the cursor moves away, the button returns to the image on the left. This mouse action is called "mouse out."

On Mouse Out ———  ——— On Mouse Over

Before you create a rollover effect, you need to create the buttons you want to use. When these buttons appear depends on the position of the cursor or the action of the mouse. Rollover effects are defined through the Image Slicer dialog or the Image Mapper dialog. For a single button, however, it is best to use the Image Slicer. Open the File menu, select Export, and click Image Slicer. If you have the Web toolbar displayed, click the Image Slicer button.

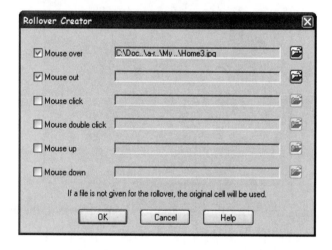

To the right of each mouse action is a text box and a folder button. If you click the folder button, you can browse to the image you want displayed. If you leave the box empty, as shown for the Mouse Out action, it is assumed you want the current image displayed.

The mouse actions are defined as follows:

- **Mouse Over**   Cursor hovers over the image
- **Mouse Out**   Cursor moves away from the image

- ■ **Mouse Click**   Left mouse button is clicked

- ■ **Mouse Double-click**   Left mouse button is double-clicked

- ■ **Mouse Up**   The left mouse button is released

- ■ **Mouse Down**   The left mouse button is held down

Producing a Rollover Effect

For this project, you are going to create two buttons and save them as JPEG files. The first button will appear when the mouse cursor moves over the button image. The second button appears first, and then reappears when the cursor moves away from the image.

To produce a rollover effect, complete the following steps:

1. Select File | New, or click the New Image button in the Standard toolbar.

2. In the New Image dialog box, enter a height and width of 75 pixels and a resolution of 72 pixels per inch and click OK.

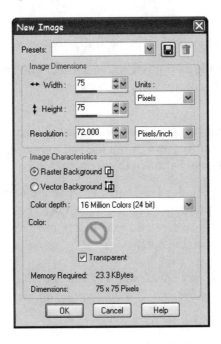

12

3. Click the Picture Tube button in the Tools toolbar.

4. In the Tool Options palette, click the Image Select button and select the Marbles picture tube object.

5. Click inside the center of your button canvas. If necessary, use the Move tool to position the marble in the center of the canvas. Your button should resemble the following illustration:

6. Make sure your Web toolbar is visible. If it is not, open the View menu and select Toolbars | Web.

7. In the Web toolbar, click the JPEG button.

TIP *If you want to preserve the transparent background, save the image as a GIF file. You may have to adjust the optimization settings to achieve the right quality.*

8. For now, accept the defaults in the JPEG optimizer. Click OK.

9. Save the button file as Button2.jpg in a folder you can easily find. Remember the location of this file because you will need it later in this project.

10. Now you are ready to create the button that will appear first and reappear when the cursor moves away from the button image. Select File | New, or click the New Image button in the Standard toolbar.

11. In the New Image dialog box, enter a height and width of 75 pixels and a resolution of 72 pixels per inch and click OK. The size should be identical to the first button you created so the button image won't jump around as it changes from one to the other.

TIP *To ensure the images are identical in size and placement, change the original image and save it as a different filename.*

12. Click the Picture Tube button in the Tools toolbar.

13. The Marble picture tube object should already be selected. Click inside the center of your button canvas twice to ensure you paint a different marble than the first button you created. If necessary, use the Move tool to position the marble in the center of the canvas. Your button should resemble the following illustration.

14. Click the Image Slicer button in the Web toolbar.

15. In the Image Slicer dialog box, click Rollover Creator.

16. In the Rollover Creator dialog box, select the Mouse Over check box and click the file folder to the right of the empty box. Find and select the Button2.jpg file you saved and click Open.

17. Select the Mouse Out check box, but leave the file location box empty so that the current image will be selected. The Rollover Creator dialog box should look like the following illustration.

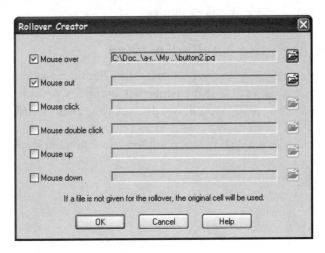

18. Click OK to close the Rollover Creator dialog box.

19. In the Image Slicer dialog box, change the format to JPEG and click Optimize Cell.

20. For now, accept the defaults. Click OK.

21. Back in the Image Slicer dialog box, click Save.

22. In the Save As window, navigate to the folder where your Button2.jpg file is saved and name the rollover file Rollover.htm. Click Save. Click Close to close the Image Slicer dialog.

23. To see the results of your rollover effect, open the folder where you saved the rollover file and double-click the Rollover.htm file. Move your mouse over the button and move it away from the button to see it change.

Creating Navigation Bars

Navigation bars are the side bars you see in many web pages. Typically, they are on the left of the page and offer several buttons that point to other pages. These bars can be fairly simple, or they can be dynamic. For example, the buttons can have rollover effects defined, or they can produce pop-up menus when the cursor hovers over an option. Once you understand the basics of how web elements work, there is no limit to your creative possibilities.

Creating a Metallic Navigation Bar

In this project, you are going to create a navigation bar that resembles metal. You can get fancy in creating your web elements, but simplicity provides better results. The page will load faster and you will not distract your visitors with stimulation overload.

To create a metallic navigation bar, complete the following steps:

1. Select File | New.

2. In the New Image dialog, change the width to 150 and the height to 300 pixels. Change the resolution to 72 pixels per inch and click OK.

3. In the Materials palette, click the Foreground Properties tile to open the Material dialog box. Click the Gradient tab.

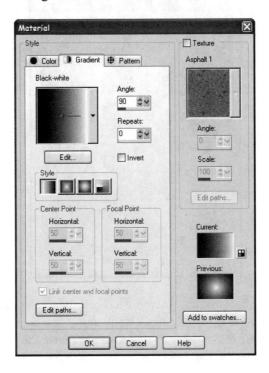

4. Configure the following options on the Gradient tab, and then click OK:

   ■ Under Style, click Linear, which is the first box on the left.

   ■ Change the Angle setting to 90 degrees. This will cause the lines to run vertical as opposed to horizontal.

5. Set the foreground color to black and the background color to white.

6. Click the Flood tool, and then click inside your image to flood it with a gradient fill.

12

7. Now you are going to give your image a metallic look and feel. Open
the Effects menu and select Artistic Effects | Chrome. The Chrome
dialog opens, as shown here:

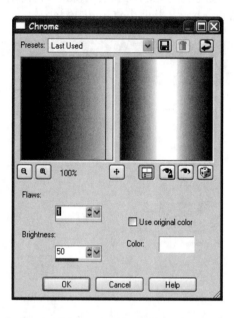

8. To make your background resemble a shiny sheet of metal that has a bit of
a curve, you need to give it one flaw, meaning one bend or change of light.
As you increase the number of flaws, you increase the number of dark and
light bands. Change Flaws to 1 and Brightness to 50 and click OK.

9. Your image should now look like a shiny sheet of metal, as shown in the
following illustration:

10. Now you can add some text that your visitors can click to open other pages. Click the Text tool and click inside the navigation bar.

11. Make sure the background color is still set to white. In the text box, type **Home**, since this will be the first link on your navigation bar. Adjust the text options, if necessary, and then click Apply.

12. Use the Object Selection tool to move the text to the right location.

13. To make the text look as if it is engraved in the metal, you can add an embossed effect. Open the Effects menu and select Texture Effects | Emboss. When asked to convert the layer, click OK. The text needs to be converted to a raster object before any effects can be applied.

14. Repeat the last four steps to create the following links:

- ■ Company
- ■ Products
- ■ Contact Us

15. Your navigation bar should resemble the following illustration:

16. Save this image as a Paint Shop Pro file. For now, call the file Nav1.pspimage. You'll use it again for the image slicing project later in this chapter. (To make this navigation bar functional, you'll have to create an image slice.)

Defining an Image Map

Image maps are used to define areas of a larger image as links to other pages, or as something dynamic, such as a rollover or a pop-up menu. It is a way of making one image behave like several separate images. To illustrate this a little better, imagine displaying a map of the United States on your page. When your visitor points to a particular state, you may want that state to stand out somehow, or have information about that state appear on the page. Creating an image map enables you to define the area or boundaries of that state.

To open the Image Mapper dialog box (Figure 12-1), click on the Image Mapper button in the Web toolbar, or open the File menu and select Export | Image Mapper.

The tools enable you to define the areas of your map. Select a tool and draw an area border around the area you want to map in the image. The shape tools make it easy for you to define a mapped area. If you make a mistake, click the Eraser tool and erase the area border you want to remove. Use the tool buttons to perform the following functions:

■ **Pan tool**   Selects and resizes a map area.

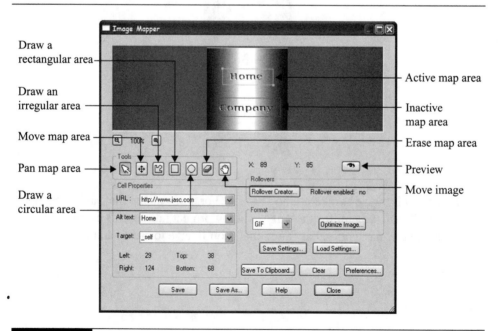

FIGURE 12-1   The Image Mapper dialog box

- **Move tool**   Moves a map area.

- **Irregular Shape tool**   Draws an irregular shape. Each click begins a new line segment.

- **Rectangle Shape tool**   Draws a rectangular shape.

- **Circle Shape tool**   Draws a circular shape.

- **Eraser tool**   Removes an area border.

- **Hand tool**   Moves the image in the display area.

The Cell Properties section lets you define how a mapped area behaves. Each selected area can have the following properties defined:

- **URL**   Causes the link to open another page. The address in this field can either be a complete URL address, such as http://www.jasc.com, or a web page file that is part of the same website, such as home.htm. When your visitor clicks this area of the image, the page specified in this field will open.

- **Alt Text**   If the visitor has chosen to disable graphics on their web browser, all they will see is a blank box with an "X" in the corner. If you want them to see text that describes what the image portrays, you can enter that text in this field.

- **Target**   Defines the window that the specified URL will use. You have a choice of the following options:

  - **Blank**   Opens a new browser window.

  - **Parent**   Loads the page in the parent frame, if frames are used. If frames are not used, the image loads in a full window.

  - **Self**   Replaces the current page with the new page in the same window.

  - **Top**   Removes all frames, if any are defined, and loads the page in a full window.

12

Rollovers were discussed earlier in this chapter. The Format area enables you to save the image in a specific format.

The buttons in the Image Mapper dialog perform the following actions:

- **Save Settings**   Saves the map.

- **Load Settings**   Loads a map you have saved.

- **Save to Clipboard**   Copies the html code to the clipboard so that it can be pasted into an html editor or authoring application.

- **Clear**   Removes all map borders from the image.

- **Preferences**   Defines the map border colors.

- **Save**   Saves the mapped image as an html file that can be viewed in a browser.

- **Save As**   Enables you to save the file as a different name.

Slicing an Image

The difference between slicing an image and mapping it is how the image is saved. In a mapped image, the image is saved as one file. In a sliced image, each slice is saved as a separate file. This enables large images to load much faster, without seams or mismatches. Unlike mapped images, slices can only be rectangular in shape. Image mapping enables you to define areas in an image that link to a target or URL. You can slice an image symmetrically, or asymmetrically, depending on how you want each slice to behave.

To open the Image Slicer dialog box (Figure 12-2), click the Image Slicer button in the Web toolbar, or open the File menu and select Export | Image Slicer.

If you are merely slicing a large image to make it load faster, it makes sense to use the Grid tool. This tool lets you define how many rows and columns to use to break the image up. The smaller the grid size, the faster the image will load. Keep in mind, however, that each slice is saved as a separate file that loads one slice at a time. Depending on the speed of your visitor's Internet connection, this can either be very noticeable, or so quick the visitor sees it as one image instead of several images.

If you are slicing an image to create specific click points, as in the navigation bar project, you should use the Slice tool because it enables you to slice the image in logical chunks. Each slice cell can be configured to perform various actions. For example, if your visitor clicks the slice, the page can redirect the visitor to another page, or you can define rollover effects for that slice.

The tools enable you to define each slice. Select a tool, and then click where you want to slice the image or define the grid size. If you make a mistake, click the Eraser tool and erase the slice you want to remove. Use the tool buttons to perform the following functions:

- **Pan tool**   Selects and moves the slice borders

- **Grid tool**   Defines the grid size

- **Slice tool**   Draws a slice across the image

- **Eraser tool**   Removes a slice border

- **Hand tool**   Moves the image in the display area

The Cell Properties section enables you to define how the active slice behaves. Each slice can have the following properties defined:

- **URL**   Causes the link to open another page. The address in this field can either be a complete URL address, such as http://www.jasc.com, or a web page file that is part of the same website, such as home.htm. When your visitor clicks this area of the image, the page specified in this field will open.

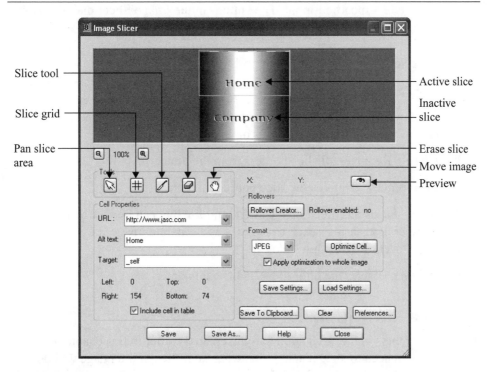

FIGURE 12-2   The Image Slicer dialog box

- **Alt Text** If the visitor has chosen to disable graphics on their web browser, all they will see is a blank box with an "X" in the corner. If you want them to see text that describes what the slice portrays, you can enter that text in this field.

- **Target** Defines the window that the specified URL will use. You have a choice of the following options:

  - **Blank** Opens a new browser window.

  - **Parent** Loads the page in the parent frame, if frames are used. If frames are not used, the image loads in a full window.

  - **Self** Replaces the current page with the new page in the same window.

  - **Top** Removes all frames, if any are defined, and loads the page in a full window.

Rollovers are discussed earlier in this chapter. The Format area enables you to save the image in a specific format. The buttons in the Image Slicer dialog perform the following actions:

- **Save Settings** Saves the slice grid.

- **Load Settings** Loads a slice grid you have saved.

- **Save to Clipboard** Copies the html code to the clipboard so that it can be pasted into an html editor or authoring application.

- **Clear** Removes all slice borders from the image.

- **Preferences** Defines the slice border colors.

- **Save** Saves the sliced image as an html file that can be viewed in a browser. It also saves each sliced area as a separate image file in the same location as the html file.

- **Save As** Saves the html file as a different name.

Slicing a Navigation Bar

To make the labels in the navigation bar you created earlier in this chapter do something, you need to slice it and define what each slice in the image will do when your visitors click on a defined area.

To slice your navigation bar, complete the following steps:

1. Open your Nav1.pspimage file.

2. Open the File menu and select Export | Image Slicer. Or, if you have the Web toolbar visible, you can click the Image Slicer button.

3. On the Image Slicer dialog box, click the Grid tool, and then click inside the image area. The following dialog box will appear.

4. In the Grid Size dialog box, change the number of rows to 4 and the number of columns to 1 and click OK.

5. You should now have four even slices. Because your labels may or may not be evenly spaced, you may need to adjust each slice so that it adequately encompasses your label.

6. Click the Pan tool and click the slice that surrounds the Home label. The slice border turns green, indicating that it is the active slice. If necessary, adjust the slice area by dragging the lower border up or down.

7. Click inside the URL box and type **home.htm**. This is what you are going to name this slice image file so when you test it later, you will return to your original page.

8. It is always good practice to define an alternate text, just in case a visitor has disabled graphics on their system. Click inside the Alt Text box and type **Home**.

9. If you do not specify a target window, the current window is assumed. For testing purposes, click inside the Target box, click the arrow to the right of the box and choose _blank. This will open a new window for the linked page.

12

10. In the Format section, choose JPEG as the format of choice and select the Apply Optimization to Whole Image check box to save each slice in the same format. Do this to preserve consistency in your image. See the following illustration:

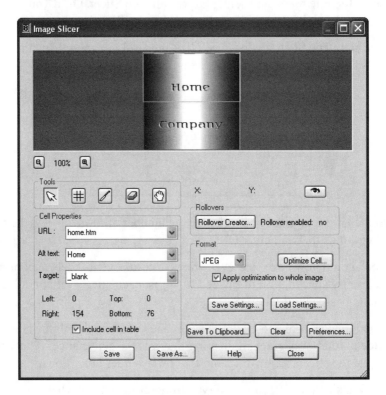

11. Make sure your Pan tool is still selected and click the Company slice. The slice border turns green, indicating that it is the active slice. If necessary, adjust the slice area by dragging the lower border up or down.

12. Click inside the URL box and type **http://www.jasc.com**.

13. Click inside the Alt Text box and type **Company**.

14. Click inside the Target box, click the arrow to the right of the box, and choose _blank. This will open a new window for the linked page.

15. In the Format section, choose JPEG as the format of choice and select the Apply Optimization to Whole Image check box, as shown in the following illustration:

16. If you want to define the other slices, do so now, following the same steps you used for the first two slices.

17. When you are done defining your slice properties, you are ready to save your settings to an html file that can be interpreted by a browser. Click Save.

18. In the Save As dialog box, create a folder for your website, open that folder, and then name your file home.htm. Click Save.

19. Click Close to close the Image Slicer dialog box.

Now you are ready to test your file out. See the next sections for detailed instructions on how to test and preview your web elements.

Testing and Previewing Web Elements

After you have created some web elements, you will want to test them and see how they will appear to your visitors. To test the navigation bar you created in the previous projects in this chapter, complete the following steps:

1. Right-click Start, and then click Explore to launch Windows Explorer.

2. Open the folder where you saved your navigation bar and double-click the home.htm file, as shown in this illustration:

3. This will open the navigation bar, including the sliced images, in your default web browser. Adjust the size of your browser window so that it doesn't take up the whole screen.

4. On the image of the navigation bar your created, click Company. Another browser window should open and the Jasc home page should be displayed.

5. Again, on the image of the navigation bar your created, click Home. Another browser window should open and the page containing your navigation bar should display.

6. Close the browser windows.

How to ... Preview a Web Element

If you just want to preview the web element to see how it displays in a browser, without the associated code, complete the following steps:

1. In your Paint Shop Pro window, open the View menu and select Preview in Web Browser. If you have the Web toolbar visible, click the Preview in Web Browser button. The following dialog box displays:

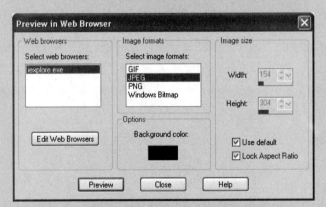

2. If you have more than one browser, from the Select Web Browsers list, select the browser you want to view the image in.

3. Under Image Formats, click the formats you want to view the image in. This is a great way to determine the best format for the image.

4. Select the background color that best matches the background for your website and click Preview.

5. For future reference, you may want to print the preview. When you are done, close the preview window.

12

Chapter 13

Create Animations with Animation Shop

How to...

- Create frames
- Use the Animation Wizard
- View an animation

Animations are nothing more than several images displayed in rapid succession. If you had a pad of paper with an image drawn on each sheet, you would have something similar to an animation file. Flip through the sheets of paper and watch the images move. An animation file combines a series of images and displays them one after the other at any interval you specify. You can even create more of a slide show effect by using slower transition speeds and methods.

If you are new to animation, the Animation Wizard can walk you through all of the steps required to build an animation file. This chapter introduces you to the basics of using Animation Shop and shows you how to build a simple animation file using the Animation Wizard.

Creating the Image Frames

Before you can build an animation file, you need to create the images for each frame. Each image must then be optimized and saved in a common location. The method illustrated in this chapter is only one of many ways an animation can be generated. The goal here is to provide you with the basics of what an animation file is and how it is created.

Generating Image Frames

What you are going to do in this example is create an animation of a marble that bounces against the sides of the image frame. This is a rather lengthy process, but it's worth the time invested. Make certain you perform each step in the order listed.

To create the image frames, complete the following steps:

1. In Paint Shop Pro 8, open the File menu, and then click New.

2. In the New Image dialog box, change the width to 300 and the height to 300 pixels. Change the resolution to 72 pixels per inch, and then click OK.

3. Click the Picture Tube tool, and then select the Marble object.

4. Click inside your image once to paint a single marble.

5. Click the Move tool and drag the marble to the upper-left corner of the image frame.

6. In the Layers palette, click the Duplicate Layer button and drag the marble slightly to the right and below the previous marble. Repeat this step until your image looks like the following illustration:

TIP *If you spread your images out, your animation may look choppy. Try to keep them a half distance apart to create a smoother animation.*

7. Save your file as a Paint Shop Pro file.

8. In the Layers palette, click the Visibility Toggle button for each layer until only the background and the first marble is visible. All other layers should have a red X through the eyeball icon.

9. Make sure your Web toolbar is visible and click the JPEG button.

10. Accept the defaults by clicking OK.

11. In the Save Copy As dialog box, create a new folder just for this animation. Name this first file 1.jpg and click Save.

12. In the Layers palette, click the Visibility Toggle button to hide the first marble, and then click the Visibility Toggle on the next marble layer to make it the only visible marble.

13. Click the JPEG button in the Web toolbar as you did with the first marble. Again, accept the defaults. Name the file 2.jpg.

14. Continue to optimize the remaining layers as JPEG files until all of them have been saved in sequential order.

15. After you have optimized each of the individual layers, you are ready to build your animation. This procedure is explained in the next section.

13

Using the Animation Wizard

Like Paint Shop Pro, Animation Shop offers toolbars, menus, a workspace, and even palettes. Although you can actually build your images in Animation Shop, that subject requires a book of its own. Our goal here is only to introduce you to the basics of generating a simple animation.

If you have installed Animation Shop, you can access it right through Paint Shop Pro 8. Open the File menu, select Jasc Software Products, and then click Launch Animation Shop. To familiarize yourself with Animation Shop, see Figure 13-1.

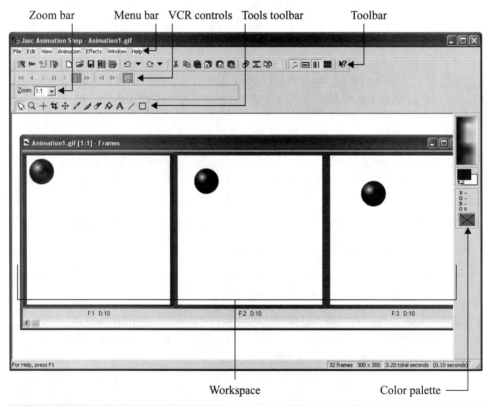

FIGURE 13-1　Welcome to Animation Shop

Building an Animation with the Animation Wizard

Using the frames you created earlier in this chapter, you are now going to build an animation file with the Animation Wizard, which walks you through the basic steps for creating an animation. Once the animation is created and you see how it looks, you can make a few adjustments.

To create an animation file, complete the following steps:

1. Start Animation Shop.

2. Click the Animation Wizard button in the toolbar. The first screen of the wizard appears, as shown next:

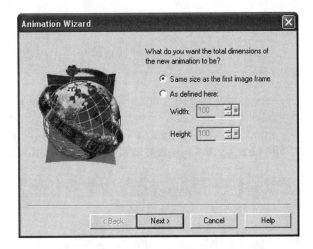

3. You are asked to define the overall size of the animation you are about to create. This screen is helpful if you have several images of different sizes. In this case, you want to choose a size that is the same as the smallest frame. In the example, you created all of the frames the same size because they are really part of the same image broken into separate frames. There is no reason

13

to change the size for this particular animation. Click Next. The next screen appears, as shown in the following illustration.

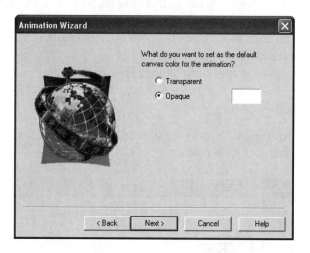

4. If you have created your images on transparent backgrounds, you can choose to keep the background transparent, or choose a color for the background. Since your background was white, accept the default, and click Next. The next screen appears, as shown in the following illustration.

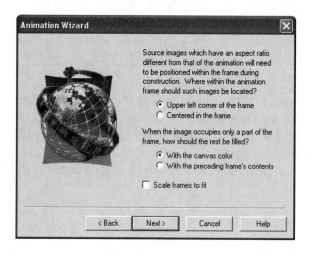

5. Again, this screen is helpful if you are using images of a different size and orientation. To make the animation appear to be one image that moves, you need to orient the individual objects so they look like one image, and the

options in this screen help you do that. However, because the objects in this example have already been arranged appropriately, you can accept the defaults and click Next. The next screen appears, as shown in the following illustration.

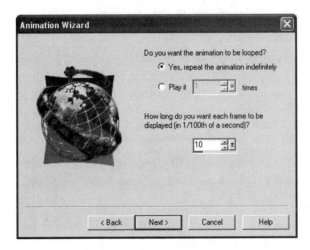

6. In this screen, you define how many times you want the animation repeated. Because this is a bouncing marble, you can choose to play the animation Indefinitely. You Can Also Define How Quickly Each Frame Is Displayed. For now, leave this value at the default of one tenth of a second. This value, along with all the others you are setting, can be adjusted later, if necessary. Click Next. The next screen appears, as shown in the following illustration.

13

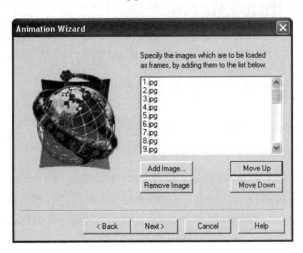

7. Here you add the frames you want to include in our animation. In the previous project, you saved each layer as a separate JPEG file and numbered them sequentially. Click Add Image.

8. In the Open dialog box, open the folder containing the images you have saved. Click 1.JPG, hold the SHIFT key, and then click the last image in the sequence. This will select all of your images. Click Open.

9. If the images do not display in the order you want them played, select the image that is out of sequence, and then use the Move Up or Move Down buttons to move it to the right sequence order. When the images are in the right sequence, click Next.

10. Now you are ready to build your animation file. Click Finish.

11. When prompted to save your file, open the folder containing all of your frames, name the file Animation.gif, and then click Save.

12. The animation file will open in your Animation Shop workspace. To view the animation, click the View Animation button in the toolbar, or open the View menu and click Animation.

There are a couple of different ways you can view an animation file. You can open the .gif file in Animation Shop, and then click the View Animation button in the toolbar, or you can double-click the .gif file from Windows Explorer.

Adding Transition Effects

Once you build your animation file, you can add several transition effects. This is a fun feature to play with because you get a chance to view the effect immediately without having to apply it first.

To add a transition effect, complete the following steps:

1. Open an animation file in Animation Shop.

2. Click the frame you want to affect.

3. Open the Effects menu, and then click Insert Image Transition. The following dialog box appears.

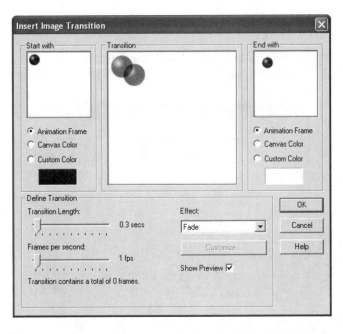

4. Under the Start With section, you can choose to transition the background or the animation frame itself. The same holds true with the End With section.

5. Under the Define Transition section, you can adjust how long you want the transition to last and the number of frames per second you want it to take to complete.

6. From the Effect list, you can choose one of many types of effects. Select one and watch an example of that effect in the Transition pane.

7. When you have defined the transition you want, click OK.

Adding Special Effects to an Image Frame

There are two ways you can add effects to your animation. You can insert an effect, or you can apply an effect to the selected frame.

13

Applying an Effect

When you apply an image effect, you change the selected image. To do this, open the Effect menu and select Apply Image Effect. The following options are presented.

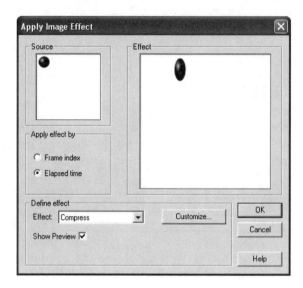

- ■ **Frame Index** Increases the intensity of the effect relative to the frame's index value or position.

- ■ **Elapsed Time** Increases the intensity of the effect relative to the sum of the delay times of each selected frame.

- ■ **Effect** Offers several effects from which to choose. When you select an effect, a sample of that effect is shown in the Effect pane, if the Show Preview check box is selected.

Click Customize to fine-tune the selected effect. When you are done, click OK.

Inserting an Effect

When you insert an image effect, you use the selected image as a base for the frame that's inserted. To do this, open the Effect menu, and then click Insert Image Effect. The following options are presented.

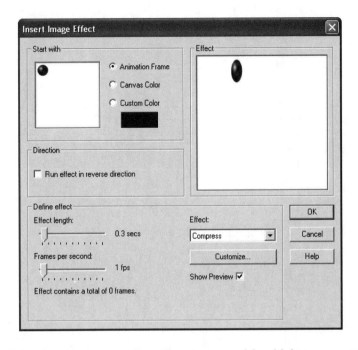

In this dialog box, you can choose the element with which you want to start the effect. To add a bit of interest, click the Run Effect in Reverse Direction check box, and see what happens. If you select the Show Preview check box, you can see the effects of your settings right away, without having to apply them first.

Click the Customize button to fine-tune the selected effect. When you are done, click OK.

13

Appendix

Digital Image Fundamentals

As the field of digital imagery expands, many people with little or no background on the subject are getting deeply involved with computer graphics. While there are many books about graphics, most of them assume that the reader knows the terminology and the technical material that serve as the foundation of computer graphics. The end result is a frustrated user. This appendix will help you fill in some of the gaps you might have in your graphics background.

Digital Imaging Terminology

Before I dive into computer terms and acronyms, there is something you must understand: There are many terms in the computer industry that are nonstandard, colloquial, or just plain dumb. This has led to one of my theorems regarding computer terminology: *The only thing that is universally accepted in the computer industry is that nothing is universally accepted in the computer industry.*

I don't expect the Pulitzer prize for that one, but it helps explain why there are so many different terms to describe the same thing in the computer industry. I am also a strong believer in using the common terminology rather than the technically correct term. When it comes to communicating ideas, the popular or commonly used term is more important. In this book, I try to always use the commonly used term (even if it isn't accurate) as well as the technically correct term. Here are a few terms you need to know something about.

Raster and Vector Images

Computers can only understand 1's and 0's. When it comes to displaying art on computers, it is necessary to convert the images into something the computer can understand: 1's and 0's. There are two ways to display images: *bitmap* (sometimes called "paint" or "raster") and *vector* (also called "freehand").

The photograph of a hamburger shown in Figure A-1 is a typical example of a raster image. The image file is composed of millions of individual parts called *pixels* (picture elements). The color or shade of each part is determined by a numerical value assigned to each pixel. This photograph is small, yet it contains 289,224 pixels. Because each of these pixels requires a number of bits to define its shade or color (some require up to 32 bits), you can see why raster files tend to be large. The original image is color and it weighs in at 1.3 megabytes (MB). These raster images are displayed by using the pixels in the raster image to control the intensity of individual pixels on the monitor.

FIGURE A-1   A raster image is composed of millions of tasty pixels.

NOTE   *Adobe refers to black-and-white images as "bitmaps." For the rest of us on the planet, a raster is any image composed of pixels.*

The other way to display images involves creating a series of instructions for the output device (a computer display, a printer, and so on) to follow. The hamburger shown in Figure A-2 is a relatively simple *vector* image. The image contains no pixels. The file it was created from contains hundreds of lines of instructions that define where each line segment and curve is to be placed in the image, as well as the type, size, and color of fill for each object. If the instructions were in English (they're not), they might look like the following:

```
001 Go to row 00, column 00
002 Draw a line (direction 090) to row 00, column 80
003 Draw a circle at row 23, column 22, radius 34
004 Fill circle with a radial fill
```

This means each time the vector image is opened, the software application must read the instructions and create the image on either the display or the printer. The advantage of this approach is that the image can be changed to almost any size. After it is resized, the application re-creates it based on the modified instructions. When a raster image is made larger or smaller, however, pixels must be added or subrated, and the resulting image is distorted.

Vector images tend to be complex—meaning they may be composed of thousands of individual objects—and yet they have a much smaller file size than their raster

A

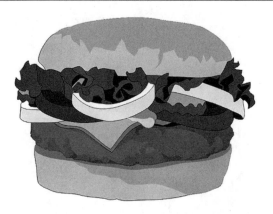

FIGURE A-2   A vector image is made of less tasty vectors and curves.

equivalent. The file containing the hamburger vector image is only 17 kilobytes (KB). Figure A-3 shows a comparison of the resulting file sizes of the two hamburgers shown in Figures A-1 and A-2.

What have you learned so far? Vector images can easily be resized, and their file size is smaller than an equivalent raster image. If I limited my comparison to the two hamburgers previously shown, you might assume that vector images are limited in their ability to look realistic. Actually, if you are willing to put in the time and effort, vector images can look like photographs, such as the image of the car created in CorelDRAW by James L. Higgins III shown in Figure A-4.

FIGURE A-3   Which burger is the light burger? The one made with vectors.

FIGURE A-4   Is it real or a drawing? Complex vector drawings approach vivid realism.

The complexity of the vector-based image necessary to create the illusion is shown next in a zoomed-in view of a portion of the image as it appears (wireframe view) in CorelDRAW. Paint Shop Pro works with both vector and raster images; some other image editors do not support vector-based image files and must first convert (or "rasterize") them to a raster image to load them.

A

Similarly, before effects can be applied to a vector layer, it must be first converted to a raster layer.

Pixels

Pixels are not little elf-like creatures found in Harry Potter books. As I said before, raster images are composed of pixels. A *pixel* is the smallest variable element on a computer display or in a computer image. The term "pixel" is short for "picture element" and is used to describe several different items in graphics. At this point in this appendix, I'll use pixels as a way to describe the number of discrete horizontal and vertical elements in an image. As shown next, a pixel is one of several units of measure in Paint Shop Pro.

NOTE *The term "pixel" replaced an earlier contraction of "picture element," "pel."*

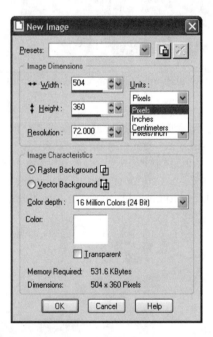

Pixel Size and Resolution

Unlike other units of measurement—centimeters, inches, and so on—a pixel is not a fixed size. A combination of resolution and the physical size of the image determine the size of the individual pixels that make up an image on a computer screen or on a hard copy. Display resolution is how many pixels your screen displays for a given dimension, and the dimensions, such as 800×600 (SVGA), refer to the number of pixels, meaning your monitor screen will have 800 pixels on the long horizontal side and 600 pixels on the short vertical side. Other popular sizes are 1024×768 (XGA) and 1280×1024 (UXGA). More display resolution, such as 1024×768, means smaller pixels and finer detail.

To give you a more explicit example, a 17-inch monitor has a usable area of 12.5 inches across, 9 inches high, and 15.75 inches on the diagonal. Running this monitor at a resolution of 800×600 means 800 pixels will be displayed across 12.5 inches, or about 64 pixels per inch. A 15-inch monitor may be about 10.75 by 8 inches, with a diagonal of 13.25 inches. This monitor, running at the same 800×600 resolution will display images at about 75 pixels per inch.

NOTE   *All pixels are square and can only display one color at a time.*

One way to understand pixels is to think of a mural created with mosaic tiles. When you get close to a mural made of mosaic tiles, it looks like someone had a bad Lego day. This is because you are so close that you are looking at individual tiles. But step away a few feet from the mosaic, and the individual tiles begin to lose their definition and visually merge. The tiles have not changed their size or number, yet the farther back you move, the better the image looks. Pixels in raster images work much the same way.

You can examine how pixels make up an image by enabling the Paint Shop Pro Magnifier (F11), which opens a small window (see Figure A-5) that shows the pixels in this close-up photo of an old carved horse I took in Mexico. As you move the cursor arrow around the image, the pixels under the point of the cursor are magnified by the amount shown in the Magnifier window. As you zoom in on an image, the individual pixels begin to stand out more in the small window; the image they produce becomes less and less evident. Returning to my mosaic tile analogy, there are, of course, major differences between pixels and mosaic tiles. Pixels come in a greater selection of decorator colors (more than 16.7 million), and pixels don't weigh as much as tiles. However, mosaic tiles and pixels operate in the same way to produce an image.

Color Depth

Color depth is the number of bits necessary to describe an individual pixel color. Each of the three primary computer colors (red, blue, and green) has a number of

A

Cursor   Magnifier window ——

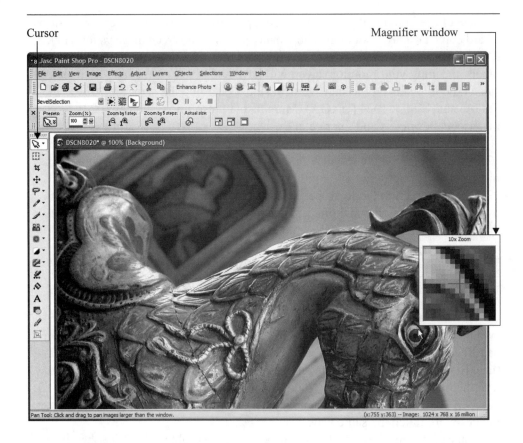

FIGURE A-5   The pixels that make up the image become apparent at high zoom levels.

bits that describes its color depth, or the number of shades of that particular color that can be displayed. The more bit depth a color has, the more shades of that color can be displayed. If a color image has a depth of 4 bits, that means there are 16 possible combinations of bits ($4^2 = 16$) to describe the color in each pixel. In other words, there are 16 possible colors available, or the image has a 16-color palette.

"True" color is also called 24-bit color. Here, each color is 8 bits, for a total of 24 bits. Because each color has 256 shades, you multiply red's 256 colors times green's 256 colors times blue's 256 colors and get millions of colors, ($256 \times 256 \times 256 = 16,777,216$). Millions of colors are pretty much what's needed for a monitor's colors to look "true" to the human eye.

There are several different color depths available with Paint Shop Pro. The choices are as follows:

- 2 colors (1-bit)

- 16 colors (4-bit)

- 256 colors (8-bit)

- 256 shades of grayscale (8-bit), called grayscale

- 32KB colors (24-bit)

- 16.7 million colors (24-bit)

In addition to these, there are some other color depths that you should be aware of. Most Windows operating systems support 32-bit color, which offers the same number of colors as 24-bit but uses a different color model to express the colors.

Some scanners can send 48-bit color. This may sound like it can produce even better color but the truth is, if you saw a 24-bit color image next to a 48-bit color image, you would not be able to tell them apart. There is also a 32-bit color used for prepress that essentially represents 16.7 million colors using a different type of color model using four colors: cyan, magenta, yellow, and black (CMYK).

The greater an image's color depth, the more shades of color it contains, as shown in Table A-1. In turn, as the color depth of an image changes, the file size changes. An image whose color depth is 8-bit (which is also called *paletted*) and has a size of 400KB becomes almost 800KB when converted to 32-bit CMYK. Color depth is explored in more depth (pardon the pun) in the section "Basic Color Theory."

Color Depth	Type of Image	Color(s) Available
1-bit	Black and white	2 colors
8-bit	Grayscale	256 shades of gray
4-bit	Color	16 colors
8-bit	Color	256 colors
16-bit	Color	65,000 colors
16-bit	Grayscale	65,000 shades of gray
24-bit	Color (also called RGB color)	16.7 million colors
32-bit	Color	16.7 million colors
48-bit	Color	281 billion colors

TABLE A-1   Color Depth for the Different Image Types

A

Paint Shop Pro does not support conversion of an image to 16-bit color depth, although it will allow 16-bit color images to be opened and saved as 24-bit color images.

All image file formats have some restrictions regarding the color depth that they can accommodate, so it's necessary to know what color depth you are working with in order to recognize what kinds of colors and other tools you can use with it. Don't worry about memorizing this information; Paint Shop Pro already knows these limitations and will only let you use file formats that can accommodate the attributes of the image you want to save.

If the concept of color depth is new to you, you may be wondering, "Why do we have all these different color depths? Why not make all the images 24-bit and be done with it?" There are many reasons for the different image types. One of the major factors of color depth is the physical size of the file that each type produces. The greater the number of bits associated with each pixel (color depth), the larger the file size. If an image has a size of 20KB as a black-and-white (1-bit) image, it will become more than 480KB as a true-color (24-bit) image. If an 8 × 10-inch color photograph is scanned in at 600 dpi (don't ever do it!) at a 24-bit color depth, the resulting 64MB+ file will probably not even fit in your system. Not to mention that every operation performed with this image will be measured in minutes instead of seconds. There are other factors associated with the different color depths.

All monitors made in the past few years are capable of displaying 24-bit color, which can contain almost 17 million different colors (16,777,216 to be exact). The result is vibrant, continuous-tone, photographic-quality display. Nevertheless, 24-bit images used to pose certain size problems for the World Wide Web—no one wanted to spend 10 minutes downloading your really cool photos. This issue has been resolved to a degree with the increasing popularity of the JPEG and JPEG 2000 file formats.

If you're not sure how many colors your monitor displays, try this: right-click your Desktop and select Properties. A dialog box similar to the one shown next opens. Click the Settings tab to display your current monitor settings. This Display Properties dialog box is from Windows XP, so yours may look slightly different.

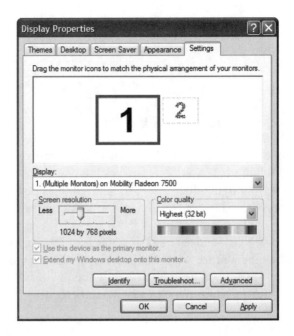

Black-and-White Images

The term "black and white" has caused some confusion in the past because old movies and television shows are referred to as being in black and white. They are actually grayscale, not black and white. Don't try to educate anyone on this subject. Just remember: the old *Andy Griffith* and *Dick Van Dyke* shows are really in grayscale, not black and white.

In real black-and-white images, one bit of information is used per pixel to define its color. Because it has only one bit, it can only show one of two states, either black or white. In actuality, the term black and white is a little misleading as "black" is whatever color is defined and "white" is the color of the paper (generally white). The pixel is turned either on or off. It doesn't get any simpler than this.

Black-and-white images are more common than you would imagine. It is common to associate black-and-white images with old Victorian woodcuts, but as you can see next, black-and-white is still in use today. Probably one of the most common forms of black and white now is for logos on business cards. They are

A

usually very small, and the business card that you have been asked to scan is wrinkled, stained, and…never mind. Where were we?

A lot can be done with a black-and-white image, also called *line art*. Adobe refers to black-and-white images as raster images; no one else does. This can be confusing since most photographic images are referred to as raster images. To best understand how Paint Shop Pro converts images to black and white, see "How Screening Works."

It is possible to use black-and-white (1-bit) images to produce photographs that appear to be grayscale by a process called *dithering*. Dithering can be thought of as pseudo-grayscale when it comes to black-and-white images. While dithering can simulate grayscale, quality suffers greatly if a dithered image is resized later.

How Screening Works

Printing is simple. A given spot on a printed page either has ink (or toner) or it doesn't. Printing does not understand shades of gray. Therefore, photographs and other material containing shades of gray must be converted to spots of pure black on a field of white.

The traditional method of doing this is called *screening*. Screening essentially simulates shades of gray by converting light grays (like regular grays with only half the calories) to tiny black dots on a white background (the paper color). Conversely, dark grays are represented by large black dots. Because of the way our eyes work, these dots or, in the case of more sophisticated screening techniques, these configurations of dots, appear as various shades of gray to the viewer.

Screened continuous-tone images, like the photographs used in most print publications, are known as *halftones*. If you look at a halftone in a newspaper or magazine under a magnifying glass, it consists of a regular grid of dots. The grid is made fine enough so those individual dots are inconspicuous to the viewer. (The exception to this definition is the late Roy Lichtenstein, who made a fortune creating large comic-strip panels with the dots very visible.)

If an area in the photograph is 90 percent black, the halftone would be a white area occupying 10 percent of the area and black dots filling the remaining

90 percent. If another area is 30 percent gray, there would only be 30 percent of the image filled with black dots while the rest is white. Magnified, this area would look like a checkerboard, but to the viewer it appears as a gray area.

The quality of the halftone image depends on both the fineness of the grid of dots and on the number of possible dot shapes for each dot. Yes Virginia, the dots come in different shapes.

The printing industry measures the grid of dots using the term *screen ruling or line frequency.* Screen ruling is equivalent to dots per inch (dpi), but it is measured in lines per inch (lpi). Screened photographs in your local paper are typically 85 lpi, while the halftones you see in magazines are typically 150 lpi. It's not that the newspapers don't like quality pictures; the screen ruling is determined by the paper type and the printing presses used.

Now that you know something about screening, you can understand how Paint Shop Pro converts images to black and white a little better.

In addition to line art, there used to be only three different types of dithering available for black-and-white images: ordered, error diffusion, and halftone. Not anymore. Now Paint Shop Pro offers a multitude of ways to convert an image into a 1-bit black-and-white image.

Selecting 2 colors (1-bit) from the Image menu opens the Decrease Color Depth 2 Colors dialog box shown next. Selecting the buttons in the Palette Component, Reduction Method, and Palette Weight (if it's not grayed out) allows you to get the best possible black-and-white image.

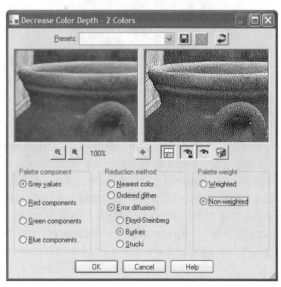

Why Use Black and White in a World of Color?

With color printers becoming so common, a question that I hear a lot is, "Why would I want to convert an image to black and white?" The answer is because many times the images that you produce will end up in publications that will be reproduced using older photocopy machines. If you convert photographs to black and white using error diffusion you'll achieve a better looking image that will reproduce well. The alternative may be that your photo will look as if it went through a fax machine, which is pretty ugly.

The image shown below was converted from a color photograph to a two-color black-and-white image.

Understanding Grayscale Images

As I said previously, what most of us call black-and-white photos are in fact grayscale images. Film photographs (color and grayscale) are *continuous-tone* images, so called because the photo is composed of continuous areas of different colors or shades. This is unlike a digital image, which is composed of square pixels. To represent a black-and-white photograph in a digital format requires dividing the image into pixels using 8 bits of information for each pixel, producing 256 possible shades of gray. The shade of each pixel ranges from a value of white (0) to black (255). Grayscale is used for many other things besides "black-and-white" photos. The selections that you create in Paint Shop Pro are actually grayscale images.

4-Bit and 8-Bit Color

With the explosive growth of the use of web pages on the Internet, 256-color (8-bit) images have become very popular. If you are using Paint Shop Pro to create images for the Web, you may be using 8-bit color depth a lot (4-bit color is rarely used). Referred to as *paletted* or *256-color,* an 8-bit color image can only have one out of 256 combinations of color assigned to each pixel. This isn't as limited as you might imagine.

Many people think that 8-bit color is markedly inferior to 24-bit color. That used to be true, but the process of converting the image from 16- or 24-bit to 8-bit color has been so dramatically improved that in many cases it is difficult, if not impossible, to tell the original image from the paletted one.

16-Bit Color (Thousands of Colors)

Using 16 bits to define the color depth provides approximately 65,000 colors. This is enough for almost any color image. I have seen 16- and 24-bit images side by side, and it is almost impossible to tell them apart. All things being equal, most of

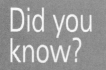
Did you know?

Why 256 Colors Is Really 216 on the Web

For images that will appear on web pages, you will usually want to choose from a palette that is limited to the 256 colors that most computer users can display. Users with very high-quality display monitors and adapters that provide a 24-bit variation for each pixel can view more than 16 million different colors. However, most web surfers have displays that can only handle 8-bit colors. If your images use a range of colors or a palette that is larger than the viewer's display or browser can handle, the browser will dither the colors. In other words, the browser will find colors within its palette that it can substitute for any color that is outside its palette. The result can get downright ugly.

When an image is converted to 8-bit, Paint Shop Pro creates a *reference palette* (also called a "table") to which all the colors used in the image are assigned—hence the term "paletted."

A

the photo-editing public could work with 65KB color from now until the Second Coming and never notice any difference. What are the advantages of 16-bit color? Faster performance on video cards with less video RAM, because you are moving one-third fewer bits. When will you use 16-bit color? Even though Paint Shop Pro doesn't export images in 16KB color, it can open them and save them in a different color depth. You may discover that your video card is set to display in 16-bit color. This is usually the case with video cards with a limited amount of video RAM when you increase the resolution setting of your monitor. When that happens, the display adapter will change the display color depth from 24-bit to 16-bit to conserve the limited amount of video RAM.

If your display adapter is set to display 16-bit color, it does not change the image color depth of the image being viewed, only the display of the image.

24-Bit (True Color)

True-color images may use up to 16.7 million colors. They are so closely associated with the RGB color model that they are sometimes referred to as RGB 24-bit. (I will talk about color models in the "Color Models" section.) "RGB" stands for red-green-blue. Your monitor displays all its colors by using combinations of these three colors. Your eye perceives color the same way: red, green, and blue. The three colors that make up the RGB models each have eight bits assigned to them, allowing for 256 possible shades of each color. Your CRT monitor creates colors by painting the images with three electronic beams from a device in the CRT called a *gun*. The new flat panel uses the same principal except instead of phosphers it turns combinations of electronic elements on and off; it is the mixing together of three sets of 256 combinations that produces a possible 16.7 million color combinations. While True Color doesn't display every possible color, it gets pretty close. It is the model of choice for the desktop computer artist.

32-Bit Color

Back in Table A-1, did you notice anything unusual about 32-bit color? Although the color depth is increased by 25 percent over a 24-bit image, the number of colors remains the same. Why is that?

There are two answers, because there are two types of color depth that involve 32 bits: a 32-bit image and an image using 32-bit color. The first is more commonly seen on the Mac side of the world. A 32-bit image uses a 24-bit RGB model with an additional 8-bit *alpha channel*. Apple reserved the alpha channel, but it never specified a purpose for this data. The alpha channel has come to be used by most applications to pass grayscale mask information. The second use of 32-bit color is to represent the four colors that are used in printing: cyan, magenta, yellow, and black, or as they are more commonly known, *CMYK*. (*K* designates the color black because the letter *B* already designates the color blue.)

> **NOTE** *Most graphic processors advertise that they offer 32-bit, 64-bit, and now 128-bit graphic processor boards. This has nothing to do with color depth. It is a reference to the width of the data path. The wider the data path, the greater the amount of color data that can be moved, and therefore the faster the screens are redrawn.*

48-Bit Color

The availability of 48-bit color can be blamed on the people who market scanners. Many of the scanners today scan color depths greater than 24 bits, then extract the best information out of the scan and send it to the computer in 24-bit format. In their headlong rush to make scanners bigger and better, someone came up with the idea of making all the unprocessed digital information available to the computer. The result is huge files of questionable worth, and you still must convert to 24- or 32-bit color to print the image.

Gamma

Gamma is an important component of an image. *Gamma* can be intimidating, but just think of it as a brightness control with attitude. How bright or dark an image appears on a computer display depends on several factors, including the software gamma setting on the computer, the physical brightness setting of the monitor, and ambient light (the light in the room).

Before we all started displaying our pictures on the Internet, life was simpler. I never thought about how to display my photographs on a Mac, just as my Mac counterpart never thought about making his creations grace a PC screen. The Internet has changed all that. Because of different gamma settings inherent in the hardware, images prepared on a Mac will look too dark on a PC, and images prepared on a PC will look too bright on a Mac. One option is to adjust the gamma so the resulting image is somewhere in the middle. This way, images will appear just a little too bright on the Mac, and a little too dark on the PC. The common gamma setting on the Macintosh is 1.8, so a good compromise is to set it to 2.0 when images will be displayed on the Web.

A

Resolution: A Term with too Many Definitions

Without an understanding of resolution and its effects, you may find yourself creating beautiful images that fill the entire display screen in Paint Shop Pro, yet appear to be smaller than postage stamps when you print them. Resolution is a misunderstood concept in desktop publishing. The confusion is compounded because this term has entirely different meanings depending on the device you are talking about. In this appendix, you will learn what resolution is and what it does in Paint Shop Pro, although this information applies to all image-editing applications, not just Paint Shop Pro.

Resolution and the Size of the Image

As I said, the term "resolution" represents one of the more elusive concepts of digital imaging. In a vector-based program, we describe an image's size in the popular unit of measure for the country we live in. For example, in the United States, we refer to the standard letter-size page as being 8½ × 11 inches. Image size in photo-editing programs is traditionally measured in pixels. The reason for using pixels is that the size of an image in pixels is fixed: when I speak of an image being 1,200 by 600 pixels, I know (from experience) approximately how big the image is. If I use a unit of measure other than pixels—say, inches—the dimensions of the printed image are dependent on the resolution of the image.

So What *Is* Resolution?

Resolution takes the density of pixels per inch (ppi) that make up an image and describes it in dots per inch (dpi). In other words, it is a measure of how many pixels in an image exist in the space of a linear inch.

Say I have an image that is 300 pixels wide by 300 pixels high. How big will the image be when I import it into another application? This is a trick question. Without knowing the resolution of the image, it is impossible to determine the size when it is imported into another application. If the resolution of this image is set to 300 pixels per inch, then the image dimensions are 1 × 1 inch when imported. If the resolution is *doubled* (set to 600 dpi), the image would be *half* the size, or ½ × ½ inch. If the resolution is *reduced by half* (150 dpi), the image size *doubles* to 2 × 2 inches. You can see that resolution exhibits an inverse relationship. The physical size of an image in Paint Shop Pro is most accurately expressed as the length (in pixels) of each side. Resolution tells you how many pixels are contained in each unit of measure.

To show the effect of changing resolution, I duplicated a photo of an old café sign with Paint Shop Pro and made three copies of it. Next, I changed (*resampled*) the resolution of each of the copies so that I had three photographs at three different resolutions. Even though each of the images in Figure A-6 is a different resolution, they appear the same size in Paint Shop Pro because Paint Shop Pro only cares about how many pixels are in the image. When all three files were imported into a PowerPoint slide, the results were as shown in Figure A-7. Why do the photos appear to be the same size in Figure A-6, you ask? Because the physical size of the images (in pixels) remained unchanged—only the resolution changed.

Screen Resolution

No matter what resolution you are using, Paint Shop Pro displays each pixel onscreen according to the zoom ratio. That is why all the photos in Figure A-6 appeared to be the same size even though they were at different resolutions. At a zoom ratio of 100 percent, each image pixel is mapped to a single screen pixel. The display's zoom setting has no effect on the actual image file. If you are a little fuzzy on monitors and pixels, read on. If you know them cold, skip ahead to the "Resolution and Printers" section.

A

FIGURE A-6   Although each photograph is a different resolution (size), they appear the same size displayed in Paint Shop Pro.

FIGURE A-7   When the same photos are displayed in PowerPoint, the image resolution causes them to be displayed at the size they would appear if printed.

When you bought your monitor and/or display card, you may have been bewildered by such terms as "640 × 480," "800 × 600," and so on. These figures refer to the number of screen pixels that the monitor can display horizontally and vertically. For example, let's say you have a plain-vanilla VGA monitor. The minimum resolution for this monitor is now 800 pixels wide by 600 pixels high (600 × 800). If you open a file that is over 1,000 pixels wide, the image at 100 percent zoom (actual pixels in Paint Shop Pro) is too large to fit into the screen, as shown in Figure A-8. With the screen resolution changed to XGA (1024 × 768), the same display area now contains a width of 1024 pixels by a height of 768 pixels. Because the physical size of the display didn't change, the pixels must be getting smaller. The image, shown in Figure A-9, appears smaller than the photograph in the previous figure, but it is still too large to fit into the screen area. The size of the photograph hasn't changed, but the screen (or display) resolution has. To make more pixels fit into the same physical screen dimensions, the actual pixels must be smaller. With the resolution changed to UXGA (1280 × 1024), most of the original photo can be seen on the screen (Figure A-10). Again, the photograph remains unchanged; only the screen resolution has increased. Screen or display resolution operates under the same principle I discussed in the previous paragraph. As the screen resolution increases, the image size decreases proportionally.

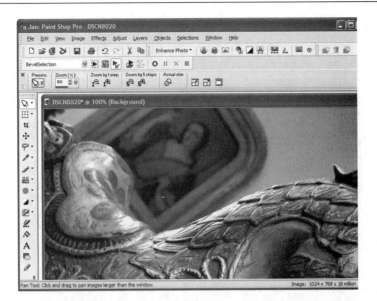

FIGURE A-8 Displaying a photograph that is 1,400 pixels wide using a SVGA (800 × 600) screen resolution.

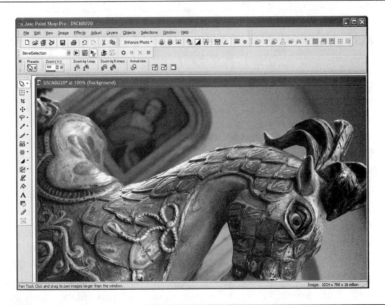

FIGURE A-9 Increasing the resolution to XGA (1024 × 768) makes the pixels smaller, and more of the photograph can be seen.

A

FIGURE A-10 Only by increasing the resolution to UXGA (1280 × 1024) can all of the image be seen.

Many people are surprised to discover that after spending a lot of money to get a high-resolution monitor, their screen images appeared smaller rather than sharper. Now that you know the secret of the screen resolution game, have your friends buy you lunch and you can explain it to them, too.

Screen Setting Recommendations

With all the exciting ads for high-resolution displays and graphics adapters, it is difficult not to get caught up in the fever to upgrade. If you have a 14- or 15-inch monitor, you should be using the Super VGA screen resolution setting on your graphics card. If you go for a higher resolution on a 14- or 15-inch display, even if your monitor supports it, your friends may start calling you Blinky, because you will be squinting all the time to read the screen. Also, be cautious about recommendations from the retail clerk/computer expert at your computer superstore. Remember that last week your "expert" might have been the tropical fish expert at the local pet superstore and may know less about computers than you do.

With the price of CRT (cathode ray tube) displays dropping, more people are investing in a few extra inches on their display. Just because you have a 17- or a 19-inch monitor does not mean you have a moral obligation to run it at the highest resolution that your display adapter will support. Using the wrong resolution for your monitor can sometimes damage the monitor. I use a setting of 1280×1024 most of the time with my 21-inch monitor and it works very well.

Resolution and Printers

If this were a perfect world, image resolution would be the same as printer resolution (which is also measured in dpi). Then if we were printing to a 600-dpi printer in our perfect world, we would be using a 600-dpi-resolution image, because each image pixel would occupy one printer dot. However, it is not a perfect world. First of all, pixels are square and printer dots are round. When we talk about printer resolution, we are talking about the size of the smallest dot the printer can make. If you are using a 600-dpi laser printer, the spacing between the dot centers is 1/600th of an inch. The dot it creates is either on or off—there is either a black dot on the paper or there isn't. If you are displaying a grayscale photograph, you know that each pixel can be 1 of 256 possible shades. So how does the laser printer create shades of gray from black-and-white dots? Using halftone cells. What? Read on.

Creating Halftones

If I take an area on the paper and create a box that has a width of 10 dots and a height of 10 dots, it would have a capacity to fit 100 dots in it. If I were to place printer dots on every other dot, it would only hold 50 printer dots. The result when printed on paper would appear to the eye as gray, or 50 percent black. This is the principle behind the *halftone cell*. The halftone cell created by the laser printer is equivalent to the pixel—not exactly, but close enough for the purposes of discussion. The number of halftone cells a laser printer can produce is a function of its *line frequency,* which some of us old-timers still refer to as "screen frequency." Companies that produce advertisements to sell their printers to the consumer marketplace never discuss line frequency, expressed as lpi (lines per inch). And why not? Because, in this hyper-advertised computer marketplace, bigger is better (except for price). And which sounds better—a 600-dpi printer or a 153-lpi printer? The 153-lpi printer would have a resolution of around 1,200 dpi, but names and numbers are everything in selling a product. This resolution-specification hype also confuses the scanner market as well.

A

So what resolution should you use? I have included the values in Table A-2 as general guidelines to use when setting up the resolution of an image in Paint Shop Pro.

Basic Color Theory

Color is everywhere. Even black and white are colors. Really. Color has a greater and more immediate effect on the viewer than any factor in graphic design. Psychologists confirm that color has an enormous capacity for getting our attention. To use color effectively, you must have a basic understanding of it.

If you were looking for a detailed discussion on the complex mathematics of color models, you won't find it here. What you will find here is a nontechnical discussion of the basic concepts and terminology of color.

Knowing how color works in the natural world and how this "real-world" color operates in a computer will help you when dealing with the complexities of the color models. It will be simple, and I think you will find it interesting.

Color Models

Color is made up of light components that, when combined in varying percentages, create separate and distinct colors. You probably learned this in elementary school when the teacher had you take the blue poster paint and mix it with the yellow paint to make green. Mixing pigments on a palette is simple. Mixing colors on a computer is not. The rules that govern the mixing of computer colors change, depending on the color model being used.

Color models fall into one of two basic categories: *additive color* and *subtractive color*. Additive color (also known as RGB) is the system used by color monitors,

Image Type	Final Output	Recommended Resolution
Black-and-white	Laser printer (600 dpi)	600 dpi
Black-and-white	Display screen	Convert black-and-white image to grayscale and use 72–96 dpi
Grayscale	Laser printer	150–200 dpi
Grayscale	Imagesetter	200–300 dpi
Grayscale	Display screen	72–96 dpi
Color	Color inkjet printer	100–150 dpi
Color	Imagesetter	150–200 dpi
Color	Display screen	72–96 dpi

TABLE A-2 Recommended Resolution Settings

scanners, photography, and the human eye. Subtractive color (also known as CMYK) is used in four-color publishing and printing. Let's take a closer look at both.

Additive Color (RGB)

This model is said to use the additive process because colors are produced by adding one or more colors. RGB (red-green-blue) involves transmitted light as the source of color. In the additive model, color is created by adding different amounts of red, green, and blue light.

Pure white light is composed of equal amounts of red, green, and blue. For the record, red, green, and blue are referred to as the *additive primary colors,* so called because when they are added (combined) in varying amounts, they can produce all the other colors in the visible spectrum.

Subtractive Color (CMYK)

The subtractive model is so named because colors are subtracted from white light to produce other colors. This model uses the secondary colors: cyan, magenta, and yellow. You have already learned this is called the CMYK model, because combining equal amounts of cyan, magenta, and yellow only produce black, in theory. When printed, they produce something closer to swamp mud than black; so, to create a vivid picture, black is added to compensate for the inability of the colors CMY to make a good black. As noted earlier, K is used as the designator for the color black because the letter *B* already designates the color blue.

CMYK is a printer's model, based on inks and dyes. It is the basis for almost all conventional color photography and commercial color printing. Cyan, magenta, and yellow dyes and inks simply transmit light better and are more chemically stable than red, green, and blue inks.

Describing Colors

If someone were to ask me to describe the color of my son's Ford pickup, it would be easy. It is black. The color of my wife's car is more difficult. Is it dark metallic green or deep forest green? The terms generally used to describe color are subjective. Even for simple classifications involving primary colors like red and blue, it becomes difficult to describe the exact color. Is it deep-sea blue or navy blue? In the world of color, we need a way to accurately describe the *value* of color.

When creating or picking out a color in Paint Shop Pro, you can specify the color either by defining values for its component parts or by using a color-matching system. When using the RGB model in Paint Shop Pro (it is the default color model), color values are expressed in shades of RGB. The maximum number of shades a color can contain is 256. For example, the value of red in an RGB model is defined as 255, 0, 0. In other words, the color contains the maximum amount (255) of the red component and a value of zero for the green and blue components. Let me interject here that in Paint Shop Pro, you still pick colors from color palettes that contain recognizable colors like red, green, and blue. You won't have to sit with a calculator and figure out the value of puce.

In CMYK, the component values are traditionally expressed as a percentage, so the maximum value of any color is 100. It should be noted, however, that Paint Shop Pro allows you to express CMYK values in both percentages and shades (0–255). The color red in the CMYK model is 0, 100, 100, 0. In other words, mixing the maximum values of magenta and yellow with no cyan and no black creates the color red.

Color Matching

While defining colors as either a number of shades in the RGB model or percentages of tint in CMYK is accurate, it is not practical. Given that we cannot assign names to the millions of shades of color that are possible, we need a workable solution. The use of color-matching systems like the Pantone™ Spot colors provides a solution. In this case, the designer and the printer have identical books of print samples. The designer wants to use red in a two-color publication and specifies PANTONE Red 032 CV. The printer looks up the formula in the Pantone™ book for the percentages of magenta and yellow to mix together and prints the first sample. The output is then compared with the book of print samples, called a *swatch book*. Most corporate accounts use one of the popular color-matching systems to specify the colors they want in their logos and ads. Color matching in the digital age is less than 10 years old. It has come a long way in its short life and is now finding its way into the design of Internet websites. No longer restricted to four- and six-color printing, the color-matching systems are dealing with the important issues of colors looking correct on the Internet, too. Color correction on the Web is critical for companies selling products. For example, if the color of the sweater you saw on the Web isn't even close to what arrives in the box, the product will probably be returned. To accurately display colors in images has become invaluable.

RGB Versus CMYK

Each color model represents a different viewpoint. Each offers advantages and disadvantages. If you are using Paint Shop Pro to create multimedia and web pages, or just printing to inkjet or color laser printers, knowing how to get what you need out of RGB will more than satisfy your requirements. If you must accurately translate color from the screen to the printed page, you must get more deeply involved in CMYK.

Hue, Saturation, and Brightness

The terms hue, saturation, and brightness (also called "luminosity") are used throughout Paint Shop Pro. *Hue* describes the individual colors—for example, a blue object can be said to have a blue hue. *Saturation* is technically the purity of the color. In practical terms, it is the balance between neutral gray and the color. If an image has no saturation, it looks like a grayscale image. If the saturation is 100 percent, it may look unnatural, since the image's midtones, which the gray component emphasizes, are lost. *Brightness* is the amount of light reflecting from an object determining how dark or light the image appears.

Color Gamut

It may come as a surprise to you, but there are a lot more colors in the real world than photographic films or printing presses can re-create. The technical term for this range of colors is *gamut*. There are many gamuts—for monitors, scanners, photographic film, and printing processes. Each gamut represents the range of colors that can actually be displayed, captured, or reproduced by the appropriate device or process. The widest gamut is the human eye, which can see billions of colors. Further down on this visual hierarchy is the color computer monitor, which can display 16 million colors. Photographic film can only capture 10,000 to 15,000 colors, and a high-quality four-color printing process can reproduce from 5,000 to 6,000. We won't even discuss the limitations of color ink on newsprint.

Congratulations

If you have read through this appendix, you should have enough background to understand how the tools and commands in Paint Shop Pro work. The good news is, there won't be a test.

A

Index

INTERNATIONAL CONTACT INFORMATION

AUSTRALIA
McGraw-Hill Book Company Australia Pty. Ltd.
TEL +61-2-9900-1800
FAX +61-2-9878-8881
http://www.mcgraw-hill.com.au
books-it_sydney@mcgraw-hill.com

CANADA
McGraw-Hill Ryerson Ltd.
TEL +905-430-5000
FAX +905-430-5020
http://www.mcgraw-hill.ca

GREECE, MIDDLE EAST, & AFRICA
(Excluding South Africa)
McGraw-Hill Hellas
TEL +30-210-6560-990
TEL +30-210-6560-993
TEL +30-210-6560-994
FAX +30-210-6545-525

MEXICO (Also serving Latin America)
McGraw-Hill Interamericana Editores S.A. de C.V.
TEL +525-117-1583
FAX +525-117-1589
http://www.mcgraw-hill.com.mx
fernando_castellanos@mcgraw-hill.com

SINGAPORE (Serving Asia)
McGraw-Hill Book Company
TEL +65-6863-1580
FAX +65-6862-3354
http://www.mcgraw-hill.com.sg
mghasia@mcgraw-hill.com

SOUTH AFRICA
McGraw-Hill South Africa
TEL +27-11-622-7512
FAX +27-11-622-9045
robyn_swanepoel@mcgraw-hill.com

SPAIN
McGraw-Hill/Interamericana de España, S.A.U.
TEL +34-91-180-3000
FAX +34-91-372-8513
http://www.mcgraw-hill.es
professional@mcgraw-hill.es

UNITED KINGDOM, NORTHERN,
EASTERN, & CENTRAL EUROPE
McGraw-Hill Education Europe
TEL +44-1-628-502500
FAX +44-1-628-770224
http://www.mcgraw-hill.co.uk
computing_europe@mcgraw-hill.com

ALL OTHER INQUIRIES Contact:
McGraw-Hill/Osborne
TEL +1-510-420-7700
FAX +1-510-420-7703
http://www.osborne.com
omg_international@mcgraw-hill.com

Know How

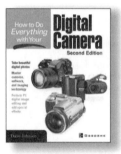

How to Do Everything with Your Digital Camera
Second Edition
ISBN: 0-07-222555-6

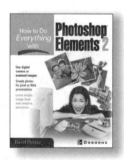

How to Do Everything with Photoshop Elements 2
ISBN: 0-07-222638-2

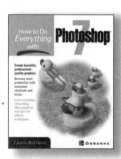

How to Do Everything with Photoshop 7
ISBN: 0-07-219554-1

How to Do Everything with Your Sony CLIÉ
ISBN: 0-07-222659-5

How to Do Everything with Macromedia Contribute
0-07-222892-X

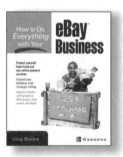

How to Do Everything with Your eBay Business
0-07-222948-9

How to Do Everything with Your Tablet PC
ISBN: 0-07-222771-0

How to Do Everything with Your iPod
ISBN: 0-07-222700-1

How to Do Everything with Your iMac,
Third Edition
ISBN: 0-07-213172-1

How to Do Everything with Your iPAQ Pocket P
Second Edition
ISBN: 0-07-222950-0

OSBORNE DELIVERS RESULTS!

OSBORNE
www.osborne.com